1991

HISTORY
&
MYTH

HISTORY
&
MYTH

Essays on
English Romantic
Literature

Edited by

Stephen C. Behrendt

 WAYNE STATE UNIVERSITY PRESS   DETROIT   1990

Library of Congress Cataloging-in-Publication Data

History and myth : essays on English romantic literature /
  edited by Stephen C. Behrendt.
      p.   cm.
  Includes bibliographical references.
  ISBN 0-8143-2009-0. — ISBN 0-8143-2010-4 (pbk.)
    1. English literature—19th century—History and
criticism. 2. Romanticism—Great Britain. 3. History in
literature. 4. Myth in literature. I. Behrendt, Stephen C.,
1947– .
PR468.H57H57 1990
820.9'145—dc20   89–16728
                                                 CIP

The editor gratefully acknowledges the permission of A.P.
Watt Ltd., on behalf of Michael B. Yeats and Macmillan
London Ltd., to quote from W.B. Yeats's "Lapis Lazuli."

Lines from "Lapis Lazuli" are reprinted with permission of
Macmillan Publishing Company from *The Poems of W.B. Yeats:
A New Edition*, edited by Richard J. Finneran. Copyright 1940
by Georgie Yeats, renewed 1968 by Bertha Georgie Yeats,
Michael Butler Yeats, and Annie Yeats.

Contents

Contents

Contributors

STEPHEN C. BEHRENDT is Professor and Graduate Chair of English at the University of Nebraska. He is the author of *The Moment of Explosion: Blake and the Illustration of Milton, Shelley and His Audiences,* and articles on eighteenth-century and Romantic literature and art. His poetry has been widely published.

LYNN BYRD is Assistant Professor of English at Centenary College of Louisiana. She is working on an extended study—in which Byron figures prominently—of the Romantic theory of pleasure.

JEFFREY N. COX, Associate Professor of English at Texas A & M University, is the author of *In the Shadows of Romance: Romantic Tragic Drama in Germany, England, and France.* He is currently working on the Gothic drama.

P. M. S. DAWSON, of the Department of English Language and Literature at the University of Manchester, is the author of *The Unacknowledged Legislator: Shelley and Politics.* He has written numerous articles on Shelley and on the political context of the later Romantics.

MINNA DOSKOW is Dean of the School of Liberal Arts and Sciences and Professor of English at Glassboro State College in New Jersey. She is the author of *William Blake's "Jerusalem": Structure and Meaning in Poetry and Picture* and of several articles on Blake. Her research interests also include feminist utopias.

MICHAEL FERBER, Associate Professor of English at the University of New Hampshire, is the author of *The Social Vision of William Blake* and several articles on Blake, Coleridge, Simone Weil, and the causes of Romanticism. A former lobbyist and researcher for the Coalition for a New Foreign Policy, he has also written widely on political and social issues.

EDWARD DUFFY is Associate Professor of English at Marquette University. He has written about the Romantics in *Studies in Romanticism* and elsewhere, and is working on a book about Shelley.

BROOKE HOPKINS is Associate Professor and Director of the Graduate Program in English at the University of Utah. His articles have been published in *South Atlantic Quarterly, American Imago,* and *The International Journal of Psychoanalysis.* He is working on a study of the "uncanny" in Romantic literature.

NICHOLAS ROE, Lecturer in English at the University of St. Andrews, Scotland, is the author of *Wordsworth and Coleridge: The Radical Years* and editor of *Coleridge's Imagination.* His articles on politics and English poetry in the 1790s have been published widely.

CHRISTINA ROOT is Assistant Professor of English at Saint Michael's College. She is working on a long study of representations of Napoleon in English Romantic poetry.

SHIRLEY CLAY SCOTT is Professor and Director of Graduate Programs in English at Western Michigan University. She is writing a book on the relations of the Romantic poets to their Classical predecessors.

ERIC C. WALKER, Associate Professor and Director of Graduate Studies in the English Department at Florida State University, is a specialist in eighteenth-century and Romantic literature. His articles on Wordsworth have been published in such journals as *Studies in Romanticism, Studies in English Literature,* and *Philological Quarterly.*

Preface

This collection of essays has grown out of the intersection of a number of lines of interest among both the contributors and modern scholarship and criticism generally. One of these is the rise of what has been termed the New Historicism, whose most immediate effects have been visible in the work of Stephen Greenblatt and others who have brought to Renaissance studies in particular a refreshing interdisciplinary perspective in keeping with the cultural and intellectual expansiveness of that remarkable period in Western culture. Another is the persistence in intellectual inquiry of myth, myth studies, and myth criticism whose origin is ancient and whose concerns received perhaps their most significant modern airing in the work of Northrop Frye and those who followed him—whether they have seconded his methodology and his conclusions or not. Still another is the culturally integrative impulse that informs structuralist criticism, among whose luminaries one thinks almost instinctively of Claude Lévi-Strauss and Michel Foucault. Finally, there is the diverse post-structuralist enterprise, which, even as it has generated its fervent adherents, has at the same time forced those who have found its various subschools uncongenial to redefine their own beliefs and practices in clear relation or contradistinction to it. In all these cases, the common activating impulse has generally been the compulsion to fashion "lenses" through which one may view not just specific textual materials, in the conventional sense of physical artifacts, but also texts in the wider sense in which semiotics understands the term "text." Moreover, the study of *contexts* has assumed greater significance in recent decades as the whole nature of "history" and historical consciousness has come under ever greater scrutiny by an increasingly diverse range of disciplines, and from a salutary diversity of cultural perspectives.

This volume results most immediately from the response to a call for papers for a session at the 1985 MLA convention. The proposal for a session which would investigate the complex relation of history and myth among the Romantics elicited expressions of interest from a far greater number of scholars and critics than those whose names and work appear in the essays which follow. The enthusiasm with which all these people responded to the idea of detailed examination of both the mythologizing and the demythologizing tendencies of particular Romantic artists and works suggested from the outset the desirability of a collection of essays like this one. This volume, then, is a response to that interest. It is also an invitation to dialogue on the issues that the various contributors raise in these pages. Just as the contributors have in the process of composing and revising their work engaged in an ongoing dialogue with one another, they are in general agreement that the matters addressed here—as well as the many other matters to which these discussions must inevitably point—deserve still further critical investigation and discussion. Plato gives us a Socrates whose contribution and commitment to the intellectual centrality of informed discussion is sometimes lost despite the dialogic form of Plato's works. In the Romantic period, William Godwin was not alone in advocating discussion—extended dialogue—as a vehicle for the improvement not only of individuals but of entire societies, and indeed of the entire processes of thought and action. Shelley, too, joined enthusiastically in the Reform movement's advocacy of public discussion, even as the expansion of the print media provided still another vehicle for such ongoing discussion in the dialogues inscribed by editorials, published letters to editors, and published responses to both.

The conviction that there is much to be gained from extended conversation is, of course, central to the Western intellectual tradition, even at those historical moments when social, political, or intellectual establishments seem most reactionary in their resistance to the formation of communities which such conversation entails. The right of free speech is a jealously guarded one which safeguards as well the right of dissent. Blake wrote in *The Marriage of*

Heaven and Hell that "Opposition is True Friendship," and the diversity of viewpoints represented in this collection of essays should, we all hope, underscore the essential accuracy of Blake's view. This is the sort of friendly opposition from which all parties draw both fire and strength, and from which some more clearly delineated view of relative truth ought ideally to emerge, along with a clearer sense of both one's own position and the positions occupied by those whose views differ. To that end, the authors of these essays have devoted their efforts.

I want to express my thanks to all the authors whose work appears here. They have been both diligent and cooperative in preparing and revising their work. In responding to me and to one another with consistent good will, they have made my own task as editor immeasurably easier. At the same time I would thank those others whose work is not present here in the form of essays, but whose interest in this enterprise has from the first been sincere and keen. They know who they are, and their part in this collection, though less immediately visible, is no less important.

I want to thank Wayne State University Press, too, for its interest in, and enthusiasm for, this volume from the very start. In particular, I thank Lee Schreiner, whose editorial assistance at all stages of this project has been as invaluable as her advice and encouragement.

Finally, I wish to acknowledge here also the substantial contribution to this volume and to all aspects of my own work of Patricia Flanagan Behrendt, whose critical sensitivity and insight remains for me at once both an irreplacable stimulus and a model of creative interdisciplinary thinking.

Introduction:
History, Mythmaking, and
the Romantic Artist
Stephen C. Behrendt

Aristotle distinguished between the historian and the poet on the grounds that the former describes "the thing that has been," the latter, "a kind of thing that might be."[1] Poetry, says Aristotle, is thus both more philosophical and more important than history, since it deals not with "singulars" but rather with "universals." But Plato banished poets from his *Republic*, however reluctant Book 10 makes Socrates sound about the decision. Socrates excludes poetry and its makers, as Jerome McGann has recently observed, precisely because his "reason" tells him he must; for "although its function is seen as a social one, its benefit to society has never been demonstrated by the poets or the friends of poetry."[2] In other words, the consuming interest of poets in the imaging and shaping of virtual futures, which Aristotle regards as their greatest distinction, constitutes for Socrates their greatest liability: they appear to be caught up in an attractive but seductive and potentially dangerous world of ideals and unreality.

The essays in this volume contend, along with the English Romantic authors whose works they examine, that Plato's hard line with poets offers an early indication of the extent to which their social function in "real" society—in the day-to-day affairs of a temporal and contemporary public world—is often significantly misunderstood and undervalued. Although the perceived social, political, and intellectual function of both historian and poet had changed radically from its classical roots by the later eighteenth century, the Romantics nevertheless envisioned for themselves a central role in the shaping of present and future alike. They saw in the past—in history, both recent and remote—a resource upon which they might draw effectively in their very public enterprise.

Hayden White argues in *Metahistory* that, in order to understand the intellectual point of any given history, we must first distinguish between the "chronicle" and the "story" that together constitute that history. The chronicle is simply the linear, temporal record of events, whereas the story is an arranged construct that provides the chronicle with the appearance of continuity—with a beginning, middle, and end.[3] This is what Aristotle's historian writes. Arranging their materials after the fact, historians of the Aristotelian mold conclude with an "ending" whose actual achievement or performance predates the composition of the history. The poet, on the other hand—and the Romantic poet (or artist), in particular—composes in the relative "middle" of the history, looking forward to an "end" that has not yet occurred and that can only be discerned, as Shelley observes, in the "gigantic shadows which futurity casts upon the present."[4] This is the point at which the Romantic artist draws upon myth as a means of shoring up his or her view of that future ending, arguing by overt or implied analogy in an effort to give shape to the present so that the future may *be* shaped by a public acting in enlightened partnership with the visionary artist.

Technological advancements in the publishing industry in the later eighteenth and early nineteenth centuries led to a mass dissemination of writing, under which name I include not merely "literature" but indeed all published and therefore public writing.[5] This print media explosion inevitably first increased and then subdivided (or compartmentalized) the reading public into a multiplicity of publics whose interests, aspirations, and values—not to mention "tastes"—have subsequently tended to be at ever greater variance. One inevitable result of the division of readerships along lines of special interests was the displacement of literature (and "fine" art generally) from relative cultural centrality to an increasingly peripheral position. Both the works emanating from this now seemingly tangential line of art and their authors became increasingly inaccessible to the general reading public, who, not surprisingly, responded defensively to the intimidating effect of such unfamiliar work by labeling works and artists alike as elite, "high

14

brow," and so forth. Adopting language at once judgmental and prejudicial, they rhetorically relocated the source of—and hence the responsibility for—their own intellectual and imaginative shortcomings not in themselves but in others. To take this position is to assert the superiority of one's own more familiar preferences, to the increasing chagrin of the ostracized artists, who remain almost evangelically convinced of both the cultural significance and the ultimate rectitude of their vision.

The response to their unappreciative audiences of these voices crying in the wilderness of modern culture is perhaps epitomized in the opening lines of Yeats's "Lapis Lazuli":

> I have heard hysterical women say
> They are sick of the palette and fiddle-bow,
> Of poets that are always gay,
> For everybody knows or else should know
> That if nothing drastic is done
> Aeroplane and Zeppelin will come out,
> Pitch like King Billy bomb-balls in
> Until the town lie beaten flat.[6]

Yeats's real concern is not with the apparent disjunction between art (and artists) and the "real" public world in which wars are fought and citizens die, but rather with the plain fact that this disjunction is illusory, not real, and that the very notion of its existence is fallacious, grounded not in reality but in hysteria. As the remainder of Yeats's poem demonstrates, though art transcends temporal reality in its timeless vision *and effects*, it also holds the potential to transform that temporal present, and hence to alter the future, by engendering a restorative activity that involves not only artist, work, and audience but also the entire social superstructure in a dynamic interchange. In short, Yeats restores art to the position of centrality from which a century of Western culture and criticism had gradually banished it.

Yeats, the first major critic to appreciate the sophistication of Blake's mythology and whose own work bears the unmistakable influence of Shelley's, shared with his Romantic predecessors the impulse to integrate art with temporal society and hence with history. Like them, Yeats understood the complex relation that inheres between, on the one hand, literature and history, and, on the other, myth, which plays a significant part—whether explicitly or implicitly—in both. Yeats's practice recalls the classical Greek view that regularly conflated history and myth without the insistence upon

strict chronological and temporal fidelity that had come to characterize, especially in Germany, later eighteenth-century empirical historiography. Yeats's energetic embrace of the invigorating function of
myth in his art is in many ways reminiscent of the project undertaken by all the major writers of the Romantic period who endeavored to compose works that were at once timely—directly relevant
to contemporary events and phenomena—and timeless—apropos
of the most enduring and universal aspects of human experience. In
a real sense, these artists sought to mediate between, and ultimately to transcend, the apparently contrary imperatives that govern empirical historicism and creative mythmaking. As White
observes, the poet, unrestricted by the limitations imposed by mere
"facts," enjoys far greater freedom in her or his work: the poet "is
free to invent 'facts' as he sees fit."[7] White's Hegelian model is strik-
ingly appropriate for the manner in which the artists of the English
Romantic period treated history in their works, in whatever medium. For the Romantics, history was no mere record of "things
that have been," but a vast storehouse of materials that the artist
might employ in an effort to resurrect the past in service to the
future.

Despite popular misperceptions of the Romantic artists as im-
practical, ethereal dreamers wandering in endlessly blooming fields
of flowers, or as egotistical rebels self-destructively defying the status quo, the Romantics were committed social reformers who regarded their public art not just as prophetic but also as distinctly
patriotic. From the arguments by analogy against war with France
embedded in both Wordsworth's early "An Evening Walk" (published in 1793 by the radical London publisher Joseph Johnson) and
Blake's *America: A Prophecy* (also 1793) to the corresponding argument by analogy on Liberty's behalf nearly 30 years later in Shelley's *Hellas*, the Romantics regularly invoked history in service to
politics, in an effort to let historical phenomena speak their own
counsel within works intended to expand and significantly *shape* the
social, political, and moral conscience of a diversifying contemporary English reading public. Blake and Shelley were in agreement
on the prophet's role, each seeing in the prophet not an "Arbitrary
Dictator" (as Blake puts it) but rather a keenly observant and public-
spirited activist and student of history able to predict, in general
terms, the shape and spirit of the future by examining the past and
the present.[8] The Romantic prophets had in common with religious
and secular prophets of all ages both an abiding conviction of
the essential correctness of their vision and an often painfully diffi-

cult mission of presenting unpopular views to a typically hostile audience.

Part of the public resistance to the Romantic prophet's message—whether that message was eminently practical (like Shelley's *Proposal for Putting Reform to the Vote throughout the Kingdom,* 1817) or visionary and idealistic (the same author's *Prometheus Unbound,* 1819)—stemmed from the prophet's assault upon the status quo embodied in the values and belief system of the very public the prophet sought to recall to the "straight and narrow" path from which it had apparently strayed. The Romantic prophet echoes the biblical injunction from on high, "Return, ye backsliding children" (Jer. 3.22), chastizing the nation or public for its own good, as Wordsworth does in his sonnets of August and September 1802. No one enjoys being told she or he is wrong, however, nor being corrected—especially in public, so the prophet necessarily begins at a disadvantage. Moreover, openly to criticize the state or its representatives during and shortly after the nearly quarter-century of hostilities with France was to risk both physical and financial hardship, as we see from the experiences of journalists like Daniel Isaac Eaton, John and Leigh Hunt, and Richard Carlile, of reform activists like Sir Francis Burdett and Henry "Orator" Hunt, and of less socially and politically powerful figures like Samuel Bamford and his Manchester acquaintances or—more pointedly—the Derbyshire rebels Jeremiah Brandreth, Isaac Ludlam, and William Turner, executed under questionable circumstances by the government in 1817.[9]

One recourse for the Romantic artist was to turn to history, and to employ the materials it afforded as a means of addressing current, pressing issues. The occurrence of the French Revolution even as England was still congratulating itself on the centenary of its own Glorious Revolution lent early impetus to this sort of "recycling" of past history to present purposes, as did the wave of millennialism that swept England at much the same time. Blake's early prophecies—*America, Europe,* and *The Song of Los* in particular—demonstrate the complex process by which that artist reformulated history and elevated it to the status of myth. In treating George III (about whom he could not write explicitly) first as Albion's Angel and later, in broader monarchical and patriarchal terms, as Urizen (about both of whom he *could* write), Blake abandoned the position of Aristotle's historian for that of his poet, "inventing" the universals by which *all* kings, *all* "fathers," might be recognized and repudiated by a public ready to embrace genuine liberty. That Blake's mythology became increasingly complex, increasingly internalized, as his vision of what was possible in the mortal world of the Napoleonic ascendency darkened, should not distract us from its demonstrable origins in temporal history and in the verbal and visual art that both celebrated and manipulated that history.

Indeed, for all his idiosyncrasies, Blake is in fact representative of his period's interest in investing history with the properties of myth. As the historian J. H. Plumb writes, "the more literate and sophisticated the society becomes, the more complex and powerful become the uses to which the past is put."[10] Eighteenth-century history painters (like the Americans-in-England Benjamin West and John Singleton Copley) had become accustomed in works like *The Death of General Wolfe* (1770) and *The Death of Major Peirson* (1783) to grafting contemporary fallen military or political figures onto the near end of a visual tradition of fallen warriors (and Depositions and Pietàs), thereby conferring upon their subjects a complex mythic and typological status that the sophisticated viewer could recognize and assess. The Romantic verbal artist often undertook something of the same sort, with the most frequent mythic types being Prometheus and Jesus Christ, on the positive side, and Satan (especially Milton's Satan), on the negative. Cain (and his fictional descendants) supplies a sort of middle ground of spiritual and psychological torment, from works like Schiller's influential play *The Robbers* (1781) through Byron's *Cain* (1821). The Romantics' frequent invocation in their works of a specifically Miltonic context complicates matters further still, for it invested the mythmaking process with a specifically *literary* dimension, as well as with a nationalistic one that reflects both the growing nationalism of eighteenth- and early nineteenth-century art generally and the lionizing of Milton that figured increasingly in eighteenth-century English art. Milton's works—reputation, in fact—offer an example of how the convergence of art, history, and myth can overleap the normally rigid boundaries between "fine art" and popular culture. James Gillray's famous caricature *Sin, Death, and the Devil* (1792), for instance, presses into immediately topical political service the famous and frequently illustrated confrontation of Satan, Sin, and Death from *Paradise Lost*. Only recently, through reassessments of history painters like Benjamin West and James Barry and through interdisciplinary cultural studies like Ronald Paulson's *Representations of Revolution*, has it begun to be clear just how large a part this same mythologizing impulse played in the visual arts of the later eighteenth century and the

Romantic period.[11] History proved to be a singularly well-suited host and vehicle for Romantic mythmaking, which operates by building upon a common ground (ostensibly shared by artist and audience) of widely known (or reputed) and accepted facts and pseudo facts.

Although myths, as culturally encompassing (and empowering) "stories," are themselves seldom strictly historical in nature or even in substance, they do provide, as Northrop Frye contends, a "kind of containing form of tradition" that frequently results in "the obliterating of boundaries separating legend, historical reminiscence, and actual history."[12] Frye's view is that myth performs an ultimately social (or socializing) role in art, engendering among the audience members the consciousness of community (as happens in the performance of an epic, for instance).[13] That is, myth functions actively in the "making" of a universe in human terms. It participates in a creative activity shared by artist (who both formulates and "forms" the work), the audience (who "re-forms" it in apprehending it within the context of individual and social sensibilities, expectations, and belief systems), and the work itself (which embodies or objectifies in a formal object of perception both determinate and indeterminate signifiers for actual and virtual phenomena). The universalizing organic nature of myth assumes (or presupposes) a fundamental unity in human experience; remove a sufficient number of particularizing temporal details (Blake's "Minute Particulars") and the underlying mythic pattern will emerge. Hence for Frye, the real value of what Aristotle calls the "discovery" *(anagnorisis)*— which Frye terms "recognition"—lies in the gradual dawning of personal, social, or cultural identification it precipitates among the audience; at some point previously concealed truth emerges into full view, full consciousness.[14]

The social function served by the telling and retelling of the "story" that the myth generates in endless, ever-related versions is central to Frye's view of myth, as it is to the structuralist enterprise with which it shares so many important features. This shared act of "making" is an act of community that simultaneously validates the roles played in the dis-covering of "truth" by storyteller, "listener," *and story*: by just such countless repetitions across time and space do actions become ritual, stories become myth. Their fundamental "truths" are built up by a process of accretion that increasingly locates them, socially and culturally, within the realm of what the audience comes to believe "has always been known"—within a belief system that both permeates and shapes the community. McGann's observation about the myth of Socrates that Plato presents in the *Lesser Hippias* is applicable in the present discussion: "the content of the myth is neither allegorical nor empirical, it is functional."[15] Functional—operative not simply within a text per se, but in the wider human context of a social community, because knowledge (or "discovery," or "recognition") is not an absolute but rather a function of any individual's daily personal and social interaction within that community. If "truth must be understood in relation to one's social investments," as McGann argues,[16] then we must accept with the Romantic artists that truth—like the myths that provide its vehicles—exists in both a personal and a *social* context, subject to the vicissitudes of the times in which it is manifested in works of art and apprehended there by its audiences. Paradoxically, the ahistorical nature of myth is determined and revealed within the context of historical time, whose temporal Minute Particulars it subsumes in its timeless universality. To this matrix of history and myth Romantic artists and works like those examined in this volume insistently return for their characteristic force. This matrix is the real source of their urgency: they are inextricably interwoven with a public world and driven by the artist's conviction of the significance of his or her own peculiar contribution to "a redemptive and transforming artistic practice"[17] for which the work of art is both a temporal and ultimately an atemporal vehicle.

If myth may be pressed into service to enhance history and historical consciousness, so also may history function to enhance myth. Outfitting modern phenomena—whether strictly contemporaneous or not—with the trappings of myth updates that mythological context, lending it increased and particular modern relevance. Encasing a historical personage or event within a shell of mythic allusion locates the individual or incident within a tradition, a continuum, making it difficult any longer to treat that person or event as a fluke of history, as a unique and inexplicable phenomenon. The mythologizing impulse faces, Janus-like, in two directions at once. Hence the danger faced by the possessors of power when they attach to their opponents the labels supplied by the mythology of orthodox belief systems. In, for instance, Blake's *America: A Prophecy*, whose complex Preludium Michael Ferber examines in this volume, Albion's Angel effectively legitimizes the revolt of Orc by his very attempt to discredit it through the litany of appositives he hurls at Orc:

> Blasphemous Demon, Antichrist, hater of Dignities;
> Lover of wild rebellion, and transgresser of Gods Law.[18]

Each of these names locates Orc, either explicitly ("Antichrist") or implicitly ("Lover of wild rebellion") within particular mythic contexts, thus establishing for Orc a complex lineage. He is not, now, a mere aberration, a monstrous abortion of an otherwise properly functioning system. Rather, he is the latest manifestation of a type whose presence has been felt sufficiently often in human affairs to have defined a mythic heritage.

What Albion's Angel *intends*, of course, in thus naming his opponent, is to validate his own credentials. He castigates Orc in terms that indicate how he conceives himself: if Orc is the violator of God's law, then Albion's Angel is of course God. Just how absurdly inverted is Albion's Angel's view of things is underscored by Blake's telling illumination to plate 4, in which we see Albion's Angel, just before he begins to rail at "serpent-form'd" Orc, metamorphosed before our eyes from human to dragon form in an ironic inversion of the familiar English trope of Saint George and the Dragon. In the context of 1793, George proves to be not "Saint" but dragon; England's "guardian angel" devastates the nation rather than protecting it.

The act of naming is central to both the mythologizing and the demythologizing projects undertaken by the Romantic authors. As Eric Walker argues here, Wordsworth's *refusal* to name Wellington in the aftermath of his part in the events leading up to, and devolving from, the Convention of Cintra denies Wellington a place in the pantheon of mythic heroes—of "liberators"—that poems like the "Thanksgiving Ode" (1816) and "Dion" (1816) laud. This antonomastic impulse stems from the poet's own understanding of the memorializing power of myth: to deny Wellington a name is to exclude him from the community simultaneously created and addressed in nationalistic poetry of the sort that contemporaries like Southey were composing. In countering that mythologizing tendency, however, Wordsworth in fact relies upon his readers' familiarity with its conventions. Readers are expected to recognize in the poet's refusal to satisfy (and therefore reinforce) their expectations the point of his antonomastic enterprise. Generating a paradoxical, unconventional myth of anonymity, Wordsworth relocates the heroic to the sphere of ordinary human affairs, much as Byron does in quite another context, as the essays in this volume by Edward Duffy and Shirley Clay Scott show.

Duffy demonstrates how Byron explores and exploits the conventions of Romantic mythology, frequently appropriating to his own authorial posture the context of Miltonic prophecy and deploying it against the lesser verbal powers of contemporaries like Southey. In a work like *The Vision of Judgment*, Duffy argues, Byron undercuts and subverts the Romantic mythological conception of human experience. But he does so by adopting and adapting strategies and tropes familiar to more conventional mythmakers, turning them against themselves—and against those who employ them—in poems that serve not to gather the universalizing energies of mythology but rather to disperse them. In *The Vision of Judgment*, Scott contends further, Byron deliberately invokes the myth-*demolishing* power of poetry systematically to reduce the stature of contemporary historical figures and events. Instead of converting history into myth, Byron follows in the steps of Seneca in the *Apocolocyntosis* and transforms history into humor, a transformation as devastating as it is delightful.

Nicholas Roe's essay takes up still another aspect of names and naming among the Romantics. Focusing upon the image of the "Star" (both in its astronomical sense and in the sense in which the word has subsequently been applied to celebrities), Roe traces how Milton functioned as political icon for Wordsworth in the period from 1792 to 1802 and how Wordsworth subsequently functioned as icon of the "lost leader" for Shelley in 1816. This imagistic connection between the two subjects carries through to Keats's poems of 1819, Roe argues, where the presence of this pattern of images in an apparently apolitical context proves to be very political indeed. Again, the catalyst is the act of naming, directly or indirectly, an act inextricably bound up with the story-telling aspect of myth.

In a related light, Brooke Hopkins's essay demonstrates how the naming of Robespierre in *The Prelude* functions in Wordsworth's historically grounded self-analysis. A particularly striking representative of the Satanic failure to channel creative energy and power into constructive activities, the "sea-green Incorruptible" to whom Carlyle would likewise devote considerable attention functions in *The Prelude* as a contrary to the sort of creative liberator Wordsworth aspired, as poet and prophet, to be. By creating in his narrative a complex overlaying of historical and mythic (Miltonic as well as biblical) elements, Wordsworth elevates the supposedly personal and decidedly historicizing activity of poetic autobiography to the extrapersonal level of the mythic. He traces in his relationship with the man to whom he initially had been attracted a mythic and historical analogue for the perils of social, political, and intellectual seduction to which Wordsworth believes his audience is just as susceptible as he had been.

Christina Root discusses a similar phenomenon in Byron's poetry, examining in *Lara, Manfred,* and *Don Juan* the complex interweaving of the myths of Napoleon and of the Byronic hero as Byron himself epitomized it. Byron engineers this parallel intentionally, she argues, to highlight the dramatically different results of these two figures' impact upon the destiny of Europe. Viewed both as historical and as archetypal figure, Napoleon is a crux in Byron's speculations on the possibilities and purposes of individual striving, and on the personality of the overreacher. Whereas Root considers a contemporary analogue, Lynn Byrd details Byron's choice of the historically distant figure of Sardanapalus for his presentation of an archetypally androgynous hero. Byrd's discussion of the Assyrian king's refusal to conform to his subjects' expectations reveals a surprising parallel to the situation of the most striking contemporary prince of pleasure, the Prince Regent. If the poised and witty Sardanapalus is ultimately a "timeless" figure caught between the historical past that has produced him and the line of mighty kings that would succeed him, so too may the Prince Regent inhabit an analogous *present* moment out of time. And so too may Byron and his Byronic heroes.

Myth helps establish through the work of art a broader context within which to examine persons and events. Thus the history of a particular family disaster, like that Shelley explores in *The Cenci* (which my own essay considers), may be viewed not as an isolated case but rather as a particular temporal manifestation of a universal pattern in human experience. J. Peter Euben has pointed out that classical Greek tragedy provides a vehicle for the juxtaposition of familiar stories and contemporary politics.[19] These plays offer analogues that facilitate discussion of present issues, present crises, by removing them momentarily from the immediacy of what is current, by distancing them somewhat from the temporal reality of the audience's own personal, social, or political reference system. Thus insulated from the threatening "now-ness" of immediately topical discussion, individuals may publicly articulate feelings and fears that might otherwise be expressed only awkwardly and obliquely, if at all. This is precisely the didactic purpose that underlies *The Cenci.* Shelley's great tragedy is a dramatic argument by historical analogy intended to caution an increasingly restive English public against the self-destructive nature of revenge as a means of redressing real or perceived wrongs. Intended for the Covent Garden stage, Shelley's play was meant to serve as an eleventh-hour appeal for moderation and humane justice, as a brake upon the accelerating cycle of domestic repression, violence, and retaliation the bloody culmination of which was the Manchester massacre (derisively dubbed "Peterloo" by the radical press) of 16 August 1819.

As Euben observes, classic drama offers a means of expanding the political agenda by "bringing before the public issues, such as mortality, madness, piety, and passion, that are usually consigned to specialists or private life."[20] The Romantic artists were, for the most part, the first to have to come to grips with the growing divisions among both social *and reading* (or art-consuming) publics. The increasing privatization of discussion about compelling moral, ethical, social, and political issues posed an enormous threat not only to an informed society generally but especially to artists, who found themselves being edged out of the discussion by the "specialists," a trend that has continued virtually unabated in the modern world. If the Romantic artists perceived the beginnings of a sort of academic division that undermined their traditional function, it was up to them to eliminate the intrusive middlemen, to carry the case back to the people. This democratizing impulse informs Wordsworth's advertisement to the *Lyrical Ballads* of 1798 and shapes the more elaborate philosophical and aesthetic program delineated in his Preface to the second and subsequent editions. It is the power, too, that drives Shelley to conceive *The Cenci* as a play for a largely undifferentiated popular audience, a truly "general" public. Yet even before setting out in 1819 to address this mass audience, Shelley had already recognized the need in his prose and poetry to define multiple and often mutually exclusive audiences, and to address them in forms and language appropriate to—even limited to— what he conceived to be the nature and disposition of those readerships.[21]

Myth offered the Romantics a way to get around—at least temporarily—some of these difficulties. It provided a means for examining contemporary phenomena, a vehicle that by its very nature lent artist and audience alike a measure of security from immediate physical or psychological threat and hence a greater degree of freedom to assess and discuss. Enlightened public discussion was the foundation of the renovation of human institutions advocated in William Godwin's philosophy, as it had been in Plato's and as it would be in Shelley's:

> If we would arrive at truth, each man must be taught to enquire and think for himself. . . . The indefatigable votary of justice and truth . . . will mix at large among his species; he will converse with men of all orders and parties. . . . Truth, and above all political truth, is not hard

of acquisition, but from the superciliousness of its possessors. It has been slow and tedious of improvement, because the study of it has been relegated to doctors and civilians. It has produced little effect upon the practice of mankind, because it has not been allowed a plain and direct appeal to their understandings. Remove these obstacles, render it the common property, bring it into daily use, and we may reasonably promise ourselves consequences of inestimable value.[22]

The appeal of such a democratization of public discourse is reflected not just in Godwin's great influence upon artists, thinkers, and leaders of his time but also, and perhaps more significantly, in his popularity among that more "general" public who bought (often by pooling their meager resources), read, and discussed *Political Justice* so widely that there was probably much truth in Godwin's characteristically egotistical remark that by October 1794 it appeared that he "was nowhere a stranger."[23]

The British Romantic artists whose work is considered in this volume saw in the intersection of history and myth a means of elucidating present issues by exposing their relation to past ones, both in their temporal manifestations in actual events and in their deeper presence in the archetypal patterns underlying and informing human experience. Fully appreciating the legitimizing power of history in the construction and perpetuation of myth, they would probably have concurred in Hans-Georg Gadamer's observation that "the classical is what resists historical criticism because its historical dominion, the binding power of its validity that is preserved and handed down, precedes all historical reflection and continues through it. What we call classical does not require a separate act of overcoming historical distance. In its constant communication it does overcome it."[24] Gadamer's point is that the "classical" work (by which I here mean, in broad terms, a work that has established itself across time within the culture, whether it has entered a more or less officially recognized canon or not) is essentially timeless. Classical works ultimately divest themselves of the Minute Particulars of immediate topical and temporal reference because their audiences perform that divestiture for them in the acts of contemplating and judging, of perceiving the similarities that outweigh the differences. In this process these works approach the simultaneous universality and autonomy we associate with myth, coming to reflect the organic expansiveness Coleridge, Keats, and Hegel all associated with the highest forms of art, the capacity to possess expressive and generative power of greater scope and significance than any particular statement made within an individual work.[25]

History and myth, then, are mutually enhanced through the expansion of public consciousness that is the logical product of their confluence in individual works of art. As the person or event is elevated to greater cultural significance through the mythologizing process, so is the myth (or mythic pattern) likewise both expanded and extended. Especially during a period of momentous social, political, or economic upheaval (such as the period of 1789–1820, dominated by the French Revolution and its repercussions), the increased interest in history reflects society's instinctive search for the reassuring explanations that history is assumed to provide.[26] But these historical answers are in fact part of a cumulative mythology in which they serve as analogues, as "stories" replete with topical, temporal relevance. In the two-line passage from Blake's *America* that I cited earlier the religious and secular mythologies Blake invokes work in concert with the details of the actual historical event, so that a mutually productive cross-fertilization occurs. The myth is brought up to date and made relevant to the audience's immediate experience by the artist who reveals its persistence in temporal reality.

The realization that the archetypal patterns of human experience that underlie Western mythology are in fact timeless, that their periodic particularizations in certain worldly events, persons, *or works of art* are in fact merely manifestations in temporal form of eternal realities is at the heart of Blake's project in his historical prophecies, as it is in Shelley's in works as diverse as *The Revolt of Islam* (under which title the altered *Laon and Cythna* was published), *Prometheus Unbound*, and *The Cenci*. Their art grounded in this conviction, artists like Blake and Shelley recognize that the real significance of the past—of history, the record of the past—lies not in the great differences it reveals between "then" and "now," but rather in the instructive similarities it discloses. Echoing Margaret Leslie's vigorous apology for historical consciousness, Euben observes that "insistence on the radical otherness of the past precludes the perception of similarity in otherness that is the lifeblood of analogical thinking."[27] Analogical thinking grew ever more attractive to English artists in the increasingly dangerous and repressive atmosphere of post-French Revolution England, just as it had, for different reasons, proved of great utility to English history painters during the previous century. It offered an effective way to embody in apparently historical works statements immediately relevant to contemporary affairs.

26

As Jeffrey Cox demonstrates briefly in this volume, and in greater detail in *In the Shadows of Romance,*[28] the employment of the past—especially the recent, Revolutionary past—in service to present crises and future states was also a notable feature of English Romantic theater. There we encounter increasingly mythologized treatments of the French Revolution, ranging from early documentary works like John Dent's *The Bastille* (1789) to fully mythologized works like Shelley's *Prometheus Unbound* and *The Cenci,* which translate the historical event into the realm of mythic romance. Indeed, Shelley himself documents this progression in the arts generally, remarking that his poem *Laon and Cythna* represents a revolution of which the French Revolution is "the *beau ideal.*"[29] The common thread in such mythologizing of history is the rhetorical device of the argument by analogy.

Of course, as M. H. Abrams pointed out long ago, "the endemic disease of analogical thinking is hardening of the categories."[30] The essays in this volume illustrate in their diversity the flexibility of the categories toward which analogical thinking ideally tends, even as they recognize the efficacy of analogical argument as an instrument for the manipulation of public consciousness. The various contexts for individual works and authors formulated by the contributors to this volume point to a broader range of virtual contexts that, in their agreements and their disagreements alike, demonstrate the healthy resistance of both history and art to the imposition of absolute values and judgments. For the definition of contexts is ultimately as much an act of interpretation as is the explication of texts. It is an attempt to formulate on a flexible and constantly expanding continuum a set of relative values and points of reference for those who would understand the relation of the texts in question to the periods from which they arose and in which they are now assessed. Something of this pluralistic view of interpretation informs Gadamer's view of historical inquiry. Gadamer sees interpretation as "a fusion of horizons in which, like participants in a Socratic dialogue, we seek to understand a text, action, or culture and ourselves as understanders, actors, and cultural beings."[31] This view accords with McGann's wish to return literary (and artistic or aesthetic) inquiry to social centrality, which position both McGann and Gadamer believe is indicated and occupied by the dialogues of Socrates as Plato records them.

What we seek in attempting to uncover the relative truth of the past is neither absolute Truth nor any absolute reconstitution of the Past, but rather, as McGann contends, a greater awareness of the complex and often self-contradictory body of ideas and images whose forms, formulations, and reformulations make up "an eventual (performative) history."[32] But we should acknowledge too the danger inherent in historicist studies: the tendency to discover not the actual nature of the past, its artifacts, and its contexts but rather a projection of our own expectations and presuppositions upon the objects of our contemplation. Viewing our material through lenses of our own making, we run the risk of distorting even as we claim to focus and to clarify. Truth necessarily resides in a diversity of viewpoints, and in the energizing dialogue those viewpoints institute with one another and with both the reader and the historical and textual materials themselves. In other words, *e pluribus multum*—a potentially liberating dynamism.

Typically, the Romantic artist is far more didactic than is generally recognized. The question for such an artist is not whether or not to be didactic, but rather "how to be didactic most tellingly."[33] The mythological formulations involved in the treatment of history and historical analogues in a significant number of works by these artists tells us much about their sense of myth's universalizing potential, and about their commitment to harnessing that potential in service to the identification and eradication of what they perceived as pervasive and pernicious errors of human behavior.

In *A Vision of the Last Judgment* (ca. 1809–10), Blake wrote,

Error is Created[;] Truth is Eternal[.] Error or Creation will be
Burned Up & then & not till then Truth or Eternity will appear[.]
It is Burnt up the Moment Men cease to behold it.[34]

Public art provides a vehicle by which Error may be given concrete form (objectified) so that it may be recognized and repudiated. This conviction forms the foundation of Blake's verbal and visual work and significantly informs the works of his Romantic contemporaries. Minna Doskow examines one example of this mythic objectification in Blake's work, showing how that radical mythologizer treats several key figures in the history of ideas (Newton, Locke, and Bacon in particular), transforming them into symbols of crushing mechanistic power and archetypal figurations of the eternal oppressors, the "Restrainers of Desire" who labor to limit humanity. But if art may facilitate this repudiation of the false, the outworn, the devastating, so too may it objectify or project Truth so that it may be embraced either consciously (as in *Prometheus Unbound*) or unconsciously (as in the community response to the old Cumberland beggar, in Wordsworth's poem of that name). The poet's task is, as Judith Chernaik writes concerning Shelley, "to reaffirm the eternal principle of freedom surviving the repeated secular (hence temporary) triumphs of tyranny, and to prophesy for present struggles the eventual breaking of the cycle" of history in a final, definitive triumph of liberty.[35] The tragic impasse in which Shelley's *Cenci* concludes exposes the faulty nature of the entire conventional patriarchal social and political structure. Here is the embodiment, in the form of a historical analogue, of the Error which must be repudiated so that Truth may assume its sway. That impasse need persist only so long as society fails to discover the truth whose embrace would resolve it. To this moment of public discovery, this social *anagnorisis*, the Romantic artists committed their efforts. This raises one final issue: the artist's social responsibility in "forcing the issue" within the public forum.

As should be clear from this introduction—and as becomes clearer still in the essays that follow—all the artists considered here were acutely aware that their art might possess (actually or potentially) significant public impact in social, political, moral, and ethical terms. Hence all of them inevitably question at least occasionally both the immediate public efficacy and the ultimate epistemological validity of their undertaking. Works that are most fully engaged in making history into myth therefore often examine at the same time both the nature and the consequences of that transformation and elevation of materials.

In large measure, English Romantic mythologization of history is nothing more (or less) than a complex refocusing of perspective, a pulling back from a close-up view—to adopt the cinematic metaphor—to a wide-angle view. In Blake's *America* the section called "A Prophecy" provides the close-up, and the "Preludium" presents the wide-angle, mythic paradigm of which "A Prophecy" constitutes a single illustration. Similar judgments might be made about the moving perspectives embodied in *Prometheus Unbound, The Prelude,* and *Don Juan.* In all of this shifting of both external and internal perspective, we may discern the influence of Skepticism, to whose fundamental premises the Romantics were irresistibly drawn even as they strove against them in their search for timeless, assertive absolutes whose names they might capitalize and whose essences they might embrace. Within this skeptical context of intellectual attraction and rejection, P. M. S. Dawson discusses *The Triumph of Life* not as a mythologization of history but rather as a thoughtful skeptical critique of all such mythologizations. Dawson argues that Shelley's last poem represents the culmination of a skeptical view of history (and its treatment by artists, as opposed to historians) whose roots may be discerned in the poet's earlier writings.

This matter of the artist's public responsibility is central to the mythmaking activity itself. Art is finally a public activity, and artists must accept the responsibility for what they set in motion through their works: this is the terrible lesson from which Victor Frankenstein flees in vain. Like the making of art, of which process it is a culturally significant portion, the mythologization of history is a seductive process whose workings are never far removed from those of propaganda, which Jacques Ellul describes as the orchestrated manipulation of belief systems in service to "the formation of men's attitudes."[36] The artist claims to work in service neither to systems nor to institutions—nor even to any particular view of truth—but to Truth itself. But Truth exists not in the quantifiable absolutes toward which empirical philosophy or empirical historiography strives. Rather, it lies in a complex, shifting, and ever-expanding dialogue. For the Romantics and their post-Romantic heirs, its essence is public rather than private, social rather than reclusive, eternal rather than temporal, a going-out of the individual self in an act of community that Shelley describes in *A Defence of Poetry.* Yet, however we may aspire to define that essential truth which is the goal of all inquiry, it must nevertheless be apprehended largely through its manifestations in temporal phenomena, which, as Kant appropriately observed, are themselves analogues: the spectacles with which we are all born and which we can never remove.[37] This process cannot go forward except in the forum of public discussion, the paradigm of which we find in the dialogues of Socrates and his contemporaries. To the continuation of that dialogical process the contributors to this volume have addressed their efforts and voices.

Notes

1. *Poetics,* in *The Basic Works of Aristotle,* ed. Richard McKeon (New York: Random House, 1941), p. 1464.

2. Jerome J. McGann, *Social Values and Poetic Acts: The Historical Judgment of Literary Work* (Cambridge, Mass.: Harvard Univ. Press, 1988), p. 23.

3. Hayden White, *Metahistory: The Historical Imagination in Nineteenth-Century Europe* (Baltimore: Johns Hopkins Univ. Press, 1973), pp. 5–7.

4. *A Defence of Poetry,* in *Shelley's Poetry and Prose,* ed. Donald H. Reiman and Sharon B. Powers (New York: W. W. Norton, 1977), p. 508.

5. See Richard D. Altick, *The English Common Reader: A Social History of the Mass Reading Public, 1800–1900* (Chicago: Univ. of Chicago Press, 1957); R. K. Webb, *The*

INTRODUCTION

British Working-Class Reader, 1790–1848: Literacy and Social Tension (London: George and Allen Unwin, 1955); Harry C. Payne, "Elite versus Popular Mentality in the Eighteenth Century," *Studies in Eighteenth-Century Culture,* Vol. 8, ed. Roseann Runte (Madison: Univ. of Wisconsin Press, 1979); Jon P. Klancher, "From 'Crowd' to 'Audience': The Making of an English Mass Readership in the Nineteenth Century," *ELH* 50 (1983); and E. P. Thompson *The Making of the English Working Class* (1963; rpt. New York: Vintage, 1966).

6. *W. B. Yeats: The Poems,* ed. Richard J. Finneran (New York: Macmillan, 1983), p. 294.

7. White, p. 89.

8. See Stephen C. Behrendt, " 'The Consequence of High Powers': Blake, Shelley, and Prophecy's Public Dimension," *Papers on Language and Literature* 22 (1986): 254–75. Blake's comment is in his annotations to Bishop Watson's *Apology for the Bible;* see *The Complete Poetry and Prose of William Blake,* ed. David V. Erdman, rev. ed. (Garden City, N.Y.: Doubleday, 1982), p. 617.

9. Eaton, the Hunts, and Carlile were all prosecuted and eventually imprisoned for their radical publishing activities. Burdett, the leading political reformer of the first three decades of the nineteenth century, was imprisoned for libel in 1810 over a public disagreement with the House of Commons. Hunt, the gentleman farmer turned powerful radical agitator, was imprisoned for his role in the "Peterloo Massacre" of 16 August 1819. This event is placed in its broader political and cultural context in *Passages in the Life of a Radical* (1845) by the radical diarist Bamford, who served a year's term for inciting riot at that extraordinary incident. Brandreth, Ludlam, and Turner, who were involved in the post-Luddite revolutionary plots in Derbyshire in 1817, fell victim in June of that year to government entrapment through the devices of the government spy and agent provocateur "Oliver the Spy." Following the abortive uprising in Pentrich, they were arrested, summarily convicted of treason, and executed. It is worth noting that Shelley much admired Burdett and took a particular interest in the affairs of all the others except Bamford (so far as we know): he wrote at various points in defense of Eaton, the Hunts, the Derbyshire rebels, and Carlile. Useful sketches of these figures appear in the first volume of *Bibliographical Dictionary of Modern British Radicals,* ed. Joseph O. Baylen and Norman J. Gossman (3 vols.; Hassocks, Sussex: Harvester; Atlantic Highlands, N.J.: Humanities, 1979–).

10. J. H. Plumb, *The Death of the Past* (Boston: Houghton Mifflin, 1970), p. 11.

11. Ronald Paulson, *Representations of Revolution (1789–1829)* (Princeton, N.J.: Princeton Univ. Press, 1983.

12. Northrop Frye, "Myth, Fiction, and Displacement," *Daedalus* (1961); rpt. *Fables of Identity: Studies in Poetic Mythology* (New York: Harcourt, Brace, and World, 1963), p. 31.

13. See, for instance, Frye's claim that "the function of the epic, in its origin, seems to be primarily to teach the nation, or whatever we call the social unit which the poet is addressing, its own traditions," traditions chiefly concerned with "the national religion and the national history" in *Fearful Symmetry: A Study of William Blake* (1947; rpt. Princeton, N.J.: Princeton Univ. Press, 1969), p. 316. This dawning of consciousness is of course related to what modern art refers to as an "epiphany"— the Joycean moment of comprehensive insight whose roots lie in the Greek oral tradition and which makes a sudden and dramatic modern reappearance in Blake's visions and in Wordsworth's "spots of time." See Ashton Nichols, *The Poetics of Epiphany: Nineteenth-Century Origins of the Modern Literary Moment* (Tuscaloosa: Univ. of Alabama Press, 1987).

14. Frye, "Myth, Fiction, and Displacement," pp. 25–26.

15. McGann, p. 30.

16. McGann, p. 29.

17. The phrase is McGann's (p. 41), but it merely distills what is implicit in the works of all the English Romantic authors, whether we consider the program of imaginative (and hence finally social) renovation that drives in different ways the poetry of Blake and Wordsworth or the sociopolitical (and likewise ultimately social) agenda that everywhere informs the work of an activist like Shelley.

18. *The Complete Poetry and Prose of William Blake*, pp. 53–54; *America* 7:5–6.

19. J. Peter Euben, "Preface," *Greek Tragedy and Political Theory*, ed. J. Peter Euben (Berkeley: Univ. of California Press, 1986), p. xi.

20. Euben, p. xi.

21. I have explored this phenomenon in detail in *Shelley and His Audiences: Reader Manipulation in the Prose and Poetry* (Lincoln: Univ. of Nebraska Press, 1989). Shelley is not unique in pursuing this strategy of defining and addressing particular audiences "on their own terms": Coleridge furnished Shelley with a timely model, as did—in another way—Jesus. Shelley's journalist friend Leigh Hunt offered the poet a graphic example of a writer whose success depended upon a clear "reading" of his intended audiences.

22. William Godwin, *Enquiry concerning Political Justice, and its influence on Morals and Happiness*, ed. F. E. L. Priestley (3 vols.; Toronto: Univ. of Toronto Press, 1946), I, 288–89, 297.

23. Godwin, III, 101.

24. Hans-Georg Gadamer, *Truth and Method* (New York: Continuum Books, 1975), p. 255.

25. Euben, "Introduction," *Greek Tragedy and Political Theory*, p. 3.

26. For further discussion of this point, which is central to the critical system of Lukacs, see especially Georg Lukacs, *The Historical Novel*, trans. Hannah and Stanley Mitchell (London: Merlin Press, 1962); Avrom Fleishman, *The English Historical Novel: Walter Scott to Virginia Woolf* (Baltimore: Johns Hopkins Univ. Press, 1971); and Richard Humphrey, *The Historical Novel as Philosophy of History* (London: Institute of Germanic Studies, 1986).

27. Euben, "Introduction," pp. 4–5. See also Margaret Leslie, "In Defense of Anachronism," *Political Studies*, 18 (1970), 442.

28. Jeffrey N. Cox, *In the Shadows of Romance: Romantic Tragic Drama in Germany, England, and France* (Athens, Ohio: Ohio Univ. Press, 1987).

29. *The Letters of Percy Bysshe Shelley*, ed. Frederick L. Jones (2 vols.; Oxford: Clarendon Press, 1964), I, 563.

30. M. H. Abrams, *The Mirror and the Lamp: Romantic Theory and the Critical Tradition* (1953; rpt. New York: W. W. Norton, 1958), pp. 34–35.

31. Euben, "Introduction," p. 19.

32. McGann, p. 7.

33. Ian Jack, *English Literature: 1815–1832* (Oxford: Clarendon Press, 1963), p. 78.

34. *Complete Poetry and Prose*, p. 565.

35. Judith Chernaik, *The Lyrics of Shelley* (Cleveland: Press of Case Western Reserve Univ., 1972), p. 115.

36. The phrase is the subtitle of Ellul's *Propaganda: The Formation of Men's Attitudes*, trans. Konrad Kellen and Jean Lerner (New York: Vintage, 1965).

37. Immanuel Kant, *Critique of Judgment* (1790).

The French Revolution in the English Theater

Jeffrey N. Cox

During the grand and terrible days of the French Revolution, history itself seemed to become theatrical. The Revolution had its stages in assembly halls, courtrooms, and scaffolds. It had its great actors in Mirabeau, Danton, St. Just. And events seemed to follow the rhythms of the drama, particularly dramatic tragedy. When Jean-François Ducis, playwright and adaptor of Shakespeare, was asked why he abandoned the drama in 1792, he responded, "Why talk to me . . . of composing tragedies? Tragedy walks the streets."[1]

Dramatists and theatrical managers were quick to seize upon the potential of these enormously theatrical events. Many of the more interesting plays of the late eighteenth and early nineteenth centuries can be read as attempts to dramatize the Revolution; as Victor Hugo proclaimed, "The physiognomy of this epoch will be determined only when the French Revolution, which personified itself in society in the form of Napoleon, personifies itself in art."[2] English writers would have agreed—with Shelley, for example, seeing the Revolution as the "master theme" of the epoch.[3] The attempt of romantic dramatists to "personify" the Revolution follows

33

an interesting path. We often think of literature arising within myth, then passing through such idealizing forms as the romance and high tragedy, before descending to such "realistic" forms as the novel and the prose drama.[4] The dramatizers of the Revolution, however, moved in the opposite direction, from the direct representation of actual events to the displacement of revolutionary acts into neoclassical and Gothic parallels and finally to the re-creation of the Revolution in mythic terms. As we will see, both governmental censors and revolutionary sympathizers had reasons for translating the representation of revolt from history to myth.

It comes as no surprise that Parisian theaters often moved events directly from the streets to the stage. Numerous plays celebrated the taking of the Bastille and the various national fêtes. Central events such as the flight of the king and his family to Varennes would throw theaters into a frenzy of competition to see which one would first and most successfully put the latest news on stage. Military victories often gave rise to such plays as *The Entrance of Dumouriez into Brussels* (L'Entrée de Dumouriez à Bruxelles; Théâtre-Français, Rue de Richelieu, 1793), which depicted a key French triumph but was a theatrical failure. We also find pieces devoted to revolutionary martyrs; Marat, who was celebrated as the "friend of the people" in a very successful play by that name (Gassier Saint-Armand's *L'Ami du peuple ou La Mort de Marat*; Variétés Amusantes, 1793), had his life and death dramatized at least six times.[5]

There was initially a parallel interest in bringing the deeds of the Revolution to the London stage, with key events sometimes being staged at several theaters at the same time. For example, in August of 1789, the Royal Circus, the Royal Grove (later Astley's), and Sadlers Wells all produced versions of the taking of the Bastille; and Covent Garden had a drama based on the events of 14 July in rehearsal only to have the play blocked by the Lord Chamberlain and his censor. The next summer found the same three "minor" theaters offering dramatizations of the national fête of 14 July 1790 in honor of the Federation. We can find less direct echoes of events in France in many plays, including popular spectacles such as J. C. Cross's *Julia of Louvain: or, Monkish Cruelty* (Royal Circus, 1797), which is taken, the published version tell us, "from a paragraph in a Newspaper during the French Revolution." Revolutionary events could even find their way into the popular harlequinade, with Charles Bonnor's *The Picture of Paris Taken in the Year 1790* (Covent Garden, 1790) mixing scenes of life under the Revolution with the antics of Harlequin and Columbine. Of course, not all these plays were sympathetic to the Revolution. For example, William Preston's *Democratic Rage: or, Louis the Unfortunate* castigated the rebels on stage in Dublin in 1793, in Charleston, S.C., in 1795, and in Boston in 1797. Coleridge and Southey joined this attempt to bring history into the theater when they wrote their *Fall of Robespierre* (1794).[6]

John Dent's *The Bastille*, which ran for 79 successive nights at the Royal Circus beginning in August 1789, provides a useful example of these early and usually popular attempts to stage the Revolution. The play's plot is simple. Henry Dubois meets with his beloved Matilda at the beginning of the play. They have a personal as well as political motive for wishing the Bastille to fall, for Matilda's father has been imprisoned after refusing to grant Matilda's hand to Henry's powerful rival. The play alternates between essentially public scenes—in which we see the people preparing to storm the Bastille—and scenes treating the private concerns of Henry, Matilda, and her father, who faces torture at the hands of the demonic governor of the prison. The people finally storm the Bastille with Henry at their head; they free Matilda's father, and the governor is led off to execution as his Cross of St. Louis is stripped from him and given to Henry. The play concludes with a grand celebration of liberty that culminates in praises of England, as an allegorical figure of Britannia descends holding portraits of the English king and queen while the statue of liberty is seen trampling the figure of despotism.

The play is in many ways a romance of revolution, with Henry snatching the imprisoned father from the instruments of torture and thus proving himself worthy of Matilda's love. The plot follows the three-part pattern Northrop Frye identifies with romance, as it moves from the preliminary minor adventures with Henry and the people readying their assault to the central struggle of the attack upon the Bastille itself and finally to the exaltation of the hero in the closing processional scene.[7]

However, Dent clearly intends this romance as in some sense documentary. Not only does he take pains to re-create actual places and events, but he also has Henry deliver in the final scene a long speech we are told is a translation of an oration delivered on 29 July to the French troops by Moreau de Saint-Méry.[8] Part of the play's appeal clearly lay in its claim to accuracy, as we can see from a favorable notice in the *Times* praising the drama as an entertainment in which "the bloody business of the Bastille . . . is dramatized into a regular story and brought to a denouement founded in truth."[9] We see similar claims in other plays where stage directions testify to the attempt to evoke revolutionary events and Parisian scenes in great detail. Covent Garden's *Picture of Paris Taken in the Year 1790*, for example, includes such sets as a "faithful representation of the celebrated Convent of the Jacobins, situated in Rue St. Honoré, part of which, according to an inscription on the Gate, is converted by the National Guard into a Guard House, or Rendezvous for the first Batallion of the Division of St. Roch."[10]

Of course, direct portrayals of actual revolutionary events were not tolerated for long by the government, as represented by the lord chamberlain and John Larpent, the examiner of plays.[11] After the success of plays such as Dent's *Bastille* at minor theaters, the patented theaters royal of Covent Garden and Drury Lane sought to offer plays that capitalized on these exciting events. In the autumn of 1789, Covent Garden prepared a play on the fall of the Bastille; but, as the author Frederick Reynolds tells us, "when the parts were studied, the scenery completed, and the music composed, the Lord Chamberlain refused his license."[12] Drury Lane was allowed to stage a play centering upon the Man in the Iron Mask—*The Island of St. Marguerite*, by John St. John (1789)—but only after allusions and parallels to the Bastille were dropped.[13] Apparently, it was felt that such performances at London's central theaters would lend a sanction to the reenactment of revolutionary events different in kind from performances at the minor theaters. Increasingly, any references to the Revolution were prohibited. For example, in November 1789 Covent Garden decided to revive a pantomime entitled *Harlequin Touchstone* and to include within the play a new scene depicting the procession of France's three Estates; the examiner of plays first banned the play and then apparently insisted that the procession be transferred to Rome while deleting several passages that might seem to embrace republican sentiments.[14] Again, *The Death of the Queen of France*, although a violently antirepublican play, was denied a license twice, in 1794 and in 1804, which suggests that the government was so squeamish about revolutionary events that any portrayal of them was suspect. Censorship was sufficiently prevalent by 1793 that almost all political comment was excluded from the drama. In fact, the lord chamberlain rarely had to exercise his power because theater managers became so sensitive about contemporary allusions that they became censors in their own right. As the author of the rejected *Helvetic Liberty* (1792) put it, the playwright who sought to bring political matters into the theater found "in that paradise . . . politics to be the forbidden fruit, lest the people's eyes should be opened and they become as gods knowing good and evil: in brief my Piece was politely returned, with an as-surance, that it was too much in favor of the liberties of the people, to obtain the Lord Chamberlain's licence for representation."[15]

Apparently, the official fear was that the theatrical re-creation of revolutionary events would lead to their reenactment on the streets. Herbert Lindenberger has noted that defenders of the drama—and of the historical drama in particular—have praised the theater's abil-ity to inspire by offering great historical figures that the audience will then desire to emulate; Lindenberger quotes Thomas Hey-wood, who says of convincing historical re-creation that "so be-witching a thing is lively and well spirited action, that it hath power to new mold the h[e]arts of the spectators and fashion them to the shape of any noble and notable attempts."[16] Similar views were ex-pressed during the Romantic period. Hazlitt, for example, in re-viewing *Coriolanus* as a play that he says includes all the ideas in "Burke's 'Reflections,' or Paine's 'Rights of Man,' or the debates in both Houses of Parliament since the French Revolution," argues that "we may depend upon it, that what men delight to read in books, they will put in practice in reality."[17] Again, John Haggit in his reactionary *Count de Villeroi* (1794) notes that the drama is "most powerfully calculated to influence the public mind" and laments that the English have not followed the French National Assembly who "by the pieces which they have ordered to be acted, as well as those composed for the purpose . . . have gained an astonishing in-crease of popularity to their cause, astonishing to those who have never considered the influence of theatrical performances." And, of course, the revolutionary government's extensive use of the drama as a means of molding opinion testifies to their belief in the power of the theater.[18]

The problem was that, if the historical drama inspired to "noble and notable attempts," it could also—at least in the eyes of the powers that be—"bewitch" audiences into imitating dangerous, re-bellious acts. The British government, concerned about any avowal of republican sentiments on the stage, was particularly bothered by the representation of mass or mob action. Although we can find crowd scenes in Dent's *Bastille* and in *The Picture of Paris,* they were prohibited in other cases, as we can see from the examiner's copies of the *Island of St. Marguerite,* which reveal the censor's anxiety to control the drama's inflammatory potential. Larpent had the theater recast the climactic scene in which a mob descends upon the evil Commandant's castle where the Man in the Iron Mask is impris-oned. In the original version, the crowd frees the prisoner and hauls the Commandant off to be executed—that is, the ending was essentially an exact parallel to the scene in which the Bastille is taken in Dent's play. In the version finally licensed, however, the Commandant comes out to the mob to tell them that the Man in the Iron Mask is within the castle and warns them not to turn "from liberty to license." He remains unharmed. Larpent also had potentially dangerous words removed from the mouths of the mob; republican sentiments were apparently less dangerous if voiced by a figure of authority, in this case an officer. As L. W. Conolly argues, giving the officer the potentially radical lines "lessens the *rapport* between gallery and stage and gives an air of respectability to the sentiments expressed."[19] If the populace was presented with the portrait of a unified and radical populace on stage, then it too might rise up. Shelley understood this potential, and tried to evoke and provoke the power of mass action in *The Mask of Anarchy,* a poem that owes much to dramatic precedent. The authorities feared the potential of communal dramatic experiences to create a revolutionary community; a vision such as that in *The Mask of Anarchy* could not be printed let alone performed.

Despite such censorship, playwrights could not ignore this revolutionary master theme; instead they sought to present it obliquely. One strategy—rarely successful, given the watchful censor—was to find historical parallels to the French Revolution in earlier uprisings. Plays were written—but not staged—about Wat Tyler and the Peasant's Revolt (e.g., Richard Cumberland's *Richard the Second*, revised as the uncontroversial *The Armorer* before the censor would allow it to be performed at Covent Garden in 1793; or Southey's *Wat Tyler*, written in 1794 but not published until 1817) or William Tell (e.g., *Helvetic Liberty*); anti-republican authors also found historical parallels, as in Arthur Murphy's unacted *Arminius* (1798). However, the writers of the romantic period did find ways to dramatize the issues surrounding the French Revolution in two more distant and more useful displacements of current events: in neoclassical tragedy they found the means to portray tyranny—not just the tyranny of individual rulers but the subtler tyranny that the past and tradition hold over the future; and in the Gothic drama, they discovered the means to explore their ambivalence toward the individual liberated by revolt.

The choice of neoclassical tragedy to represent the Revolution or revolutionary themes—a strategy we find in Goethe's *Natural Daughter* (*Die natürliche Tochter*; 1803), Byron's history plays, and innumerable, long forgotten dramas that filled the theaters of the

French Republic—might surprise us. In the age of Romanticism and revolution, neoclassicism might strike us as a preeminently conservative form. In France, however, in the works of artists such as David and dramatists such as Marie-Joseph Chenier, neoclassicism became the style of the Revolution, and this ideological tie was not without impact in England.[20] Plays on classical themes often received a political reading. We have already noted Hazlitt's comments on Shakespeare's *Coriolanus*. Sheridan Knowles's classical *Caius Gracchus* (1823; Drury Lane, 1823) and *Virginius* (Covent Garden, 1820) were both censored for their liberal ideas. This provoked Hazlitt to complain, "Is the name of Liberty to be struck out of the English language, and are we not to hate tyrants even in an old Roman play?"[21] The answer was given by George Coleman, examiner of plays after the death of Larpent, who told Bulwer-Lytton's parliamentary panel investigating the status of the theater that he would ban from the stage "anything that may be so allusive to the times as to be applied to the existing moment, and which is likely to be inflammatory." He then went on to note that the word *reform* might provoke a disturbance in a theater and that he would not permit a play about Charles the First, "because it amounted to every thing but cutting off the King's head upon the stage."[22] For him any historical incident that paralleled the Revolution was a dangerous provocation: neoclassicism could be another disguise for radical sentiments.

The most intriguing attempt to use neoclassical form to treat revolutionary matters occurs in Byron's three history plays, *Marino Faliero*, *The Two Foscari*, and *Sardanapalus* (all three 1821; *Marino Faliero* was performed that year at Covent Garden).[23] That these plays, which all center upon a struggle between tyranny and liberty, have a political, even revolutionary, theme has been noted by reviewers, both in Byron's day and our own; *Marino Faliero* was performed only in a heavily censored version; and Byron himself wrote to Kinnaird that the play "is full of republicanism."[24] Given this subject matter, readers often have been puzzled by Byron's choice of a neoclassical style. Still, we can see the appropriateness of his neoclassical form to his vision of revolt: the neoclassical form images the power of the past over the future that revolt would create. Significantly, when at the close of *Sardanapalus*, his most severely classical play, Byron wants his hero to offer a vision of the future—"a light / To lesson ages" (V, i, 440–41)—he shatters the play's neoclassical fetters in a grand romantic finale that inspired Delacroix's painting.

The power of the past over the future is asserted throughout the two Venetian plays. In *The Two Foscari*, all of the central male characters are fixated upon the past and tradition: Loredano is obsessed with revenge against the elder Foscari, for he believes the Doge to have murdered his father and uncle; the Doge himself is so tied to the traditional forms of Venetian law that he will do nothing to prevent the torturing of his son; and that son has brought this torture upon himself by an obsessive need to return to his ancestral home in Venice after he has been banished from it. The central image in the play sums up this entrapment in the past: the play opens with Loredano speaking of his account book in which he has entered Foscari's debt to him for the two lives of his kinsmen; it closes after the deaths of the two Foscari with Loredano closing out his account book over the collapsed body of the Doge. *The Two Foscari* is a play in which the present owes a debt to the past that binds the future to the patterns of violence that have marked previous history.

This vision of history—in which the future can never break free of the rhythms of the past—dominates Byron's vision even in *Marino Faliero, Doge of Venice*, which presents a revolutionary effort to free Venice from tyranny. The play analyzes a political situation in which a party of aristocrats have robbed Venice's nominal ruler, the Doge, of any power and denied the people their rights. The Doge thus joins a plebian revolt, hoping that a popular revolution will re-create Venice as a republic within which he can act freely and win the public acclaim he identifies with his heroic honor; his goal is to "free Venice and avenge my wrongs" (I, ii, 316). Yet this revolt for an ideal Venice is beset by contradictions that arise from Faliero's ultimate commitment to an idealized past rather than to a vision of the future. The heroic self-image that Faliero struggles to reassert is bound up with the city's traditional hierarchy and with the very nobles he must kill, for he is an aristocrat himself; as he realizes, "Each stab to them will seem my suicide" (III, ii, 402). If he does not act, he loses his powerful sense of himself to the political realities of a debased present. If he does act, he must move to destroy the social and political forms that in the past have been the supporters of his identity. Although he fights for the revolutionary regeneration of his society, his problems can be resolved only by a revival of a neoclassical world of honor and hierarchy.

Faliero's inability to escape the past is reinforced by the fact that the rebels come to commit the same crimes for which they condemn the aristocrats. They talk of ideals but repeat the kind of violence that has marked Venetian history. As in *The Two Foscari*, the neoclassical form becomes an image of society's inability to break free from the past and into the future. For example, in order to preserve the unities that Byron embraced as the hallmark of the "regular" drama (see "Preface" to *Marino Faliero*), he has the key elements of the political crisis—Steno's insult to Faliero's wife and the assault by a noble upon the rebel leader, Israel Bertuccio—occur prior to the opening of the play; by the end of the first act, we have already witnessed Faliero's movement toward the rebellion as he reacts angrily to the light reprimand Steno receives. The rest of the play can offer (within its twenty-four-hour limit) the rise and fall of the revolt. This structure gives the play unity and inevitability; but inevitability also arises from the sense that what occurs within the play's present has already been determined by what has occurred in the past. Largely given over to exposition, the play is firmly tied to events that occurred prior to the first act, and the conclusion appears as the fateful closing off of the future as only destruction looms for Venice. *Marino Faliero* goes further than does *The Two Foscari*, presenting not just society's entanglement in the past but that of the revolutionary himself: the tragedy is not just that man has failed to change society, but that the rebel finds himself—as in Blake's "Orc cycle"—becoming a new tyrant.

If neoclassical tragedy was a form tied to the past, and thus an appropriate choice to portray humanity's entrapment in the past, the popular Gothic melodrama seemed as immediate as the Revolution itself. The melodrama arose alongside of the Revolution; Pixérécourt, the "father" of the French melodrama, fought both for and against the revolutionary government and escaped the Terror to create the kind of dramatic fare that pleased audiences who had experienced with him the splendors and miseries of their day. The shape and mood of the melodrama were often close to such revolutionary plays as Monvel's *Cloistered Victims* (*Les Victimes Cloîtrées*; 1791) and Maréchal's *Judgment Day for Kings* (*Le Jugement dernier des rois*; 1793). The ties between the melodrama and the Revolution that saw its birth were asserted by Charles Nodier, who argued that melodrama was "the only popular tragedy appropriate to our age"; he saw the violence and moralism that marked the melodrama as an image of the chaos and restoration of order that had marked French history.[25]

English melodrama in its early Gothic form could also appear to embrace republicanism, as in Monk Lewis's *The Castle Spectre*, a smash hit at Drury Lane in 1797. As in most Gothic plays, the action centers upon the struggle of the beautiful heroine, Angela, against an evil aristocrat, Osmond, who has killed her mother and attempted to assassinate her father. Though she too will prove of noble birth, she has been raised by humble folk and comes to represent the domestic values of family, home, and purity against the amoral power of Osmond. Much of the plot concerns attempts by Angela and the heroic Percy to escape from Osmond's decaying castle, which seems to symbolize a ruined aristocratic past. In that their escape and their liberation of Angela's imprisoned father are aided by comic rustics and servants opposed to the villainous Earl, the play could be seen to embrace a republican view of natural equality; and, in fact, the drama included attacks upon slavery by the villain's black henchman that were marked for omission by the examiner.

The truly radical feature of the Gothic melodrama, however, lay not in its plot—which was finally a moralizing one—or in individual speeches—which were subject to censorship—but in its characterization of the villain, who increasingly becomes a villain-hero, a complex, inwardly divided, charismatic figure, far more attractive than the bumbling, official hero. Lewis's Osmond, for example, is much more appealing than the dull Percy; whereas Percy seems largely ineffectual (it is Angela who finally saves her father), Osmond not only controls the action but is also granted considerable sympathy as he struggles with his present love for Angela and his remorse over past crimes against her parents. That such figures were considered as "revolutionary"—and as potentially dangerous—can be seen in Coleridge's attack upon Maturin's Gothic tragedy *Bertram* (Drury Lane, 1816), in which he rejects the Gothic as the "modern Jacobinical drama," because it finds grandeur in immoral figures.[26] Within the plot the villain-hero acts as a feudal aristocrat bent upon maintaining the system of rank and power that sustains him, even if he must commit crimes to do so; but as a sympathetic character, he embraces the liberation of the self from any social code, any system of power. He may oppose social change, but he embodies a more individual revolt, a stand against all authority that would reduce the self. The Gothic villain-hero reminds us that the age of the French Revolution also had room for more personal rebellions.

Of course, the Gothic drama was not truly revolutionary. It remained escapist rather than inflammatory. Indeed, the melodrama always insisted upon a return to moral order. The domestic virtues of the hero and heroine overcome the liberated selfhood of the villain-hero. As Peter Brooks has argued, the violence that marks the melodrama thus becomes a means of reinstating order—a way of revealing the moral valence of the characters—not a path to a radically new society.[27] The revolutionary motto of Saint-Just was that the Revolution ruled through Virtue, not Terror, but the melodrama embraces terror to recover virtue. Within the melodrama the Revolution becomes a necessary and temporary testing of an eternal moral order.

Still, romantic dramatists found in the Gothic villain-hero a vehicle for exploring both the glory and the danger they discovered in the self liberated by revolt. In plays closely allied to the Gothic drama, such as Schiller's *Robbers* (*Die Räuber;* 1781) and its two descendants, Wordsworth's *Borderers* (1795–96; published 1842) and Coleridge's *Remorse* (Drury Lane, 1813), the rebel figure's revolt leads him into crime, but we still find him superior to the world he rejects. The fear raised by such plays is that his revolt severs the conventional ties that would otherwise check the revolutionary's deeds; it enables him—much like the villain-hero—to see himself as an amoral superman: Karl Moor, for example, comes to realize that two men like himself would wreck the moral universe.

The younger romantics continued to draw upon the Gothic heritage. *The Cenci* is in many ways a Gothic tragedy, and Wasserman and Behrendt among others have found in it a treatment of revolution.[28] The debt of the Byronic hero to the villain-hero is well known; in *Werner* Byron works to transform the Gothic into historical tragedy, and in *Manfred* and *Cain* he offers vastly refined examples of the Gothic self's revolt against authority. Such Gothic characters offended the government censors, whose opposition suggests the ideological import of the Gothic villain-hero. Larpent blocked the performance of a translation of *The Robbers* because, the translator tells us, "the grandeur of his [Moor's] character renders him more likely to excite imitation than aborhence" and this "conjunction of sublime virtue with consummate depravity, though it may be found in nature, should never be dragged into view:—the heroism dazzles the mind, and renders it blind to atrocity." Larpent's successor, Coleman, offered a broader objection to Gothic characters, stating that he would not license plays that "pourtray [sic] the disaffected as gallant heroes and hapless lovers."[29] Rebellious characters could be granted no sympathy lest such sympathy be extended also to actual ideas and causes.

The censors were not very successful in eliminating Gothic villain-heroes or the tragic rebels of neoclassical drama from the stage. But, then, such figures were less dangerous than direct political comment or the representation of the Revolution itself. After all, these plays did not present successful revolutionary movements; in fact, they hardly represent movements at all, despite conspiracies such as the one in *Marino Faliero*. Both the Gothic melodrama and neoclassical tragedy refocus attention upon the individual—and an aristocratic individual at that. There are no dangerous scenes of mob action in these plays. They pit an individual against a society, and it is usually a solitary such as Faliero with as little sympathy for the people as he has for tyranny. It is, thus, interesting that in what I see as the third or mythic phase of the romantic attempt to "personify" the Revolution we find playwrights creating—if not mass movements—at least archetypal human figures rather than unique individuals.

This phase is best represented by Shelley, who gave his dramas on political events a mythological frame in *Prometheus Unbound, Hellas,* and *Swellfoot the Tyrant.* Shelley is not, however, the only poet to turn revolution into myth. The ideological concerns of Byron's metaphysical plays have been noted by a number of critics; and Goethe sought in the second part of *Faust* to work out his attitudes toward the French Revolution in the struggle between "Neptunism" and "Vulcanism" in the "Classical Walpurgisnacht."

Still, Shelley provides the fullest example. His reasons for turning history into myth are complex, but in a curious way he ultimately shares with the government censors a basic objection to the direct representation of recent French history: they fear the impact that the spectacle of the Revolution might have on an audience. Like these censors Shelley believes in the ability of poetry to shape behavior. In *The Defence of Poetry*,[30] he argues that those who read Homer, for example, "were awakened to an ambition of becoming like to Achilles, Hector, and Ulysses" (486); and Athenian drama presented "that ideal perfection and energy which every one feels to be the internal type of all that he loves, admires, and would become" (490). Given this belief in the power of art, Shelley is concerned about the direct portrayal of revolutionary events: dramas of revolt might lead audiences to embrace the brand of violent political action that Shelley clearly rejects; or, more ominously, in depicting the collapse of the Revolution, the drama might inculcate despair in the remaining defenders of liberty. Shelley saw such political despair—and the quietism and conservatism it can bring—as a key problem for Restoration Europe. Wordsworth's embrace of private over public solutions and Southey's political apostasy were vivid examples for him of what could happen to men who had internalized the Terror, Napoleon, and war as despairing rejoinders to their youthful revolutionary hopes. Harold Bloom has suggested that the literal is, for the poet as poet, death.[31] I would suggest that, for the romantics as dramatists of the Revolution, the literal recreation of history was death for revolutionary hopes. It is significant that the period's two most despairing treatments of revolt turn to the literal: Musset's *Lorenzaccio* (1834) closes with the actual speech given by Cosimo de Medici as he took control of Florence, this literal re-creation signaling the end of the dreams of revolution set forth earlier in the play; and Büchner's *Danton's Death* (*Dantons Tod*; 1835) relies heavily upon transcripts of speeches by key revolutionary figures, the literal reiteration of historical documents adding to that play's sense of entrapment and inevitability. Shelley, however, set out to write dramas that would replace the literal with the mythic, that would translate events from what he saw as the "sad reality" ("Dedication" to *The Cenci*) of historical events to a visionary plane where hope for a future revolution could be nourished. From Shelley's perspective all the dramatic attempts to stage the Revolution I have been discussing fail. As Shelley knew well, the project of portraying the Revolution was beset by difficulties. Ronald Paulson has argued that the French Revolution challenged the artist to assimilate within traditional forms what were felt to be unprecedented events.[32] Simply put, playwrights faced a tension between the astonishing new content presented by the events of the French Revolution and the conventional dramatic models they might select to give shape to those events. Shelley understood this tension; in writing *Hellas*—a play about revolt and liberation in Greece—he adopted the strictures of Greek tragedy; yet in speaking of the content of the play, he apologized for relying upon "newspaper erudition" ("Preface"). Shelley outlines here two directions playwrights turned in their attempts to stage the Revolution: they adopted traditional forms into which the writers molded current events, even though they might thus discount the very novelty of those events; alternatively, they allowed contemporary content to determine form, even though this might result in the sacrifice of vision to fact—or, worse yet, to the narrow political opinions of the moment. As Paulson argues, the dramatist seemed to be caught between the poles of the present and the past.

Shelley hoped to escape this bind by creating dramas directed toward neither the past nor the present but the future. It is interesting to note that the worst thing that Shelley's Christ in the fragmentary prologue to *Hellas* has to say about Satan is that "Thou seest but the Past in the To-Come" (161).[33] For Shelley the drama of the day was trapped in patterns of repetition, tied to the past, not creative of the future. Documentary plays literally repeat the past—even if it is the recent past—and threaten to drown us in despair. The Gothic melodrama reiterates the morality of the past, no matter what its theatrical innovations or plunges into daring characterization. Neoclassical tragedies of revolt, even those of Byron, were incapable of staging any moment of liberation without shattering their form. Shelley explicitly criticizes neoclassical tragedy and the melodrama in the *Defence:*

> In periods of the decay of social life, the drama sympathizes with that decay. Tragedy becomes a cold imitation of the form of the great masterpieces of antiquity, divested of all harmonious accompaniment of the kindred arts; and often the very form misunderstood: or a weak attempt to teach certain doctrines, which the writer considers as moral truths; and which are usually no more than specious flatteries of some gross vice or weakness with which the author in common with his auditors are infected. Hence what has been called the classical and the domestic drama. (491)

Imitations of past forms and presentations of fleeting contemporary ideologies are signs of social decay, not signposts to a revitalized future.

Prometheus Unbound contains within itself a critique of these opposing attempts to "personify" the Revolution. The attempt to portray directly the true but sad tale of the Revolution receives the clearest criticism; for the staging of revolutionary failure is one of the tortures brought to bear on Prometheus by the Furies, as they call to him:

> See! a disenchanted nation
> Springs like day from desolation;
> To truth its state, is dedicate,
> And Freedom leads it forth, her mate;
> A legioned band of linked brothers
> Whom Love calls children—
>
>   'Tis another's—
>
> See how kindred murder kin!
> 'Tis the vintage-time for Death and Sin:
> Blood, like new wine, bubbles within
>   Till Despair smothers
>
> The Struggling World, which slaves and tyrants win.

(567–77)

As Prometheus himself states when the Furies first approach, the danger in watching such spectacles is that "Whilst I behold such execrable shapes, / Methinks I grow like what I contemplate / And laugh and stare in loathsome sympathy" (I, 449–51). A preoccupation with the failures of the past leads us to repeat these failures. Shelley explores more fully this possibility of becoming what one beholds in the companion piece to *Prometheus Unbound*, *The Cenci*, a sad reality counterposed to the high idealisms of his mythic drama. In his history play, Shelley's Count Cenci describes what he hopes to do to Beatrice in forcing her into an incestuous relationship:

> She shall become (for what she most abhors
> Shall have a fascination to entrap
> Her loathing will), to her own conscious self
> All she appears to others. . . .

(IV, i, 85–88)

Of course, most readings of *The Cenci* find Beatrice in fact becoming what she most abhors, that is, becoming a duplicate of her father; and Wasserman has suggested that Beatrice's decision to use her father's violence to overcome her father's tyranny parallels the course of the Revolution: *The Cenci*, then, becomes an example of what happens when man cannot free himself from the patterns of the past. Prometheus's great victory is that he overcomes the past— even the revolutionary past with its high hopes and deadly despair. He refuses to repeat the past in refusing to repeat his curse, in "unsaying" that curse. He liberates himself from historical time, just as Shelley liberates his play from the historical time of documentary reconstruction.

Shelley's objections to neoclassical re-creations of the French Revolution are partially grounded in his rejection of hackneyed forms, outlined in the passage from the *Defence* quoted above; but his reservations went further, as can be seen in his comments on Byron's use of a neoclassical model for his history plays. He remarked of *Marino Faliero* that Byron "affects to patronize a system of criticism fit only for the production of mediocrity, & although all his fine poems & passages have been produced in defiance of this system: yet I recognize the pernicious effects of it in the 'Doge of Venice.' " As Charles Robinson has argued, Shelley felt that Byron's traditional form forced him to adopt a predestined action that finds reform inevitably leading to violence; and insofar as that action appeared fated, there also seemed to be an excuse for that violence.[34] Byron's neoclassical plays can be read as embracing the two results of the Revolution that most concerned Shelley: the turn to violence as the only way to combat tyranny, and despair over what appears to be the inevitable corruption of the forces of liberty when they adopt such violence. Byron shared Shelley's liberal views, but Shelley believed that Byron's neoclassical aesthetic ultimately betrayed those views. Shelley saw, as Starobinski and Paulson have seen, that neoclassicism—even when it was adopted by the Revolution itself—could not portray the liberation of revolt, its leap toward the future. The traditional form came to embody man's entanglement in historical patterns, and thus, in Starobinski's words, "such tragedy was doomed to mere repetition."[35]

Shelley, of course, offers his own brand of classicism in *Prometheus Unbound*, but he clearly overturns classical traditions in his revisionist handling of Aeschylus. In inverting Aeschylus's ending, Shelley liberated his play from any pattern of inevitability; the play depicts not the force of fate but the power of the will and the imagination. The grand romantic finale of the fourth act stands as an emblem of Shelley's rejection of traditional versions of classicism, as he leaves behind all models to celebrate a world remade.

Even the melodrama is subsumed and transformed in Shelley's play. Stuart Curran has noted the generic label for *Prometheus Unbound*—lyric drama—which marks its ties to the opera.[36] But "lyric drama" might also remind us of the *melo-* or *music*-drama. The melodrama typically followed a four-act structure in which a virtuous hero and heroine struggle against an oppressive villain, as the action moves toward the overthrow of the tyrant and the union of the lovers; the plot was often resolved through the uncovering of some mysterious relationship—usually some question of paternity or kinship—here, the paternity of that ultimate mysterious stranger Demogorgon. I do not want to render *Prometheus Unbound* into a melodrama. What I want to suggest is that Shelley includes the outlines of that form to respond to its vision of narrow moralism, of terror issuing in virtue, a vision worthy of Jupiter. In Shelley's play terror is laid to rest, and traditional morality is overturned as man frees himself to rule the world through imagination and love.

In a sense all of these alternative dramatic forms create plays written within the language of Prometheus's curse, a language bound to past tyranny and violent resistance. In seeking to replace this language with a visionary language that will be a "perpetual Orphic song" (IV, 412), Shelley seeks to displace these rival "personifications" of the Revolution: in the place of the "sad reality" of historical chronicles, he offers the "dreams of what ought to be" provided by myth ("Dedication," *The Cenci*); to counter the restrictions of neoclassical tragedy, he offers his own romantic classicism with its open form; and rather than a moralizing melodrama, he offers his lyric drama with its celebration of "the great secret of morals," love (*Defence*, 487).

Of course, one can argue that this mythic "personification" of the Revolution is not a personification at all but an impersonation, a sublimation of the Revolution's actual violence in order to create a metaphoric or mythic "beau ideal" of revolt, to quote Shelley's own description of his *Revolt of Islam*.[37] These plays clearly participate in what Jerome McGann has called the "romantic ideology": "The poetry of Romanticism is everywhere marked by extreme forms of displacement and poetic conceptualization whereby the actual human issues with which the poetry is concerned are resituated in a variety of idealized localities."[38] The question to be asked is what is gained by such displacement. The movement away from actual historical events and issues can appear as an evasion, a turn to ideal solutions over complex human problems. Such may be the case with Coleridge's dramatic corpus. It begins with the historical *Fall of Robespierre* (1794), which treats the Revolution as an example of usurpation, then turns to *Osorio/Remorse* (1797/1813), which again depicts an example of political usurpation but now within a Gothic framework, and concludes with *Zapolya* (1817), a romance in which the usurpers are defeated and a conservative ideal of stability and succession is discovered. In moving from documentary play to Gothic parallel to romance, Coleridge seems to be fleeing the troubling historical realities of his day in pursuit of a form within which his vision of the Revolution as a simple act of usurpation can be brought to a satisfactory conclusion.[39]

However, Coleridge's development is not that of Shelley, for example. There *is* in the romantic dramatists' move to myth an increasingly ambiguous attitude toward history and politics. Romantic plays dealing with revolt—from Goethe's *Götz* (1773) and Schiller's *Robbers* to Hugo's *Hernani* (1830) and Büchner's *Danton's Death*—typically depict the rebel's involvement with the historical realm as part of the tragedy. It is, for example, because Byron's Foscari and Faliero must adopt the means available to them in their time and place—Foscari is forced to accept the rituals of the law and Faliero finds himself allied with a plebian rebellion that contradicts his own sense of himself—that they are unable to find a path of action that breaks free from Venice's doomed history. Again, it is because Beatrice Cenci lives in a particular historical reality dominated by patri-

49

archal systems of authority and the ideology of the church that she makes what Shelley calls her "pernicious mistake" and kills her father ("Preface" to *The Cenci*). The heroes of romantic drama remain time-trapped as long as they remain within the confines of the early nineteenth-century stage, the stage of John Dent's documentary romance, Sheridan Knowles's neoclassical plays, Monk Lewis's Gothic dramas. They can, however, be liberated on the mythic or visionary stage. Faliero and Foscari cannot find a mode of action that does not compromise their sense of honor, but Manfred walks through his play shunning any compromise to remain master of his fate. Beatrice must succumb to violence or react with violence, but Prometheus can move beyond violence to vision. Although in these visionary plays the historical past—and particularly the revolutionary past—is in part lost, that past is translated into a myth whose goal is to shape future history.

Notes

1. Quoted in Marvin Carlson, *The Theatre of the French Revolution* (Ithaca, N.Y.: Cornell University Press, 1966), p. 142.

2. Hugo, "Ymbert Galloix" (1833), in *Philosophie* 1, *Oeuvres complètes*, ed. Paul Meurice et al. (Paris: Albin Michel, 1904–52), p. 184.

3. Letter to Byron, 8 September 1816, in *The Letters of Percy Bysshe Shelley*, ed. Frederick Jones (London: Oxford University Press, 1964), 1:504.

4. For example, see Northrop Frye's theory of modes, *Anatomy of Criticism* (Princeton, N.J.: Princeton University Press, 1957), pp. 33–67.

5. On the drama of the French Revolution, see: Carlson, *Theatre of French Revolution*; Marie-Hélène Huet, *Rehearsing the Revolution: The Staging of Marat's Death 1793–1797*, trans. Robert Hurley (Berkeley: University of California Press, 1982); Daniel Hamiche, *Le Théâtre et la Révolution* (Paris: Union Générale d'Editions, 1973); Louis Emile Dieudonné Moland, *Théâtre de la Révolution* (1877; rpt., Geneva: Slatkine Reprints, 1971).

6. J. C. Cross, *Julia of Louvain: or, Monkish Cruelty*, in *Circusiana, or a Collection of the most favourite Ballets, Spectacles, Melo-Drames, &c. Performed at the Royal Circus, St. George's Field* (London: Lackington, Allen, & Co., 1809), p. 1. See Allardyce Nicoll, *A History of English Drama 1660–1900* (Cambridge: Cambridge University Press, 1960), 3:54; and Joseph Donohue, *Theatre in the Age of Kean* (Totowa, N.J.: Rowman & Littlefield, 1975), p. 34.

7. Frye, *Anatomy*, pp. 186–206.

8. Dent, *The Bastille* (London: n.p., 1789), title page: "The Celebrated Speech Delivered the 29th of July to the French Troops, by Mons. Moreau de St. Merry, on the Destruction of the above Fortress."

9. *Times*, 8 August 1789, p. 3, col. D.

10. Charles Bonnor, *Airs, Duetts, and Chorusses, Arrangement of Scenery, and Sketch of the Pantomime, entitled The Picture of Paris Taken in the Year 1790* (London: T. Cadell, 1790), scene 2.

11. The best treatment of dramatic censorship during the period is L. W. Conolly, *The Censorship of English Drama 1737–1824* (San Marino, Calif.: Huntington Library, 1976); he gives an account of Larpent, pp. 34–45. My comments on the censorship of the dramas of the day are based on a review of the examiner's records and his notations on the licensing copies of the plays, held by the Henry E. Huntington Library and Art Gallery, San Marino, California; this material makes up the Larpent Collection, abbreviated here as LA with the appropriate manuscript number.

12. *The Life and Times of Frederick Reynolds* (1826; rpt., New York: Benjamin Blom, 1971), 2:54.

13. John St. John, *Island of St. Marguerite* (London: J. Debrett, 1789), "Advertisement." See also LA 845 and 848.

14. *Harlequin Touchstone*, LA 851, contains two manuscripts, one marked "forbidden" and one licensed with material cut; the original pantomime was for Charles Dibdin in 1779. The *Morning Post* of 1 December 1789 indicates that the procession was moved from Paris to Rome.

15. *Helvetic Liberty, an Opera in Three Acts by a Kentish Bowman* (London: Wayland, 1792), p. vi of postscript.

16. Quoted in Herbert Lindenberger, *Historical Drama: The Relation of Literature and Reality* (Chicago: University of Chicago Press, 1975), p. 24.

17. *Hazlitt on Theatre*, ed. William Archer and Robert Lowe (New York: Hill & Wang, n.d.), pp. 113, 117.

18. John Haggit, *Count de Villeroi; or, The Fate of Patriotism* (London: T. Cadell, 1794), "Preface," p. vi, vii n. The kind of French propaganda play that Haggit is referring to is well represented by Sylvain Maréchal's *Le Jugement dernier des rois* (1793).

19. Conolly, *Censorship*, p. 90. For the various versions of the play, see n. 13 above.

20. See Marilyn Butler, *Romantics, Rebels, and Reactionaries* (Oxford: Oxford University Press, 1982), esp. pp. 179–82; and Ronald Paulson, *Representations of Revolution (1789–1820)* (New Haven, Conn.: Yale University Press, 1983), pp. 1–36.

21. *Hazlitt on Theatre*, p. 172.

22. George Coleman, "Testimony," in *Report from the Select Committee Appointed to Inquire into the Laws Affecting Dramatic Literature*, reprinted in the Irish University Press Series of British Parliamentary Papers, Stage and Theatre (Shannon: Irish University Press, 1968), 1:66.

23. All quotations from Byron are from *Poetical Works*, ed. by Frederick Page and rev. by John Jump (London: Oxford University Press 1970). I offer a fuller discussion of Byron's plays and the drama of the period in general in my *In the Shadows of Romance: Romantic Tragic Drama in Germany, England, and France* (Athens, Oh.: Ohio University Press, 1987).

24. Byron, letter to Douglas Kinnaird, 1 October 1820, *Byron's Letters and Journals*, ed. Leslie Marchand (Cambridge: Belknap Press, 1977), 7:190.

25. Nodier, "Introduction," in Pixérécourt, *Théâtre choisi* (Paris: Tresse, 1841), 1:vii.

26. Coleridge, *Biographia Literaria: Edited with His Aesthetical Essays*, ed. J. Shawcross (Oxford: Oxford University Press, 1907), 2: 188.

27. Peter Brooks, *The Melodramatic Imagination* (New Haven, Conn.: Yale University Press, 1976), p. 15.

28. Earl Wasserman, *Shelley: A Critical Reading* (Baltimore: Johns Hopkins University Press, 1971), pp. 94–97; Stephen Behrendt, "Beatrice Cenci and the Tragic Myth of History," in this volume.

29. J. G. Holman tells us of the examiner's reactions in the preface to his adaptation of *The Robbers* as *Red Cross Knights* (London: Cawthorn, 1799), pp. i–ii. Coleman's comment is found in a letter to Sir William Knighton, 29 February 1824, in Richard Brinsley Peake, *Memoirs of the Coleman Family* (1841; rpt. New York: Benjamin Blom, 1971), 2:400.

30. Quotations from Shelley's works are taken, wherever possible, from *Shelley's Poetry and Prose*, ed. Donald H. Reiman and Sharon B. Powers (New York: Norton, 1977).

31. Bloom, *Map of Misreading* (New York: Oxford University Press, 1975), p. 91.

32. Paulson, *Representations of Revolution*, pp. 1–36.

33. This prologue is not in Reiman and Powers. See *Poetical Works*, ed. by Thomas Hutchinson and rev. by G. M. Matthews (Oxford: Oxford University Press, 1969), p. 452.

34. Charles E. Robinson, *Shelley and Byron: The Snake and Eagle Wreathed in Fight* (Baltimore: Johns Hopkins University Press, 1976), pp. 144–60; Shelley's comments come in a letter to Mary Shelley, 7 August 1821, *Letters*, 2:317.

35. Jean Starobinski, *1789: The Emblems of Reason*, trans. Barbara Bray (Charlottesville: University Press of Virginia, 1982), p. 122.

36. Stuart Curran, *Shelley's Annus Mirabilis: The Maturing of an Epic Vision* (San Marino, Calif.: Huntington Library, 1975), p. 232 n.11.

37. In letter of 13 October 1817, *Letters*, 1:564.

38. Jerome J. McGann, *The Romantic Ideology: A Critical Investigation* (Chicago: University of Chicago Press, 1983), p. 1.

39. For a fuller discussion of Coleridge's development along these lines, see Janet Tvetan, "Vision and Revision in Coleridge's Dramas," Master's Thesis, Texas A&M University, May 1987.

William Blake and
the Wheels of Compulsion
Minna Doskow

William Blake was very much a man of his particular time and place, as his involvement with political events and the many historic references in his poetry demonstrate. He was equally involved in the intellectual life of his time, reacting to the philosophic, scientific, and artistic ideas around him in satiric writings, in marginalia, and above all, in poetry and picture. However, he saw both events and ideas through the lens of imagination, thereby transforming them from history and philosophy to poetry, myth, and visionary art. In *The French Revolution* and *America*, revolutionary events are portrayed in the clash of archetypal figures engaged in mythic actions. Similarly, throughout Blake's poetry, contemporary philosophical ideas are transformed in the crucible of his imagination to symbols of crushing mechanistic power or to archetypal figures waging wars to limit humanity. It is important then, if we are to understand Blake's relation to the history of ideas—his reactions to, and his understanding and transformation of, philosophic thought—to look closely at the use he made of particular philosophic ideas in his poetry.

Since Blake is concerned primarily with those philosophers who were most influential in shaping eighteenth-century thought, the names of Newton and Locke naturally figure prominently in his poetry. Universally recognized as jointly shaping British empiricism, modern science, and European thought generally in the eighteenth century, they were the intellectual giants of the time. Hardly a contemporary or subsequent early nineteenth-century philosopher writing in England, France, or Germany, fails to acknowledge intellectual debts to one or both. Newton introduced a deductive system of science based on analytical methods that presented nature as a rational and harmonious order ruled by natural law. As he tells the reader in the introduction to the *Principia*, "I offer this work as the mathematical principles of philosophy, for the whole burden of philosophy seems to consist in this—from the phenomena of motions to investigate the forces of nature, and then from these forces to demonstrate the other phenomena."[1] Locke extended that observationalist deductive method from natural science into social science. He also extended Newton's atomism into psychology by treating ideas as irreducible ultimate elements in the mind. The rest of the eighteenth century followed these thinkers, extending natural law into natural rights, natural religion, and natural morality. Simultaneously they applied the mechanistic model of the universe to society and the individual.

What is startling, at least initially, is to see in Blake's work the names of these two influential thinkers almost invariably coupled with that of Bacon. Writing in the sixteenth century, and not as generally recognized in his time as Newton and Locke were in theirs, Bacon at first seems an odd triplet. If, however, we see Bacon as establishing a break with earlier scholasticism, with medieval conceptions of knowledge based on Aristotelian methods, and as clearing the way for modern philosophy (as he was perceived in the eighteenth century), the connection becomes clearer. It is thus as a precursor of empiricism and the foremost philosopher of science, as the "father" of the inductive method that the eighteenth century and Blake alike generally saw and exemplified Bacon. This father "achieved his doubtful paternity at the hands of Voltaire and Diderot, and was canonized in D'Alembert's *Discours préliminaire* to the *Encyclopédie*.[2] Having advocated an empirical and experimental method that moved from particular observation of things to broad generalizations, Bacon was a natural third in the company of Newton and Locke. Moreover, the English citizenship of the triumvirate is significant. Throughout his work Blake is preoccupied with Albion (and Britain) both as individual character and place, and as symbol of everyman and every place. Blake presents Britain as the universalized microcosm, archetypal in its significance; consequently its philosophers assume a similar function. Coming together as Hand, Urizen, Reuben, the Spectre, or the fallen Sons of Albion, their pernicious doctrines are firmly anchored in British soil and given a local name and habitation, but their effects are universal.

This specifically English orientation may help explain the absence from Blake's text of Descartes, whose emphasis on reason and mathematics as a model certainly marked as much of a break with the past as Bacon's. Although it has been argued that Blake had Descartes in mind and was implicitly criticizing the French philosopher in all his attacks upon "Doubt" as philosophic or scientific method,[3] he never mentions Descartes by name, and we have no direct evidence that Blake had read or was familiar with Descartes. Blake seems to be referring rather to empirical skepticism, the mode that led Hume to question the nature of causality itself, than to Descartes's method of a priori reasoning leading to unshakable truths as exemplified in the *Discourse on Method* or the *Meditations*. Though Blake used the Cartesian term "vortex,"[4] he used it in a far different sense than Descartes, and may very well have acquired it elsewhere.

The figures of Bacon, Newton, and Locke are thus embodied in the looming menacing giants of Blake's myth. They form the unholy triumvirate that represents for Blake the epitome of English empiricism, the dominant philosophy of his time. They emerge as the myth character Hand in *Jerusalem*, the three-headed monster pictured in plate 50 who functions as a rationalistic Cerberus in the epic poem and illustrations. They appear individually as oppressive characters under their own names or as Urizen, Albion's Spectre, or the fallen Sons of Albion, the archetypal characters of Blake's myth who spout empiricist doctrines. They also combine to keep Albion from inspiration in *Milton* and to oppress humanity in *Jerusalem* in the compulsive wheels originating from the Universities of Europe in *Jerusalem*. Nevertheless, they emerge in the final Chariot of the Almighty with Milton, Shakespeare, and Chaucer at the end of *Jerusalem*, demonstrating the usefulness of philosophy when coupled with imagination. Taken alone, however, they have the power to destroy humanity, and Blake shows them repeatedly in the attempt.

Looking at Blake's choice of philosophical targets, one is startled at the presence there of the political liberals of his time. It is not immediately obvious why he chooses Locke, Voltaire, and Rousseau to symbolize human repression and the oppressive forces rampant in Europe when these philosophers, like Blake himself, object to the reigning tyrannical European monarchies, enunciate democratic principles, and justify rights of political revolution. Why should the author of *Songs of Experience, America,* and *The French Revolution* condemn the author of the *Two Treatises of Government, Philosophical Letters,* or of *Social Contract?*

There seem to be two answers to this apparent inconsistency. First, it may have appeared to Blake, as it has to modern historians such as E. P. Thompson or John Herman Randall, Jr., for example, that the political liberalism of Locke, Voltaire, Rousseau, and others was too closely tied to the interests of the rising middle class. Randall sees the Enlightenment as

> the first thoroughgoing attempt to reconstruct the traditional ideas and institutions of Western society in the light of the demands of the triumphant business spirit, by means of the intellectual method presumed to have led to the triumphs of Newtonian science. The middle class at last possessed a powerful, well-organized instrument for criticism, and an adequate intellectual basis on which to erect a new type of social organization. . . .
>
> So the Enlightenment really meant the rapid spread of the aims and ideal of business enterprise and of the intellectual tests and method and model of Newtonian mechanics. It meant the emergence of a rounded middle-class culture, an ideology capable of satisfying most of the intellectual needs of those it served.[5]

Locke's works in particular furnished the intellectual foundation for eighteenth-century middle-class aspirations to economic and political hegemony. His attack on innateness and his appeal to experience as the foundation of all ideas constituted an implicit criticism of hierarchical society based on landed interests, a critique advanced on behalf of the emergent bourgeoisie. Locke's wide influence on subsequent French thought, the deep respect in which he was held by Voltaire and his followers, was in large measure due to his furnishing as well the ideology needed by the rising bourgeoisie in France for economic advancement. Locke, following Newton's example in natural science, demanded that these reconstructions take place on a "scientific" basis. He described social and political institutions as reflections of a natural order, following natural laws applied to human society. He was later followed in this science of society by Bentham in England, and Voltaire, Montesquieu, the Physiocrats, and Rousseau in France.

Blake recognized the partiality of such social science and political philosophy, and although he also opposed the tyrannical monarchies of the time, he separated his vision from the reigning liberal political ideology. He briefly recognized the revolutionary role of Voltaire and Rousseau in *The French Revolution*, where they are portrayed as driving out superstition and the entrenched authority of the established church, and as inspiring Lafayette's heroic words of liberty (ll. 274–76; 282–84). However, this is a unique instance of praise in his work, which is otherwise almost completely devoted to the condemnation of these philosophers. In all his later works, he notes the futility of limited political revolution that changes the forms of government but leaves the imaginative condition of humanity untouched.

Blake symbolizes that futility in *America* when he pictures her at the end, in the final dismal illustration (plate 16), kneeling, bent double, and praying, unseeing as her hair flows down over her face in a waterfall of despair while small figures expressing both the positive hope and implicit betrayal of her revolution appear along her bent body, and four bare ruined human trees reach out behind her. The poem's triumphant celebration of the glorious American Revolution that successfully defeated repressive English monarchy is mitigated by that final illustration.[6] It is also limited by other dark hints of revolutionary failure in the poem as Orc, the spirit of the revolution, gives heat without light (4:11), and as the Bard smashes his harp in shame after having sung the song of America (2:18–20). Disappointed in his hopes for imaginative renewal and thereby silenced and shamed, he acknowledges the limitations of Lockean politics. These limitations are equally illustrated by the terrified human family who are never visibly relieved of their terror (pl. 3).

He also demonstrates that futility mythically by showing the metamorphosis of Orc, the young radical revolutionary spirit, into his oppressive opposite, Urizen, the old repressive tyrant, when revolution limits itself to political forms. Northrop Frye describes this movement that typifies both historical political change and natural vegetative change as the Orc cycle: the cycle of birth, youth, aging, death, and rebirth seen in *The Mental Traveller*, the cycles of history in *Europe*, and the story of Luvah and Vala in the *Four Zoas*. He notes that in Blake's poetry "history exhibits a series of crises in which a sudden flash of imaginative vision (as in the French Revolution) bursts out, is counteracted by a more ruthless defense of the status quo, and subsides again."[7] The potential for Orc to turn into Urizen, or revolutionary fervor into oppression, is represented pictorially in *America,* where Orc and Urizen are depicted as mirror images of each other differentiated by age, clothing and surroundings but in similar attitudes and poses (plates 8 and 10).

Second, Blake rejects the political philosophers of the Enlightenment because their writings are grounded in an appeal to nature: natural phenomena, natural laws, the state of nature, and natural rights. Although Blake throughout his works emphasizes the importance of the natural world of time and space as a foundation upon which to build and without which humanity would be condemned to mere chaos, he is even more insistent on the primacy of imagination and oppressive dangers of limitation to nature alone. As early as *There is No Natural Religion,* Blake warns against limiting one's knowledge to the senses and the merely natural; *The Marriage of Heaven and Hell* notes the limitation in a proverb: "Where man is not nature is barren";[8] and *Jerusalem* embodies the idea in the character of Reuben, the merely natural man whose fate it is to become what he beholds. Pictorially, these ideas are illustrated as men and women grow roots and branches in the plates of *America* or *Jerusalem.* For Blake, the locus of control is with human beings who shape nature. Or as Michael Ferber puts it, " 'nature' is the Other, the 'not-human,' which must be reclaimed or reabsorbed into the human. It is congruent with Hegel's doctrine that nature is Spirit estranged from itself, a doctrine derived through Schelling from Boehme and his 'exhalations' or 'emanations' of Soul and God (these ideas coming in turn from the Kabbalah and more ancient sources)."[9] Thus any political doctrines based like Locke's on human law and social institutions that reflect natural law and natural rights, or, like Rousseau's on man's original position in the state of nature, must be anathema to Blake.

Blake's major quarrel with Locke, however, is epistemological rather than political. The objects of his attack are the sensationalist theories of *An Essay Concerning Human Understanding* rather than the political ones of the *Treatises.* His criticisms of both particular ideas and passages and the general doctrines in Locke's *Essay,* are ironically similar to criticisms leveled by subsequent British empiricists and their German successors. Hume, for example, whom Blake equally condemns, also rejects Locke's notion of primary and secondary qualities and "the absurdity of all the scholastic notions with regard to abstraction and general ideas."[10] He rejects as well Locke's split between subjective perceptions and objective reality, as does Berkeley. Kant, working off Hume's reformulation, also heals the Lockean split between the outer world of observed phenomena and the inner one of the observer by locating the structuring of experience within human thought and perception. Although the similarity of objections to Locke is apparent, the alternatives proposed by Blake and these philosophers are vastly different.

Blake's opposition to Locke's notion of human experience as the passive reception of sense impressions and mind's reflection upon those impressions resulting in combination and abstraction has been cited often by critics (e.g., Northrop Frye, Peter Fisher). Indeed, these processes describe Urizen, Blake's mythic transformation of Lockean man. As Locke sees it,

> All ideas come from Sensation or Reflection. . . . Our observation, employed either about external sensible objects, or about the internal operations of our minds perceived and reflected on by ourselves, is that which supplies our understandings with all the *materials* of thinking. These two are the fountains of knowledge, from whence all ideas we have, or can naturally have, do spring.[11]

> The mind makes the particular ideas received from particular objects to become general; which is done by considering them as they are in the mind such appearances, separate from all other existences, and the circumstances of real existence, as time, place, or any other concomitant ideas. This is called *Abstraction*, whereby ideas taken from particular beings become general representatives of all of the same kind, and their names general names applicable to whatever exists conformable to such abstract ideas.[12]

Blake's *Book of Urizen* criticizes many elements of Locke's theory of knowledge as it is incorporated in Urizen's character and creation. Urizen represents both the analytical and abstracting power of mind as

> . . . unknown, abstracted
> Brooding secret, the dark power hid.

> Times on times he divided, & measur'd
> Space by space in his ninefold darkness
> Unseen, unknown!

(3:5–9)

Demonstrating Lockean sensation, reflection, and abstraction, he forms a mathematical universe and moral laws. "Urizen's world is at once a metaphysical projection and a critique of Locke's distinct ideas of solidity, body, extension and motion."[13] It is the "wide world of solid obstruction" (*BU*, 4:23), the world of science and mathematics, of lines, plummets, and rules, of weights, scales, and quadrants (*BU*, 19:9; 20:33–40), the world of Bacon, Newton, and

Locke. The torturous and oppressive nature of that world reflects and exposes Urizen's limited and distorted consciousness, which is Blake's visionary presentation of Lockean epistemology and moral philosophy, as well as of Baconian and Newtonian science. This visionary presentation extends beyond Urizen himself to Urizenic figures such as the Spectre, Reuben, or the Sons of Albion, who also closely reflect the tenets of empirical science and philosophy. In *Jerusalem*, Reuben, the merely natural man, exists with limited Lockean senses (49:32–41; 30:51–54), as does fallen Luvah (30:46–50), and all who see them "became what they beheld" (30:50, 54); that is, they become passive and dependent on outside material stimuli for their intellectual identity. They are limited to material sense impressions that the mind may only juggle, combine, or abstract from, not transform through imagination.

Blake summarizes Lockean epistemology in his early writing, *There is No Natural Religion [a]*, when he states in the first two propositions:

I   Man cannot naturally Perceive. but through his natural or bodily organs.
II   Man by his reasoning power. can only compare & judge of what he has already perciev'd.

Here we have Lockean Sensation and Reflection succinctly stated. But Blake goes on to show the limitation of such theories in his conclusion: "If it were not for the Poetic or Prophetic character the Philosophic & Experimental would soon be at the ratio of all things, & stand still unable to do other than repeat the same dull round over again."

To counter Lockean notions, he proposes his own theory of variable perception (*J*, 3:55–56) based on immortal "all flexible senses" (*BU*, 3:38) or "imaginative and immortal organs" (*DC*, E 532) that human beings exercise when they function in unfallen and truly human terms rather than in limited Lockean ones. This kind of perception brings the world to life rather than letting it persist in dead Newtonian matter or scientific mechanism (as the Fairy point out to Blake in the Introduction to *Europe*, iii:13–18) in which it repeats the "same dull round" endlessly like "a mill with complicated wheels" (*NNR*, b, IV).

Blake further criticizes specific Lockean principles when he describes the manner of Albion's sons in *Jerusalem*.

And this is the manner of the Sons of Albion in their strength
They take the Two Contraries which are calld Qualities, with which

Every Substance is clothed, they name them Good & Evil
From them they make an Abstract, which is a Negation
Not only of the Substance from which it is derived
A murderer of its own Body: but also a murderer
Of every Divine Member: it is the Reasoning Power
An Abstract objecting power, that Negatives every thing
This is the Spectre of Man: the Holy Reasoning Power
And in its Holiness is closed the Abomination of Desolation

(10:7–16)

Here Blake is directly criticizing both Locke's theory of qualities, which had been prevalent in scientific thinking from Galileo on, and his idea of abstraction. Locke distinguished between primary qualities, which are inherent in and inseparable from the objects we perceive "viz., solidity, extension, figure, motion or rest, and number," and secondary qualities, "which in truth are nothing in the objects themselves but powers to produce various sensations in us by their primary qualities, i.e. by the bulk, figure, texture and motion of their insensible parts, as colours, sounds, tastes, etc."[14] This dichotomy, which dissects the object, arranges its attributes hierarchically, and separates the object from the perceiving subject, runs counter to Blake's own doctrine of variable perception and unity between subject and object. It is parodied—or, rather, corrected—by the doctrine of contraries explicated in *The Marriage of Heaven and Hell* and elsewhere.

Lockean abstraction appears in Blake's work as negative reason responsible for the desiccation and destruction of the living natural world ("a murderer of its own Body") and of transcendent human imagination ("a murderer of Every Divine Member"). It leads to the dead, mechanistic universe of British empiricism that stretches from Bacon onward. It also forms the basis of the natural religion that empties the world of an active, participating divinity and separates the Divine to a prior condition or hereafter, leaving the natural world, in Blake's view, as an empty, desolate, mundane shell. Ironically, as Blake points out in the above passage, the denial of contraries and the process of abstraction lead to the dichotomy of good and evil in orthodox religion, the condemnation of the natural world and body, which is no longer considered good or divine, and the separation of spirit and matter, humanity and divinity. Like Blake, George Berkeley criticized Locke's definition of primary and secondary qualities in *Three Dialogues Between Hylas and Pholonous in Opposition to Sceptics and Atheists* (particularly in the First Dialogue). More importantly, he also attacked Locke's notion of abstraction. In

A Treatise Concerning the Principles of Human Knowledge, Berkeley attacks the idea that general ideas or universals can be separated from their particular existences, "that the mind can frame to itself by *abstraction* the idea of colour exclusive of extension, and of motion exclusive of both colour and extension."[15] He further denies that having perceived common elements in various particulars, the mind may single out that commonality on its own,

> making thereof a most abstract idea of extension, which is neither line, surface, nor solid, nor has any figure of magnitude, but is an idea entirely prescinded from all these. So likewise the mind, by leaving out of the particular colours perceived by sense, that which distinguishes them one from another, and retaining that only which is common to all, makes an idea of colour in abstract; which is neither red, nor blue, nor white, nor any other determinate colour. And in like manner, by considering motion abstractedly not only from the body moved but likewise from the figure it describes, and all particular directions and velocities, the abstract idea of motion is framed; which equally corresponds to all particular motions whatsoever that may be perceived by sense.[16]

Berkeley further denies being able to imagine a hand or eye without "some particular shape and colour," or, anticipating Yeats in "Among School Children," being able "to form the abstract idea of motion distinct from the body moving," or to "frame a general notion by abstracting from particulars" in a Lockean manner.[17] Instead, Berkeley claims that "a word becomes general by being made the sign, not of an abstract general idea, but of several particular ideas, any one of which it indifferently suggests to the mind."[18] Although Blake goes further in the allegiance to minute particulars and attacks the generalizing tendency completely, especially in his *Annotations to Reynolds* and *Jerusalem*, it is readily apparent that they are on the same road in objecting to Locke.

Berkeley further attacks Locke's idea of abstraction as the source of "an opinion strangely prevailing amongst men that houses, mountains, rivers, and in a word all sensible objects have an existence natural or real, distinct from their being perceived by the understanding."[19] For Berkeley sensations or ideas "cannot exist otherwise than in a mind perceiving them."[20] Similarly, for Blake natural objects are dependent on the "Perceptive Organs" and vary as the latter do (*J*, 30:55–56). Whether we see the sun as "a round Disk of fire somewhat like a Guinea" or as "an Innumerable company of the Heavenly host crying Holy Holy Holy is the Lord God" (*VLJ*, E 566) depends on the imaginative state of our corporeal eye.

The primacy of Spirit over Matter and its shaping quality was Berkeley's answer to Locke, an answer certainly compatible with Blake's ideas. For example, Berkeley writes: "From what has been said it is evident there is not any other substance than *spirit*, or that which perceives. . . . Hence it is plain that the very notion of what is called "matter" or "corporeal substance" involves a contradiction in it."[21] And Blake states: "Mental Things are alone Real What is Call'd Corporeal Nobody Knows of its Dwelling Place [it] is in Fallacy & its Existence an Imposture Where is the Existence Out of Mind or Thought" (*VLJ*, E 565).

Berkeley proceeds in his argument with Locke by denying the independent existence of corporeal substances, thereby healing the subject/object split in Locke by annihilating one half of it. He locates the source of ideas not in the external world, as Locke does, but in the human mind. Blake too heals that split between perceiving subject and independently existing object by insisting, as Berkeley does, on the ability of perception to shape the object. "Imagination" he cites as "the real & eternal World of which this Vegetable Universe is but a faint shadow" (*J*, pl. 77). But he also envisions a humanized universe in which the external world becomes subject, "All Human Forms identified even Tree Metal Earth & Stone" (*J*, 99:1). Berkeley never goes this far. He proceeds from spiritual causes to the denial of material substance and thence to the deduction of an omniscient external deity who is the original cause and in whose Mind the entire universe exists as an idea. Since, he states, "it has been shown that there is no corporeal or material substance: it remains therefore that the cause of ideas is an incorporeal active substance or spirit."[22] Thus his philosophic system postulates a God who is the final cause, who exists outside of human beings, Blake's Nobodaddy. Indeed, the human mind and human beings themselves are simply interesting notions occurring to that Mind.

Bishop Berkeley's theological doctrines, unlike Blake's, had to at least be compatible with those of the Anglican church. He saw himself in the "revealed" tradition of the church and not as an innovator like Blake.[23] His God is a separate omniscient spirit not at odds with orthodox religion and the established church. Blake's God, however, is inseparable from the human imagination at work. As he tells us in his "Annotations to Berkeley's *Siris*," "Man is All Imagination God is Man & exists in us & we in him" (*E*, p. 654). For him, the only God is incarnate in human beings, "the Human Form Divine," and this puts him in conflict with religious orthodoxy.

Blake too provides a spiritual basis for the natural world, stating:

And every Natural Effect has a Spiritual Cause, and Not
A Natural: for a Natural Cause only seems, it is a Delusion
Of Ulro.

(*M*, 26:44–46)

But he anchors that spiritual base securely within Human Imagination. The founders of the natural world, Los and Enitharmon, the spirits of time and space, are simultaneously the mercy and messengers of Eternity in Blake's vision. Though they determine the material world as a foundation for imagination to work on and as a barrier against chaos, they are not separate from the Human Form Divine but a part of it. Indeed, as soon as man begins to function imaginatively rather than in the oppressive empirical, deistic, or orthodox religious way, Enitharmon and Los become one with him as does Jesus, and he becomes fully human. We see this happen to Albion at the end of *Jerusalem* (92:7–93:18).

Like Blake, Berkeley opposed the Newtonian notion of absolute time and space with a more relativistic theory. For Newton,

I. Absolute, true, and mathematical time, of itself, and from its own nature, flows equably without relation to any thing external, and by another name is called duration: relative, apparent, and common time, is some sensible and external (whether accurate or unequable) measure of duration by the means of motion, which is commonly used instead of true time; such as an hour, a day, a month, a year.
II. Absolute Space, in its own nature, without relation to any thing external, remains always similar and immovable. Relative space is some movable dimension or measure of the absolute spaces;

As the order of the parts of time is immutable, so also is the order of the parts of space. . . . All things are placed in time as to order of succession; and in space as to order of situation. It is from their essence or nature that they are places; and that the primary places of things should be moveable, is absurd. These are therefore the absolute places; and translations out of those places, are the only Absolute Motions.[24]

For Berkeley, however, no absolute categories of time and space exist independently of our ideas of them. Distance, for example, is a function of the thoughts and sensations that accompany vision rather than a mathematical measurement of place existing in absolute space. Visible phenomena are signs of particular ideas, and we are manipulating a system of signs as we perceive the world. The same is true of time, as well as cause and effect, which are temporal phenomena. "The connexion of ideas," claims Berkeley—sounding like a modern semiologist—"does not imply the relation of *cause* and *effect* but only of a mark or *sign* with the thing *signified.*"[25] All knowledge, then, becomes a universally agreed upon symbol system based on ideas and signs derived from perception.

In Blake's view Newtonian categories of time and space are wholly false. They are responsible for the nightmares of history and geography described in *Europe* and elsewhere, and for the same dull round of the oppressive, dehumanizing Urizenic world. However, Blake's vision of flexible time or space is closer to Kant's categories than to Berkeley's signs. For Kant space and time are a priori forms of human intuition and "the determinations [not] of things in themselves but of appearances,"[26] whereas for Blake they are human imaginative creations (*M*, pl. 28–29). For both they originate in, and are determined by, the human mind. For Blake however, time is defined by each individual act of imaginative creation, and space is defined by human sight and is relative to the individual: "if he move his dwelling-place, his heavens also move." (*M*, 29:12). Although this conception is not precisely Kant's universal mode of human perception, for it is particular to each individual, it is far different from Newtonian scientific absolute space based on Galileo and other early astronomers. This last, Blake calls "false appearance which appears to the reasoner, / As of a Globe rolling thro Voidness, it is a delusion of Ulro" (*M*, 29:15–16). Though Blake agrees with Berkeley in his claim that human perceptions define objects— that is, that all we can know of an object is our perception of it—he goes even further, as Kant does, to define Time and Space as inescapable categories of human thought rather than as signs in a mutually agreed upon and God-given symbol system. Blake founds these categories in the human being's very life blood.

> The microscope knows not of this nor the telescope, they alter
> The ratio of the Spectators Organs but leave Objects untouched
> For every Space larger than a red Globule of Mans blood.
> Is visionary: and is created by the Hammer of Los
> And every Space smaller than a Globule of Mans blood. opens
> Into Eternity of which this vegetable Earth is but a shadow:
> The red Globule is the unwearied Sun by Los created
> To measure Time and Space to mortal Men. every morning.
>
> (*M*, 29:17–24)

Los, or the imagination, creates within the blood of each of us the capacity to measure time and space; that is, in Kant's terms, to order the manifold according to these forms of intuition. But every drop of blood is simultaneously the Sun itself. Thus Blake amalgamates the inner and outer universe, and the microcosm not only defines, but is identified with, the macrocosm.

Here Blake, the visionary poet, departs from the criticism of rational empirical philosophers. He parts company with Berkeley, who finally takes refuge in a religious metaphysics superimposed on his relational science. Recognizing mathematical laws of nature that explain observations but not causes, Berkeley places them within a God-given symbol system. Blake similarly parts company with Kant, for whom physics, mathematics, philosophy, and indeed all human knowledge are a product of a priori synthetic judgments that operate as universals with no trace of individual subjectivity. Newtonian physics is as necessary a truth for Kant as is morality determined by the categorical imperative. For him One Law for the Lion and the Ox is not oppression.

Blake also seconds with some of Hume's criticism of Newtonian science and Lockean epistemology, although he soundly condemns Hume's ultimate skepticism. Hume has been credited with "uncovering of the problem of induction," for revealing that though we "claim to know, yet [we] never in principle do know for certain, that any generalization based upon observed instances of phenomena remains true when extrapolated to cover unobserved instances, whether in the past or future."[27] This is the essence of Hume's skeptical attack on the concept of causation that Bacon, Newton, and Locke, for example, took for granted. Blake, seeing the same difficulties, went in a different direction. Equally aware of the limitations of empirical views of experience and the human mind, Blake went beyond Hume in recognizing the dangers of pure skepticism: "If the Sun & Moon should doubt / Theyd immediately Go out" (*Aug Inn*, 109–10). Thus he turns to the "Poetic or Prophetic character" (*NNR*, E 3), or imagination, as the only way to solve the problem.

It is, therefore, in the solution of the problem rather than its statement that Blake radically parts company with Hume, condemning his approach as soundly as Locke's, which Hume carries to a logical culmination. In order to avoid the problem of generalizations on unobserved phenomena, Hume adopts a strict observationalism. The connections between objects and events in Hume's system are not logically necessary as they are in the mathematical systems of seventeenth-century science, but are merely natural, matters of fact based on succession, "constant conjunction" and "customary connexion." This takes Newtonian and Lockean observationalism to its skeptical conclusion, marking the last step in the march of Doubt. When Blake condemns Newtonian science for its insistence on demonstration,

> Newton says Doubt
> Aye thats the way to make all Nature out
> Doubt Doubt & dont believe without experiment

(E, 501)

he is even more soundly condemning Hume, whose "doubt" puts Newton's in the shade.

Blake's solution, on the other hand, places the individual as perceiving subject simultaneously at both the center and circumference. As the creative mind shapes and humanizes the world, subject is connected with object. Blake's imaginative psychology replaces Hume's associationist psychology as it does Locke's atomistic psychology; for both limit the scope of human thought. As Hume states,

> Nothing, at first view may seem more unbounded than the thought of man, which not only escapes all power and authority, but is not even restrained within the limits of nature and reality. . . .
> But though our thought seems to possess this unbounded liberty, we shall find, upon a nearer examination, that it is really confined within very narrow limits, and that all this creative power of the mind amounts to no more than the faculty of compounding, transposing, augmenting, or diminishing the materials afforded us by the senses and experience.[28]

Hume here reaches a Lockean conclusion that places ideas in the mind like furniture in a room and limits thought to furniture arrangement. The result is equally restrictive for humanity.

Blake thus condemns Hume as well as Locke in his depiction of Reuben, the Spectre, or Urizen and his progeny. Indeed, the illustration of a Urizenic figure (J, pl. 15) who rises from the "Schools & Universities of Europe" to limit human vision by the contracting sweep of his arms and the force of his body, which pushes the vegetating and enrooting human figure into the corner, could be Blake's illustration of the above quotation from Hume as easily as it is his illustration of the ideas of Locke and Newton mentioned in the text of Jerusalem. Each limits the scope of human thought to the manipulation, through limited reason, of unimaginative sense impression.

Hume's prescription of human liberty through the operation of logical necessity in his Essay also demonstrates his Urizenic oppres-

67

sion. That liberty of mind and body which Blake extols as the essence of truly and fully human existence is symbolized by risen Albion at the end of *Jerusalem:* "I know of no other Christianity and of no other Gospel than the liberty of both body & mind to exercise the Divine Arts of Imagination" (pl. 77), Blake tells the reader.

But Hume, like Locke and Newton, grinds out his arguments denying liberty in that mechanistic logic mill with

> wheel without wheel, with cogs tyrannic
> Moving by compulsion each other: not as those in Eden: which
> Wheel within Wheel in freedom revolve in harmony & peace.
>
> (*J*, 15:18–20)

What Blake calls "compulsion," Hume terms "necessity." "It consists," Hume states, "either in the constant conjunction of like objects, or in the inference of the understanding from one object to another."[29] Both of these definitions fit Blake's description of compulsion as they do that of Dostoevsky's underground man. One sets up a chain of natural events, what Locke and Newton call causality and Hume calls constant conjunction, and the other sets up the laws of logic and reason founded on noncontradiction or negation rather than on dialectical logic founded on contraries.

Although Blake implicitly attacks Hume's epistemology and skepticism, his explicit attack centers on Hume's ideas of natural religion and history. Mentioning him four times by name, Blake consistently puts him in the company of Voltaire and Gibbon and twice in the company of Rousseau as well. In two instances, *Milton*, 40 and *Jerusalem*, 52, the references are to natural religion. Blake is condemning eighteenth-century deism, which saw God as the retired creator of the universe governed by natural laws. Mechanistic images like Voltaire's of the watchmaker creating and setting the apparatus in motion only to sit back and watch passively afterward were anathema to Blake, for whom the ongoing identity and interpenetration of human and divine was the basis for imaginative existence and fully realized human potential. His attack on Deism is clearly stated in the preface to chapter 3 of *Jerusalem:* "Your Religion O Deists: Deism, is the Worship of the God of this World by means of what you call Natural Religion and Natural Philosophy, and of Natural Morality or Self-Righteousness, the Selfish Virtues of the Natural Heart. This was the Religion of the Pharisees who murdered Jesus. Deism is the same & ends in the same" (pl. 52).

It is thus Hume's writings on natural religion and natural morality, as well as Voltaire's and Rousseau's, that are being attacked.

Hume's notion that "a miracle is a violation of the laws of nature," or that there is "a direct and full *proof* from the nature of the fact, against the existence of any miracle," and finally that "it is experience only, which gives authority to human testimony; and it is the same experience, which assures us of the laws of nature,"[30] landed him squarely in the world of the merely natural within natural religion and the nightmare of history. This puts him in the company of Voltaire and Rousseau, Democritus and Newton, futilely throwing sand against the wind upon the Red Sea shore.

It mattered little to Blake that Hume also rejected the mechanistic images of the eighteenth-century deists and entertained an organic rather than a mechanistic metaphor for the universe. Changing the metaphor does not save him in Blake's eyes. "The world," Philo tells us in the *Dialogues Concerning Natural Religion*, "plainly resembles more an animal or a vegetable than it does a watch or a knitting loom. . . . The cause, therefore," he goes on to say, "of the world we may infer to be something similar or analogous to generation or vegetation."[31] The world of generation and the vegetative world are phrases familiar to all readers of Blake and refer to that unimaginative and limited natural world that oppresses humanity and cuts human beings off from their divine imaginative nature. Whether Blake picked up these phrases from Hume, or came to them in other ways, is not clear. It is clear however, that though each writer values the natural world in a different way, both are loosening the bonds of mechanistic science and moving toward the organic metaphors of the nineteenth century.

There is no such mitigating metaphor in Voltaire, however. Idolizing Bacon, Newton, and Locke, Voltaire was responsible for spreading and popularizing in France the major tenets of English empiricism that Blake attacked. Newtonian science became the basis of Voltaire's thoroughgoing materialism based on notions of natural law. Similarly, Newtonian and Lockean natural religion together with English deism formed the basis of Voltaire's religious views. His argument from design, for example, is not very different from Cleanthes' in Hume's *Dialogues Concerning Natural Religion*, nor his criticism of revelation or miracles from that set forth in Hume's *Enquiry*. Finally, Lockean empiricism and political writings inspired Voltaire's sensationalism and political theory. Thus Blake's attacks on Voltaire are very much the same attacks that he leveled at the British empiricists, and they are launched for the same reasons. As the popularizer of Newtonian mechanics applied to the individual and the social order that included natural religion, Voltaire combines with Rousseau, who was similarly influenced and similarly affected, in the blocking figure of Blake's mythic vision. They form the wings of Albion's Spectre, his "Rational Power" who is "Bacon & Newton & Locke" and who teaches the "Doubt & Experiment" (*J*, 54:16) of British empiricism.

As the Spectre's wings, they demonstrate the flight abroad of British empiricism (Bacon, Newton, Locke), and its continental manifestations, which Blake attacks. It is not until these ideas migrate further in time and space, into Germany at the turn of the century and later, that we begin to see a philosophical kinship with Blake's poetical vision. The German rebellion against Newtonian rationalism, the different conception of knowledge as active rather than passive, "the raising of artistic creation to a primary phase of human experience, the elaboration of a systematic aesthetics and an appreciation of the active power and originality of the imagination that extended to all works of mind, led directly to the formulations of the great romantic philosophers"; Kant's redefinition of time and space, Herder's appeal to immediate and intuitive experience of the divine, Fichte's attempt to connect the Self and Not-Self, Schlegel's celebration of the "divine power of imagination," Schelling's notion that "Nature is visible Spirit, and Spirit invisible Nature,"[32] and Hegel's dialectical logic that sees the necessary existence of contraries for the development of new truths, all demonstrate the philosophical reaction to British empiricism implicit in Blake's visionary poetic response. A full analysis of those similarities, however, is the subject for another essay.

Thus, while taking his place in the historical philosophic dialogue, Blake enters the conversation in his own imaginative terms. As readers we may unfold Blake's refutation of, and dialogue with, the major philosophic ideas of his time by analyzing the meaning of his poetry and illustrations, but he presents his vision to us in mythic terms. He rejects the philosophic tools of the trade—logic, empirical reason, scientific observation and experiment resulting in discursive argument—in favor of the artisan's and artist's tools—Los's hammer, tongs, and anvil forging imaginative vision in creative fires, and the artist's pen, burin, and brush delineating word and image. Through his use of image and symbol, the structure of his poetry, and the conflicts of his mythic characters, the clash of ideas is revealed. The Urizenic forces at work present the implications and consequences of perceiving and reasoning in empirical terms, and the Eternal characters dialectically present a critique and imaginative alternative. But all do so in poetic form through character, language, and action as well as in pictorial form through image, line, and color. Philosophical argument is thus transformed into art through imaginative vision, myth, and symbolic action.

Notes

1. Isaac Newton, *Mathematical Principles,* trans. Andrew Motte (Berkeley: University of California Press, 1966), pp. xvii–xviii.

2. John Herman Randall, Jr., *The Career of Philosophy* (New York: Columbia University Press, 1962), v. 1, p. 241 (hereafter cited as *Philosophy*).

3. Donald Ault, *Visionary Physics: Blake's Response to Newton* (Chicago: University of Chicago Press, 1974), p. 22.

4. Ibid.

5. Randall, *Philosophy,* v. 1, p. 564.

6. For a full discussion of the elements mitigating the glory of revolution in *America,* see Minna Doskow, "William Blake's *America:* The Story of a Revolution Betrayed," *Blake Studies* 8, no. 2 (1979): 167–86.

7. Northrop Frye, *Fearful Symmetry* (Boston: Beacon Press, 1947), p. 260.

8. David V. Erdman, ed., *The Complete Poetry and Prose of William Blake* (Garden City: Doubleday & Co., 1982). All citations from Blake's works are from this edition.

9. Michael Ferber, *The Social Vision of William Blake* (Princeton: Princeton University Press, 1985), p. 97.

10. David Hume, "An Enquiry Concerning Human Understanding," in *Enquiries Concerning the Human Understanding and Concerning the Principles of Morals,"* 2d ed., ed. L. H. Selby-Bigges (Oxford: Clarendon Press, 1970), XII:ii, p. 155 (hereafter cited as *Essay*).

11. John Locke, *An Essay Concerning Human Understanding* (New York: Dover, 1959), II:i,2, pp. 121–22 (hereafter cited as *Essay*).

12. Ibid., II:xi, 9, pp. 206–7.

13. Harold A. Kittel, "*The Book of Urizen* and *An Essay Concerning Human Understanding,"* in *Interpreting Blake,* ed. Michael Phillips (Cambridge: Cambridge University Press, 1978), p. 127.

14. Locke, *Essay,* II:viii, 9, p. 170; and II:viii, 10, p. 170.

15. George Berkeley, *A Treatise Concerning the Principles of Human Knowledge* (Indianapolis: Bobbs-Merrill, 1970), Intro.:vii, 228.

16. Ibid., Intro.: 8, pp. 228–29.

17. Ibid., Intro.: 10, p. 230 and p. 231.

18. Ibid., Intro.: 11, pp. 232–33.

19. Ibid., I:4, p. 247.

20. Ibid., I:3, p. 246.

21. Ibid., I:7 & 9, p. 248 and p. 250.

22. Ibid., I:26, p. 258.

23. Kathleen Raine, *Blake and the New Age* (London: Allen & Unwin, 1979), p. 153.

24. Newton, *Principia,* p. 6 and p. 8.

25. Berkeley, *Principles of Human Knowledge,* I:65, p. 279.

26. Immanuel Kant, *Critique of Pure Reason,* trans. Norman Kemp Smith (New York: St. Martin's Press, 1965), p. 286.

27. Isaiah Berlin, *The Age of Enlightenment,* in *The Great Ages of Western Philosophy* (New York: George Braziller, 1958), v. 4, p. 189.

28. Hume, *Essay,* II:13, p. 19.

29. Ibid., II:75, p. 97.

30. Ibid., X:i,90, p. 114 and p. 115; X:ii,98, p. 127.

31. David Hume, *Dialogues Concerning Natural Religion,* ed. Henry D. Aiken (New York: Hafner, 1955), VII, p. 47. Although the first-person narrator of the *Dialogues* claims at the end to agree with Cleanthes, and not Philo, we cannot simply accept this as Hume's real position. Philo, a more thoroughgoing skeptic than the deistic or rational empiricist Cleanthes, gets the best arguments in the Dialogues and comes out the winner in the debates too often for us to think that Hume did not mean to make him an attractive spokesman for his position.

32. Randall, *Philosophy,* v. 2, p. 58 and p. 257.

Blake's America and
the Birth of Revolution
Michael Ferber

Blake was seventeen years old when the news came to England of the shots fired at Lexington and Concord; he was thirty-one at the time of the storming of the Bastille. The French and American revolutions decisively shaped his thought and feeling about human beings as social beings, which is to say, humanity in its essence. Even more decisive was the agonizing fact that a revolution did not occur in England: in an extension of England, perhaps, and in her nearest neighbor, but not, despite his fondest hopes, in his homeland, where it might have begun the renovation of the world. On the contrary, England fought for six years against her colonies and, after some wavering, led the reaction against France. What revolutionary ferment did take place in England (and Scotland, Ireland, and Wales), quite substantial in Blake's city and among Blake's social peers, was effectively defeated by the time he was forty. Reports, finally, of the perversion of the original revolutionary spirit of France, and perhaps of America, though not as pivotal as some critics have argued, added confusion to his disappointment and forced a rethinking of what it takes to bring about a social transformation.

To what extent a disillusioned Blake abandoned his hopes for revolution and turned instead to a more private Christian faith I must leave to another occasion. In this essay I shall dwell on Blake's idea, or ideal, of social revolution before anything resembling a crisis or conversion can be traced, when the French Revolution was still young and Blake was still working out his "continental myth" of universal renewal. I shall concentrate on the "Preludium" to *America: A Prophecy* (1793); from limitations of space, I shall look only briefly at the "Prophecy" section of *America* and at the "Preludium" to its sequel, *Europe: A Prophecy* (1794).

Historians may debate how great an impact the American Revolution made on France, but Blake had no doubts, at first, that the liberation of the world from tyranny had begun in America, was spreading to France, would soon come to England, and would ultimately reach Asia and the scene of man's original enslavement, Africa. Blake's figure of reaction in *The French Revolution* (1791), "the ancientist Peer, Duke of Burgundy," blames America for the leveling spirit now abroad in France: shall "these mowers / From the Atlantic mountains, mow down all this great starry harvest of six thousand years?"(89–90). At the end of *America*, Urizen has managed to hide the fires of the American Orc behind clouds and mist, but it is announced that he will fail after twelve years, "when France reciev'd the Demons light" (16:15). Even more striking is the continuity of the two "Preludia" to *America* and to *Europe*, as if the two narratives they introduce, set in different continents twelve years apart, are only the "historical" embodiment of the same unfolding situation in a spiritual or allegorical realm. Around both *America* and *Europe*, finally, Blake seems to have planned to put the two parts of *The Song of Los* (1795), "Africa" telling of the fall and enslavement of man, its final line identical to the first line of *America's* "Prophecy" section, and "Asia" opening with a howl rising from Europe and concluding with the resurrection of the dead. Had he engraved these in sequence instead of fusing the first and last parts inseparably, he would have had a fourfold gospel of freedom set in turn on the four continents of the world (America being one continent from Canada to Peru), moving clockwise historically from the south through the four cardinal points, and recapitulating the whole Bible from the descent into Egypt (Africa) to the return to Jerusalem (Asia). He would also have been continuing the tradition of the "westering of the spirit" begun in Virgil's *Aeneid*: the destruction of a city in Asia, the escape from gentle fetters in Africa, and the colonizing of a promised western land, Hesperia, where a new city shall rise; extended to Britain in medieval times with Brutus a descendant of Aeneas and London a New Troy; and brought to America in Shakespeare's *The Tempest*, where the voyage from Tunis (Carthage) to Italy detours, it seems, to Bermuda, where a new social order is drawn out of the old.[1]

Nowhere in *America* does Blake refer to an American *revolution;* even Albion's Angel, the voice of English reaction, never uses the word but, like the real spokesmen of the time, calls it "rebellion" (7:6). Since Blake calls his poem about the French events of June 1789 *The French Revolution,* it might seem he is drawing a distinction, like many modern historians, between the genuine social revolution in France and the less drastic America war of separation from Britain. But he is not. That he uses "revolution" of France in 1791 is in fact more interesting than its absence from *America,* for the term was only just taking on its modern sense of a large, usually violent, upheaval from below that brings about a new structure of society. The title of Edmund Burke's hostile *Reflections on the Revolution in France* (1790), which decisively shifted the term from its older meanings, suggests an unexpected readiness to part with a term Burke himself reserves for what amounts to a *restoration,* the "Glorious" Revolution of 1688.[2] This was indeed *the* English Revolution, even among those who sympathized with the doings in France in 1789. Revolution was a restoration of ancient liberties through the removal of a usurping tyrant; its exemplar was the relatively bloodless expulsion of James II and the summoning of a "constitutional" monarch to replace him. What happened in 1649—which we would today call a revolution far sooner than we would 1688—was the Great Rebellion. Indeed, "revolution" was used of the Stuart Restoration of 1660, for it returned England, in the eyes of the royalists, to its condition before the usurpation of Cromwell. I am not sure what Burke had in mind, but it is clear that, until the news of the September Massacres in 1792 and especially the regicide of early 1793, most English people sympathized with the changes in France and called them revolutionary in the older and favorable sense. France seemed to be reinstating her ancient liberties—the Estates-General was meeting for the first time since 1614—turning its once absolute tyranny into a constitutional monarchy explicitly on the English pattern. In 1790, when he probably wrote *The French Revolution,* Blake may have had doubts about just how constitutional things were in England; but in echoing

Burke's title, as others were also doing, he meant to preserve the meaning of "revolution" from the taint Burke's diatribe had given it. As early as page 1 of the poem, even the King recognizes that it is "the ancient dawn [that] calls us / To awake from slumbers of five thousand years" (7–8). The ghost of good King Henry IV himself walks through the poem, as if to say that what Fayette and the Abbé de Sieyès have in mind is a purification of the monarchy to its ancient glory.

Though Blake does not call it one, the rebellion of the colonies as he portrays it in *America* is in fact a revolution in the older sense Blake invariably uses. Like the King of France, the Angel of Albion recognizes the rebellion as a reprise of something that took place once before, though he is not so ready to see that the sun has left its blackness and found a fresher morning. With these ancient dawns, however, we enter into an aspect of the meaning of "revolution" of such importance to Blake that it is best to take it up in some detail before turning to the text of *America*.

For as long as humankind has considered anything, it has considered the stars; to "consider," of course, means exactly that in its Latin roots. Sun, moon, planets, and stars not only made up the sole reliable guides to time and space, calendar and compass, but they seemed to govern events on earth as well. Our words "consider," "disaster," "influence," and "lunatic" preserve astrology on even skeptical lips, and the majority of Americans still read the horoscope with more than idle amusement. For poets, whatever their beliefs, the heavenly bodies and their movements provided a rich and coherent system of metaphor, perhaps the foundation of all figuration of terrestrial deeds. As King Edward the Third states it in Blake's early play, "The world of men are like the num'rous stars"—some shine more brightly than others, some wander from their spheres, and so on (E 424).

All of this hardly needs repeating. It is interesting to see in Blake, however, one of the most persistent and extensive displays of astronomical and meteorological phenomena in his texts and designs to be found in any poet or painter; it is interesting because Blake, it seems clear, despised astrology, had no use for telescopes, and even thought stars, at least as the specks of light most people take them for, to be no more than a delusion, a mere "rash" (as Hegel once called them),[3] the limit of contraction and alienation of the light that once filled our being. For all that, and because we happen to be here in our "fallen" state beneath the spangled cosmic shell, Blake embodies many of his chief themes in terms of stars, moons, meteors, clouds, and nearly everything else that inhabits the sky "above" us. He is often very specific, as in a passage about Mars in *America* that we shall shortly consider, and in a fascinating note in *A Descriptive Catalogue* (E 542) where he connects King Arthur with Arcturus or Bootes, "Keeper of the North Pole."

What is most important in this context is the link between heavenly movements and political events, and for these Blake had several major precedents. One of them was the star of Bethlehem, appearing at midnight in the "dead" of winter to herald the dawn of the new age, the birth of the sun of righteousness. Some scholars have seen in this star an example of "political astronomy," arguing that the authors of the ur-gospels inserted a *nova*, or new star, and three magi or astrologers as a refutation of the magian stellar worship that was widespread in Judea.[4] Another precedent was Virgil's Fourth Eclogue, imagery from which easily assimilates to passages from Isaiah and Revelation, and which is explicitly political in a narrow partisan sense. Throughout the Bible, of course, we find wishful threats of falling stars and "spiritual wickedness in high places" deserving to be humbled.[5]

"Revolution" was an astronomical term before it became a political one; or rather, it was, and remains, literal in astronomy and figurative in politics. There were several cycles of heavenly movement: not only the daily motion of all the bodies around the pole and the yearly motion of the sun through the zodiac, but much larger cycles such as the conjunction of the sun and Sirius every 1,461 years (known to the Egyptians) and the realignment of the equinoctial points and the zodiac about every 26,000 years, which was called the Great Year. This latter cycle of backward drifting or precession of the equinoxes may have had something to do with the astral symbolism of both the Gospels and the Fourth Eclogue, for it was at about the reign of Augustus that spring no longer began in Aries but had entered the house of Pisces. Any of these cycles could be called a revolution, a restoration, an *anacyclosis* (Polybius's term for both a political and an astronomical cycle), or an *apocatastasis*.[6]

Here below, in the sublunary realm, events were subject to heavenly influences but even more subject to the fickle revolutions of the wheel of fortune, a kind of parody of the regular cosmic cycles. The moon itself is regularly changeful and irregularly eclipsed; and then there are comets and meteors, not to mention winds and clouds, to keep affairs on earth properly chaotic. Blake draws on all of this, and even occasionally suggests a unique cataclysm in the high heavens; but it is largely the great regular cycles that interest him, the kind of process evoked in the return of an "ancient dawn" after five thousand years or more.[7]

In filling his political poems with celestial objects and events, of course, Blake endows the affairs of nations with cosmic significance, like any Fourth of July orator. Since *America* is in fact about the Fourth of July, it is only appropriate that he launch some fireworks and make a jovial hullabaloo among the spheres. Americans themselves were quick to do so, declaring each new state a *stella nova* in the blue firmament of the official flag and quoting, or misquoting, the Fourth Eclogue in Latin on the Great Seal, now on the back of the dollar bill. In doing this Blake is exploiting the "revolutionary" significance of astronomy itself. Finally, following hints from Isaiah and Revelation, he is bringing the stars down to earth. The age now dawning is precisely a dawn; the returning sun, somehow hidden all these years (inside Mars, as Blake will tell us), will put out the stars of the ancient heavens as Jesus eclipsed Babylonian star-worship. Parts of the heavens will be drawn down to earth, as they are in Revelation, and the Angel of Albion will know just what that means—the dragon who took a third part of the stars of heaven (Rev. 12.4) reappears as the Orc who threatens to devour the children of heaven (7:4). But this rebellion is a repetition with a difference. It is a restoration of the "fallen" earth to its rightful height, and the angels falling from the sky are converts from the false remote heavens of orthodoxy to the original ground of all energy and delight.

The "Preludium" to *America* begins with something that sounds a little like a celestial revolution in the offing: "The shadowy daughter of Urthona stood before red Orc. / When fourteen suns had faintly journey'd o'er his dark abode" (1–2). Setting aside for a moment just who these people are, we see something red under eclipse by something shadowy, or perhaps something bright like the sun showing red through a mist or haze (a frequent image in Blake) and ready, perhaps, to burn through and shine clear. But this sun has been in total eclipse for two weeks, if that is what "fourteen suns" means and if "journey" means a day's travel, so Orc sounds rather more like a moon, about to wax, rather abruptly, from new to full. As this is not a very satisfactory conflation of symbols, and as Blake doubtless intended something pretty definite about the interval, readers have offered plenty of suggestions, but none of them quite answers the problem.[8] A cycle of some sort has reached its term, but what happens afterward hardly resembles a revolution: it is much more like a rape. What we are asked to do as we read these two plates is to ponder in what sense the events of the American struggle for independence may be considered a sexual act, a violent embrace by a frustrated boy, joyfully accepted by a speechless girl who, finding her voice at last, announces her pregnancy in woeful terms.

That we have come into a story already well advanced the two unheard-of names in the first line are enough to tell us. This may be Blake's idea of the epic entrance *in medias res;* but the classical epic always circles back to explain the opening situation clearly and at length, but Blake does not, at least not here—only in *The Four Zoas* does he place the situation in a much larger context. From *America* alone, even together with *Europe,* we can only with some difficulty infer pieces of the antecedent story; much remains unknown.[9]

We may infer that a stern father has chained Orc and set his daughter to tend him, putting her under a spell as well and arming her to prevent Orc's escape; she brings her captive his food and, it seems, falls in love with him. Except for the clouds and the pestilence shot from heaven (a meteor), which project the story onto the sky where part of it will remain for the whole poem, we are on more or less familiar ground, that of chivalric romance. Urthona is a wicked enchanter who has bound both his daughter and her liberator in magical spells or physical chains, but love conquers all; the young hero manages to break his chains and then break her spell. There is even a dragon to be slain in the "Prophecy" section, the Guardian Prince of Albion, whom we may reasonably take at first as Urthona himself (not mentioned again), and who is revealed in "A dragon form" (3:15).[10]

But this variant of the romance plot is grotesquely out of order. Orlando or St. George or any proper hero will slay the dragon first and then win the maiden (in Orlando's case, the *dragon* is named Orc!); Blake's Orc subdues the maiden to gain the power to slay the dragon, or rather face him down when he "burns" at the sight of Orc's rising. This is most unchivalrous. No doubt the pressure of the political allegory bent the story out of shape: the archetypal myth tells that the land is usurped by a tyrannous power that a young man must set to rights, whereas America is a new land, newly colonized, and perhaps only newly tyrannized by an absentee landlord (Urthona the earth-owner) who must be kept at bay. Still, there are problems. Who, or what, frees Orc? Is it the nameless female herself, by nourishing him, though on iron rations, in a fruitful land, until he simply grows strong enough to break free?

Another archetype hovering over the "Preludium" is a variant of the romance plot, Shakespeare's *The Tempest*. Orc is part Caliban and part Ferdinand, both chained by Prospero; Caliban had sought to rape Miranda, and she, at first nameless to Ferdinand, "quickens what's dead" in his slavery and out of love for him breaks her father's behest and tells him her name. Apart from his sexual nature, Orc is a cross between Caliban and Ariel, or rather a Caliban growing into an Ariel, riveted in chains "while still on high my spirit soars." Ariel had also been confined a dozen years in a cloven pine by Sycorax (Enitharmon?); "free" now, if he disobeys Prospero he will be locked in an oak "till / Thou hast howled away twelve winters." That certainly sounds like the twelve-year winter of reinslavement prophesied at the end of *America*, though there it is Urizen who does the howling (16:12–14). It also suggests the enslavement of Orc's offspring by Enitharmon in *Europe*, where they will be heard "shrieking in hollow tress" (2:6), though Dante's wood of suicides is also relevant. (Blake drew tangles of humanoid roots and branches on several of the *America* plates; there is a little Orc hunkered under a root on plate 1 and sprouting on plate 2, and a Daphne caught in a tree on plate 15.) Finally, *The Tempest*, as I have mentioned, is in some sense set in America or at least evokes it. If the *America* prologue, then, stirs up odd echoes of other romance stories, the effect of most of the echoes is to bring out the abrupt departure from the pattern—the Calibanish deed of Ferdinand, the Orc inside Orlando—while still holding the pattern before us as a guide to interpretation.[11]

By displacing the sexual consummation from the end to the beginning of the heroic action, Blake may also be summoning the original mythical basis of the romance plots themselves, a more forthright masculine tale rearranged, sublimated, and "feminized" into the stories we know. This is about the conquest and cultivation of a virgin land. The American Revolution was a twofold act, after all, the overthrowing of a dragonish tyranny, as in all the romances, and the colonization of a promised land, which we find in the Old Testament, the myth of Cadmus, and the *Aeneid* (in all of which there are dragons or serpents). The image of Israel as the "married land" and God as her husband recurs often in the Old Testament (e.g., Isaiah 54.5, Jeremiah 3:14); the term Beulah ("married"), from Isaiah 62.4, passes by way of Bunyan's *Pilgrim's Progress* into a central spiritual "place" in Blake's later symbolic system, notably in

Milton. As early as *Thel,* one finds continual references in Blake to the Song of Solomon. From the forward Thel to the forward Oothoon, "the soft soul of America" (*VDA* 1:3), and then to the shadowy female, we have a sequence useful for interpreting the four poems: *Thel* turns out to have a social theme in germ while the "dark virgin" in *America* emerges more clearly as the "black but comely" maiden of the Song of Solomon who seeks her lover. Indeed, there is a fairly clear hint in the Preludium[12] itself that the Song of Solomon is another prototype, for the "virgin cry," the first line the female ever utters, is almost a quotation from it. In the Song the beloved rises from her bed to look for her lover, and after a while "I found him whom my soul loveth: I held him, and would not let him go" (3.4).[13] The female's possessiveness has a sinister note—has Orc rent his manacles only to fall prisoner again in the arms of his supposedly disarmed guardian?—and it is sounded as well in the rest of the biblical passage: "and would not let him go, until I had brought him into my mother's house, and into the chamber of her that conceived me." In *Europe,* we learn, her mother is Enitharmon, a female tyrant who lives in a crystal house in heaven.

A similar symbolism underlies Aeneas's conquest of Italy, the promised western land of Hesperia, which includes his ceremonial plowing of the borders of the first Trojan camp and his destined marriage to King Latinus's daughter Lavinia, "Miss Italy," and his founding a new city in her name. King Latinus corresponds roughly to Urthona and to the Guardian Prince of Albion, who knows, as Latinus knew, that "now the times are return'd upon thee," or upon him (9:19). It is also relevant that Aeneas must descend to the lower world, which Virgil once names "Orcus," and emerge from it to face the wars his arrival in Italy has precipitated.

Beulah, Italia, America: the land is always feminine in name and nature. She receives her conqueror: he plants his flag, plows her field, and "marries" her in often quite literal rituals, and "she becomes his dwelling place / And Garden fruitful seventy fold," as Blake puts it in "The Mental Traveller."

What, then, is the name of the nameless female? When she is finally brought to speech, she all but announces that it is America, though she also names Canada, Mexico, and Peru (and suggests that they might be male figures, courting her like Orc). Before Orc took her, I suppose, her secret name was Virginia. But her new name, her first real name, must be the United States, and that is hardly a name. Perhaps Blake gives her a voice but withholds a name because he does not want us simply to equate her allegorically with America; she is more a potential of terrestrial embodiment of revolution and cultivation, something like nature itself. (Later Blake will settle on "Vala" and identify her with nature.) She moves, for one thing, to Europe; and in the Preludium to *Europe*, she is still nameless. In fact, she worries there that her exhausting production of sons, who are taken away by Enitharmon, will "cause my name to vanish," an odd fear in one who had no name to begin with. We are left with the idea that the name she is on the verge of acquiring (not Miss America but Mrs. Orc, that is, the Bride of the Revolution) is the name she is also about to lose because Orc has become bound again (he lies silent or asleep throughout the second Preludium) and all her sons are given other names (stamped with Enitharmon's signet) and sent away; she might at least be called Mother of the Little Orcs, but they will not carry on the patronymic. Behind all this is the story of Adam and Eve: a female who is nameless, called "Woman" until after the Fall and her punishment of bringing forth in sorrow, whereupon she is named Eve, the "mother of all living."

As we first meet her in *America*, the female seems a kind of iron maiden, with a helmet and a tongue of iron; she brings Orc's food and drink in iron implements and guards him in his tenfold iron chains. In Blake's later myth, Urthona, or Los, is a blacksmith or ironworker like Hephaestus (Vulcan), who made armor for Achilles and Aeneas and chained down Prometheus. For America it is an iron age. Washington points his companions to a bow in heaven like the female's and "a heavy iron chain" that reaches all the way across the Atlantic from Albion's cliffs (3:7–9); America is enslaved and war is in the offing. She resembles both Artemis the archer, whose brother's bow shoots pestilence on the Greeks in the *Iliad*, and the helmeted Athena, both virgins. There is something disturbing about her, however much we may blame it on her father's spell or command. It is far from certain, too, just what Orc can see of her, what she can see of him, and what hinders either view. Though the clouds seem to roll round her loins, which Orc's gaze might well seek to penetrate, it is her face, he complains, that the clouds obscure. Perhaps the clouds move upward—they "roll to & fro"— from her loins to her face. After the sexual act, she parts her clouds and smiles, and only then does she see the terrible boy. They have consummated their love in the dark: Orc could find her loins, but they still could not see each other's face until it was done and her joy came out. I am not sure how to interpret this. The helmet and bow may be more or less equivalent to the cloud, which protects her one vulnerable place (Blake likens the vagina to a wound in *FZ* I, 12:40–43): they are the physical and mental facets of her enslavement and his, the mind-forged manacles, the condition of being "bound in the dens of superstition" (*FR* 228), the clouds of ignorance that keep out the sun of enlightenment. They are also her virgin fears, like those of the dreaming maiden in "The Angel": "I dried my tears & armed my fears, / With ten thousand shields and spears" (*E* 24). The pestilential bow reminds us that Blake connects pestilence with sexual repression, with desiring but acting not. In feeding the chained Orc, she is, in the language of *The Marriage of Heaven and Hell*, almost literally nursing an unacted desire (*E* 38). One imagines her helmet as covering her face at first, preventing her speech as well as her sight, until she raises her vizor to smile; but the absurdities this idea invites are probably disallowed by the word "crown'd," which makes her more a queen (with visible hair, too) than a Woman in an Iron Mask. Maybe the helmet is meant to suggest the barrier between her mind and the reception of new heavenly ideas; enslaved, at war, she has iron thoughts in an iron time. Her mind is clouded over, she sleepwalks through her duties, silent as night herself, and unaware of the faint suns seeking like red eyes to shine through to her during this endless fortnight.

It is clear that one level of this allegory refers to ideological struggle, as indeed most of the action of the main poem consists of speeches, demonstrations of unity, trumpets of alarm, and defections, and only passingly and implicitly of "corporeal war." Orc's fierce embrace the shadowy female tenaciously returns: it is hard to resist translating this as "America embraces the revolutionary idea." Her maiden speech in the public forum is the Voice of America, the remonstrances, demonstrations, and declarations that were heard round the world. Looking ahead again to the *Europe* Preludium, we find it confirmed that Orc's sexual act represents the implanting of ideas in her head. When she has had enough of giving birth, she replaces her helmet with a turban of thick clouds around her "lab'ring" head. She will prefer the cloudy dreamworld to the bright, difficult concepts of Orc, which are labor enough to think on, let alone to give birth to their embodiments. She has "conceived" of revolution and cannot stop delivering her ideas. The angel-winged woman in the design of *Europe* plate 3, who might be the shadowy female, seems to have given birth to the little fiery baby out of her head: she holds her head as if in pain, the baby floats down directly beneath it, and four tongues of flame around him lick upward to

Michael Ferber

four snaky locks of her hair as if a fourfold umbilical cord has just
unraveled and snapped.

The laboring head metaphor is elaborate. In counting the stars,
she "considers." In seizing their power, she "grasps" or "appre-
hends" their meaning. In taking them into her abyss of sheety waters, she "reflects" (on) them. And so on.[14] These are "influences"
she cannot resist, at least until, for some reason, she stops speaking. Taking the literal action as a metaphor for thoughts helps account for the contrary states she feels drowned in, "shady woe, and
visionary joy" (2:12); the shade may be more restful, but it was vision, the sight of Orc, a conception of how the brave new world
might look, that caused her womb to joy.

The double sense of "conception" recalls another archetype, already suggested by the parallel with Adam and Eve, and that is the
creation of the world in chapter one of Genesis. The earth before
creation, though it is called "earth" in verse two, is nameless until
God formally names the dry land "Earth" in verse ten. It is originally a "deep" like Blake's nameless female, who is called a "silent
deep" and "nether deep," or in Greek (as in Milton), an "abyss,"
which is "fathomless" in both preludia. It is originally shadowy like
her, without form, dark, and void—"void as death," as she says in
Europe. The deep in Genesis has a face God moves upon, or broods
upon: Orc broods and seeks to behold her face. Like Milton's Holy
Spirit, Orc "satst brooding in the vast Abyss / And mad'st it pregnant" (*PL* 1.21–22), pregnant with what he was brooding over, his
fertile conceptions of freedom and revolution. Now Orc may seem a
poor caricature of the omnipotent Creator, but then what Blake
called Creation was the bringing about of the original void, a deed
accomplished by Urizen, Blake's deliberate caricature of the omnipotent Creator. Orc is closer to the Holy Spirit of Milton or the Jehovah "who dwells in flaming fire" and sends "Ideas to build on," as
Blake defines him in *The Marriage of Heaven and Hell* (*E* 35). "Dove-
like" does not suit Orc, though he feels love: Blake may have disliked the dove's female connotations in Milton (which Wordsworth
gives in to with his "mother dove sits brooding" in the opening of
his Prelude) and certainly its gentleness.[15] Orc is an eagle, not whis-
pering in the Virgin's ear but screaming in the sky. Whatever we
may think of the decorum of all this, the allusions to Genesis are
frequent and prominent enough to direct our reading of the preludia as, among many other things, the creation of a new world. The
creation of the New World in the west is precisely the subject of the
poem.[16]

84

There is an interesting simile in the *America* Preludium: "It joy'd: she put aside her clouds & smiled her first-born smile; / As when a black cloud shews its light'nings to the silent deep" (2:4–5). It is an odd violation of epic convention to keep in the comparison or simile proper something that belongs to what is under comparison, but a cloud has nonetheless drifted across from the tenor to the vehicle. Of course, the whole "literal" level of the action is so thoroughly metaphorical that a new figure seems almost gratuitous, but this metonymical simile is carefully placed to interfere with out distinguishing of levels and even of characters. She who puts aside her clouds to smile is likened, as we first take it, to a cloud who shows its lightnings. That is all right; a smile is a quick, bright thing like lightning, which seems to come from within or behind a cloud, though we might have expected the sun here. But the "silent deep," on this reading, stops us, for the Orc who sees her smile has hardly been silent. We are compelled to reverse the equivalents: *she* is the silent deep and Orc the cloud who shows its lightnings; had we any doubt, her speech that follows makes it clear that she thinks of herself as "the nether deep" who has received "thy fire" and "thy lightnings." The simile must refer to the entire act.[17] Her smile, then, would most likely be the reflection of his lightning in her waters, as she will later seize "the overflowing stars" as they rain down on her. There is a precedent for this image in *Visions of the Daughters of Albion* (2:17–19): Oothoon summons the eagles of her sulking "husband," Theotormon, to rend away her defiled bosom, that is, to take her sexually and undo the rape she has just undergone at the hands of Bromion, so "that I may reflect. / The image of Theotormon" (2:17–18). The eagles do so, while he severely smiles; I think the birds represent Oothoon's ideal of her lover, far above his earthbound reality. Yet he smiles; "her soul reflects the smile; / As the clear spring mudded with feet of beasts grows pure & smiles" (2:18–19).

The borrowing of a cloud across two parts of a simile is itself a kind of simile for the way the shadowy female borrows the forms of Orc. A comparable simile in *Europe's* Preludium, however, muddies the water, for there "the dark cloud disburdend in the day of dismal thunder" (1:7) can only be she, not the now silent or exhausted Orc. But, as she has come to "reflect" him, I suppose she deserves to have one of his similes.

Another reversal, a revolution in the strict sense, occurs in the locations of Orc and the female. He is chained beneath in caverns, and she seems to hover over him like night, with a bow that shoots pestilence from heaven; it is only his spirit that soars on high. After the consummation their positions switch, her cloud in the simile becomes his cloud, she becomes land or sea or "deep" (2:11) and he a fallen angel or bolt of lightning. The four forms of his soaring spirit incarnate in the lower realm, and he himself, in her eyes at least, seems the Incarnation itself, "the image of God" (2:8) who "art fall'n to give me life" (2:9). (He is also a seed here, and she the awaiting furrow.) Orc is, of course, a form of Christ, who brought a revolutionary spirit once and will come again to defeat the dragon when the times revolve. To the orthodox angels who think they still own heaven, this Orc-Christ will appear to be the Anti-Christ and eternal serpent. The serpent is the last form Orc's spirit takes before the sexual act, revolving upward to the light, and it is the first form the female recognizes afterward, when she has been revolved (or converted) herself, feeling serpentine roots writhing downward.[18] It is all too complete a reversal, for it leaves the female a bit stunned: the serpent smacks too much of the biblical prototype who "courts" Eve and plants ideas in her head. If Orc is Christ, he is also a second Adam; the Incarnation is a second Fall; Christ is also a second Lucifer, a fallen angel full of light; add the serpents, Caliban, and Prometheus, and it gets harder to cheer on Orc whole-heartedly. The female's speech grows anguished, and though we may discount the pain of labor as the inheritance of womankind, "eternal death" sounds more like hell than the beginning of a new era.

Orc has other hellish features. He is red and hairy, like the devil, and, like Esau, the devil's prototype, with whom Blake always sympathized, Jacob being the pious sneak and mama's boy who usurped Esau's rightful place. Orc comes from Africa, according to the female, a "southern" place (like Edom, descendant of Esau, south of Judea), a land of slavery in both modern times and biblical. At the end of the "Africa" section of *The Song of Los*, clouds roll round three places: the Alps, where Rousseau and Voltaire lived (Geneva); the mountains of Lebanon, where the "deceased Gods" lived; and the deserts of Africa, where the fallen angels still, perhaps, cling to life. If these are comparable forces, then the fallen angels, of which Orc is one, are humanity's liberators. The deceased Gods, which Milton in *Paradise Lost* elaborately identifies with *his* fallen angels, suggest not only the Molochs and Baalim that Milton names but the generation of Titans who reigned with Saturn during the Golden Age. The subterranean Orc, as befits one chained by a Vulcan, stirs like Enceladus under Mt. Etna (suggesting that the female is the Athena who put him there) and erupts in fire, clouds, and lightning.[19] If "darkness of Africa" is also meant to suggest Negro slavery in America, the "swarthy children of the sun" Bromion owns in Oothoon's America (*VDA* 1:21), the suggestion is raised only here. The slaves of the main story of *America* are simply Americans. It may be one source of the ominous notes we have heard in the otherwise hopeful story of a justified insurrection that Blake knew that the slaves of America gained nothing, and even may have lost something, by the Revolution.

We come at last to the end of the Preludium: "this is the torment long foretold" (2:17). The Guardian Prince of Albion takes the same view. He recognizes Orc in plate 7, and in plate 9 echoes the female's language as he wrongly predicts "now thy unutterable torment renews" (9:20). Whether the return of Orc is a torment or not is a matter of conflicting opinion;or perhaps it should be put the other way, that the conflict over his return makes it a torment for both sides. Yet it is obvious that the princely Angel has got it wrong, and much of the poem's irony lies here. He has been reading the Book of Revelation and takes for granted that he is one of the victorious angels; Blake reads the Bible "in its infernal or diabolical sense" and has bad news for him.

Blake has also been reading classical mythology in its infernal sense, and finds prophecies of the Golden Age that suited his plan very well; he has ingeniously blended them with the prophecies of Daniel and Revelation. If, as I have said, Blake is portraying an iron age at the outset of the poem, that hardly means things are hopeless. Hesiod charts a general devolution of the race through four metals from gold through silver and bronze to iron, with an interlude of heroes like those who fought at Troy. Blake recalls us to that heroic age and its disastrous conclusion in his stunning frontispiece, engraved in a different manner from the designs that follow, of a breached city wall in Greek style (though with a cannon), a monumental fallen angel chained within the breach, and a distraught woman with two children. Whatever specific historical associations it is meant to evoke, the engraving certainly suggests the ruin of Troy, the enslavement of the women, the slaughter of the innocents, and the onset of the iron age. But, as the slight echoes of the *Aeneid* may have reminded us, out of the ashes of Troy a new city arose in a promised land. It was Virgil, too, who encircled Hesiod's pessimism within a grand *apocatastasis* of the golden age: "Time has conceived," he announces in the Fourth Eclogue, in language Blake echoes everywhere, "and the great sequence of the ages starts afresh. Justice, the Virgin, comes back to dwell with us" (we may see her scales, at least, in plate 5), "and the rule of Saturn is restored. The firstborn of the new age is already on his way from high heaven down to earth"—the first-born smile, the lightning, and the "secret child" who descends at the opening of the *Europe* Prophecy. "With him the iron race shall end and golden man inherit all the world" (5–7)[20] "Time will run back, and fetch the age of gold" (135) is Milton's near quotation in his ode "On the Morning of Christ's Nativity," which Blake in turn nearly quotes in his "secret child" passage.

What is most ingenious, however, is the way Blake unites the yielding of the iron age to gold with the image of smelting and refinement in a furnace. When Orc rises over the Atlantic to confront Albion, he seems the very essence of the iron age, "a Human fire fierce glowing, as the wedge / Of iron heated in the furnace" (4:8–9), but Orc enjoys the fires of love and revolutionary energy and announces that he, and the forces he symbolizes, will be refined in fire:

> Fires inwrap the earthly globe, yet man is not consumd;
> Amidst the lustful fires he walks: his feet become like brass,
> His knees and thighs like silver, & his breast and head like gold.
>
> (8:15–17)

This, as many commentators have noted, conflates several passages from Daniel: his escape from Nebuchadnezzar's furnace (Nebuchadnezzar, mad like King George, was a favorite subject of Blake's), the king's dream of an image golden in its head and passing downward through silver and brass to feet of iron and clay, and Daniel's vision of a great man with a face of lightning, eyes of fire, and arms and feet like brass. In Revelation this last vision serves as an image of Christ, "who hath his eyes like unto a flame of fire," and "his feet like unto fine brass as if they burned in a furnace."[21] Orc, if his feet were once made of iron, or bound in iron, has already surpassed it, and has taken on the attributes of Christ (clay would be ruled out because Orc is not mortal). Daniel interpreted Nebuchadnezzar's dream as a prophecy of the kingdoms to follow his own, each inferior to the one before it, until the fourth kingdom ("iron and clay") is divided in two. In his Fast Day sermon of 1793 the Reverend Joseph Priestly hailed the French Revolution as a preparation for the events of Nebuchadnezzar's dream.[22] Whether Blake was prompted by this or similar speculations, very much in the air after 1789, he like Priestley stressed the final kingdom, the Fifth Monarchy, "which shall never be destroyed" (Dan. 2.44), but suggests it will come about as a reversal, or revolution, of the decline the king dreams. That is one reason Orc starts with the feet (with which he stamped the stony law to dust); the people are on the march and the heads of state are falling. If Orc seems to threaten to divide the empire (a king's nightmare), we know he is its only hope for unity; and if the Prince of Albion thinks he knows his man, he is as mad as Nebuchadnezzar, for in the furies of a passionate struggle for liberation, man may transcend the wars of iron and usher in a golden age. In *The Rights of Man*, Paine wrote that "the iron is becoming hot all over Europe. . . . The present generation will appear to the future as the Adam of a new world."[23]

The frontispiece to *America* obviously depicts the end of an era, however, and the new one struggling into birth is not yet evident. Erdman connects this scene with the conclusion of *America* rather than the beginning: the angel of liberty, Orc, has made a breach in the stony wall of Albion's tyranny, but that is all. "By 1793, the date on the title page, the American Revolution as a chapter in the revolt of people against monarchs and of minds against mental chains has been stopped dead as far as the people of Albion are concerned." Yet Orc is still alive, and has broken his chains at least once in recent times. His French equivalent is very active even now. Crouched in fetal position, much like the little Orc under the roots of the first Preludium design, as well as the "secret child" descending in a flaming spherical womb through the clouds in *Europe* plate 3, he is only dormant, hibernating for a season under the snows of Urizen. Reborn, he will resume his attack on this new Troy, the "Trinovantum" that London in its imperial pretensions has become.[24]

The frontispiece, then, has a double aspect: the death of Troy as Hector and Andromache felt it, and the birth of a new epoch as Aeneas came to understand it. Erdman again: "Blake now puts before us this vision of death as one we must search as he helps us replace it with a vision of life."[25] Something of that ambivalence, by 1793, Blake may have felt about France and projected back onto the American Revolution. He may well have felt doubts about the American Revolution itself. It was not, after all, nearly as drastic a social transformation as the French Revolution, and may not deserve the name "revolution" in any of its meanings. Whatever Blake may say in the Prophecy section about slaves and female spirits, blacks and women gained very little during the events he presents. Blake may also have disliked the isolationism and neutrality that determined the new nation's foreign policy, a "revolution-in-one-country" policy that made it difficult for revolution to spread to the Europe that needed it more. This American "selfishness," it has been argued, finds expression in the shadowy female's first line, "I will not let thee go."[26] Say what she may, however, she does not keep his flames from spreading to England, and only an extraordinary blizzard of English repression beats them back. In 1793, too, the revolutionary spirit is again flaming in England, ignited by France but fed by long-accumulated English grievances. The shadows of fear or doubt that we sense hovering over *America* and *Europe* have more to do with the war of England against France, I believe, than any withdrawal of enthusiasm or hope for revolution. Not until about 1797 would this particular Orc be quenched—for a while.

Part of what we may call the "preludic" level, the realm of Orc and Urizen (who replaces Urthona), continues in the Prophecy section, the main body of the poem. It is quite literally a higher level, a war in heaven parallel to events on earth. We hear no more about the shadowy female, however, and her absence suggests that she has become the historical level itself. The "revolution" that brought Orc up also brought him down to earth, and earth now groans in the issues of real men. Indeed, the last "historical" event before the final "preludic" intervention of Urizen is the liberation of real women from the bondage of religious marriage; they seem to enact the moment of joy the female feels in Orc's embrace.

The other "level" in which the realm of the Preludium survives is pictorial. In the fourteen designs for the Prophecy section, almost nothing historical or literal can be found, except possibly the old man entering death's door and the bodies left as carrion for birds and fish in plates 12 and 13, neither of which are referred to in the text. There are, of course, other levels besides these two: the various angels mediate between the heavenly doings and the earthly, and there are two strange passages about the planet Mars and the Atlantean hills that also occupy some middle space. The designs have their own intermediate elements—angels, sibyls, children riding on a serpent, and so on—but nothing on the primary level of the main text. This division of subject lets us literally see the visionary dimensions of the text we read, so that while in the midst of Boston and New York, we are also surrounded by sibyls and flaming serpents. There is lateral shifting as well as vertical, notably in the beautiful seventh plate, where a pastoral scene of a sleeping ram and children under a graceful birch housing birds of paradise frames a wrathful tirade by Albion's Angel. The constant shifting and reintegration that the illuminations ask us to do, however, are not essentially different from what we must do to make sense of the text alone.

To turn for a moment to a remarkable piece of ad hoc political astronomy (5:2–5), the red planet Mars was the old center, an empire based on war, like the Trojan and Roman empires before it. The three planets or wandering comets may allude to the three nations of England's original empire, Ireland and Scotland, and Wales, named together at 15:13 as abandoned by their frightened English oppressors; the nations threaten to go into orbit around the American sun, which has wrested itself free of England's "sphere of influence," of its eclipse by blackness, and found a fresher morning (6:13).[27]

The main plot, on the historical level, is an escalating series of challenges and responses, a little like the push and pull of events in the *Iliad;* but here the stress falls on the unity or "rushing together" of the colonists and not, for all their "warlike" generals, on their years of corporeal warfare with Britain. Blake may or may not have followed events closely during the War of Independence, but in this mythologized version, he certainly proclaims his opinion that it was the "congress" of the thirteen colonies, the concerted actions of New York, Boston, Pennsylvania, and Virginia, that brought victory and created a new nation. It is as if he were struck with the new name, the United States, and its ironic reflection on the old name, the United Kingdom, and set down his hopes for a new Atlantic "empery" of freedom.

Perhaps the most important theme, which will eventually return us to political astronomy, could be defined as the identity of revolution and enlightenment, the battle for the hearts and minds of the people, or the mutual imposition of visions. We recall that much of the Preludium is concerned with clouds and the parting of clouds, with Orc's yearning to see the shadowy female, and her response when she first sees him. The same motives govern much of the main poem. Washington tells his comrades to "look over the Atlantic sea" to a portent in the sky; the dragon's voice, locks, shoulders, and eyes "appear to the Americans," a phrase of studied ambiguity; and when Orc arises, the King of England "trembles at the vision," it being uncertain here too if what is seen is objective or subjective or both. Phrases like "in sight of Albions Guardian" or "to Angels eyes" recur insistently. It becomes a war of visions in both senses: each side stages extravagant spectacles to impress the other (or induces the other to project its extravagant fears and fancies) and at the same time makes declarations of its worldview. They show the flag, literally in Albion's case, both to warn the enemy and to see who rallies round it.

The Americans are the stronger in this visionary war.[28] Washington, Paine, and Warren turn their foreheads toward the east, that is, not only to "confront" Albion but to watch the coming dawn, but Albion, facing westward, cannot quite make out this "return" of the sun, for "clouds obscure my aged sight" (9:10–12). Albion's view of things being no match for Orc's and America's, his soldiers seek "where to hide / From the grim flames; and from the visions of Orc"; and back in England, his guardians, bards, and priests rush into caves and coverts, "hiding from the fires of Orc" (13:8–9, 15:20). Rather than lose the earth because the guardians are hiding under it, Urizen pours his snows down, "Hiding the Demon red with clouds & cold mists from the earth" (16:13). The earth, the people, have already caught the spirit of Orc, their senses have been irrevocably changed, do what the guardians will to "shut the five gates of their law-built heaven" (16:19).

Though Urizen in his later guises sums up much of what we call the "Enlightenment," it is evident here that Blake considers "reason" to be obfuscatory and repressive, precisely that combination of tyrant and priest that the great Enlightenment spokesmen strove to pry apart and destroy. From Albion's viewpoint, "heat but not light went through the murky atmosphere" (4:11), like the "darkness visible" of Milton's hell, and perhaps like Mars, red but not very bright. But then it is Albion who has made the atmosphere murky with his aged sight, and he has an interest in keeping it as murky as he can. He wants us all to take a dim view of Orc. So a blizzard of laws—the Ten Commandments Orc is stamping to dust (8:3–5), the "trade" and "science" of hypocritical morality (11:10), the "blasting fancies" and "mildews of despair" that blight this life and replace it with an allegorical heaven—tumbles onto the heads of the English people, whose eyes have seen the glory.

Blake takes "enlightenment," then, in an almost literal sense as the capacity to *see;* and the light that dawns, for all the celestial machinery, is essentially the inner light, the Holy Spirit, or the Imagination. A large part of enlightenment for Blake is just this internalizing of "external powers, the bringing of the stars down to earth. We saw this in the Preludium, and we see it in the descent of the thirteen Angels. Whether his astronomical imagery is consistent is debatable, but he gives this episode considerable weight:

> and all the thirteen Angels
> Rent off their robes to the hungry wind, & threw their
>   golden scepters
> Down on the land of America. indignant they descended
> Headlong from out their heav'nly heights, descending swift
>   as fires
> Over the land; naked & flaming are their lineaments seen
> In the deep gloom . . .

(12:2–7)

This passage summons up Turgot's famous saying about Franklin: "he wrested the lightning from heaven and the sceptre from tyrants."[29] It also recalls Milton's account of the rebellious angels' fall, which he twice calls "headlong" (1.45, 6.864), and that is certainly how Albion's Angel sees it; but Blake's transformation of this story not only reverses the values, making the rebels "good," but reverses the directional polarity as well. Up, in other words, is bad, except insofar as a redeemed slave can at least "look up into the heavens" (6:7) where he will see, in fact, no clouds, no stars, no planet Mars, but only bright days and clear nights. Down here among the people is the "ground" or source of all the celestial projections Albion demands we worship; and when the thirteen Angels join George Washington, they are not only defecting but, as their divestiture of royal trappings implies, abdicating as angels and rejoining the human race. Here indeed is the song played by Washington's troops at the British surrender at Yorktown (Orctown), "The World Turned Upside Down."

"Mental fight," we know, is a cornerstone of Blake's social vision and a concise expression of his calling as a prophetic artist. What may be less obvious is the way mental fight serves as a plan for the structure of several of his works, not only *America*, but *The French Revolution* and *The Marriage of Heaven and Hell* among his "revolutionary" writings and *Thel* and *Visions of the Daughters of Albion* among his ostensibly more psychological ones. To each creature who offers Thel its vision of self-sacrifice and joyous renewal, she replies with her own vision of fear and self-protection; in the end her own vision speaks and scares her almost to death. Oothoon pits her grandly eloquent plea for unpossessive love and sexuality against Theotormon's jealous bondage to past "facts" about her. At the council of the King of France, the Archbishop tells his dream of the terrors of heaven and the Abbe de Sieyès replies with a vision of a renovated earth. *The French Revolution* reminds us that nearly all the action of epic poetry from the *Iliad* to *Paradise Lost* is either war-

93

fare or council, and that a hero must excel at one or both. Councils are often the battlegrounds of mental fight, and many bodily battles begin with an exchange of speeches. In *Paradise Lost*, Blake may have thought, the two kinds of contention have become one because the war in heaven, for all the business about celestial gunpowder and flying mountains, is really a spiritual war fought within every human soul.

The contentions of angel and devil in *The Marriage of Heaven and Hell* issue in either of two ways, a standoff or a conversion of one contender. The fourth "Memorable Fancy" (plates 17–20), during which the devilish speaker and the angel each show their vision of the other's eternal lot, ends formally in a draw, though the angel is certainly outscored. They agree that what passed between them was a mutual *imposition* of fantasies, whereas the motto at the end proclaims that true friendship is *opposition*. The fifth "Memorable Fancy" (22–24) begins with a similar clash of viewpoints but ends differently: "This Angel, who is now become a Devil, is my particular friend: we often read the Bible together in its infernal or diabolical sense. . . . " In this friendship, presumably, imposition has become opposition: the two devils vigorously challenge each other's imaginations as they wrestle with the Bible.

We get a glimpse here of what goes on in Blake's state of Eternity. It is as important to understand the continuity of war-forms as it is to grasp their differences. The life-enhancing contentions of friendship may backslide through ideological impositions and spectacular scare tactics to the corporeal warfare of eternal death. It was Blake's great hope that revolution would put an end to wars that shed real blood by transforming them first to the ferocities of celestial fireworks between Orc and the Angels and then to spiritually loyal "opposition." However dismal the history of the so-called revolutions of the two centuries since Blake watched the first ones, I do not think his hope was based on nothing but wishful dreams. Perhaps we have yet to see a genuine revolution. In any case, Blake invites us to conceive of revolutionary violence as inessential to the main process, the enlightenment and organization of the people and their learning to refuse any longer to submit to the impositions of tyranny.

Yet the Preludium begins with an act of violence. Classical theorists of revolution, Marxist and otherwise, usually insist that the violence, if any is necessary, is only *maieutic*, only the agony of the delivery of the long-incubating new society out of the womb of the old, and not initiatory or inceptive. Orc, it is true, has been incubating for "fourteen suns," just as the spirit of revolution has been brooding in America beneath the English tyranny, and his "fierce embrace" of the shadowy female is more in the nature of a coming of age than the first sign of life. Blake has taken a risk, nonetheless, in identifying the actions of the American colonists, whose essentially nonviolent struggle he has been careful to bring out, with a violent act that initiates a new cycle, whatever it may culminate. Even though the female's womb joys at its impregnation, which may suggest that she welcomes it after the fact, Orc's act begins as a violation; and we need only look at *Visions of the Daughters of Albion*, engraved in the same year as *America*, to dispel any suspicion that Blake is soft on rapists. If anything, it may raise new doubts about Orc's potentially Bromion-like maturity. But in that poem, too, we find a theme resumed in *America*, the last theme I want to single out, which partly motivates the placing of a rape or near-rape in the Preludium.

Oothoon begins her second great speech to Theotormon with a jeremiad against parasites, those who feed off the abundance of the land without contributing to its production, the "fat fed hireling" who "buys whole corn fields into wastes" (*VDA* 5:14–15), even before she turns to her main subject of sexual freedom.[30] In *America*, Albion's Angel first complains that the soldiers already garrisoned in the colonies "cannot smite the wheat, nor quench the fatness of the earth" nor "bring the stubbed oak to overgrow the hills" now devoted to pastureland (*A* 9:5, 8). When Boston's Angel leads the defection, he gives a speech about "generosity" and idleness—the confiscation of the land or the land's surplus by the idle, who are the pestilence itself (11:6), and the displacement of the "generous" to "the sandy desert" or wilderness from their once fertile farms.[31] All this is accomplished, we may be sure, by "taxation without representation." The outcome is ruin and revolt. After the defection, Albion summons his army of plagues, the "diseases of the earth," which seem both literally and figuratively, and directly and indirectly, to blight the crops of American farmers. As Erdman says, "we must not suppose that Blake distinguished any more sharply than the Bible and the historians between plagues that killed people or crops directly and plagues that killed people by killing crops or that killed crops indirectly by causing people to destroy each other in battle."[32] That indistinction Blake inscribes in two more similes that merge the realms of tenor and vehicle: his plagues fall upon America "as a blight cuts the tender corn when it begins to appear" and "as a plague wind fill'd with insects cuts off man &

beast" (14:5–8). When the plagues rebound onto England and turn the Guardians leprous, the imprisoned young women feel their nerves and desires renew "as a vine when the tender grape appears," only to be nipped in the bud by Urizen's jealous snowstorm. But America is safe. The landlords with their tithe- and tax-gatherers have been driven off the land, which is now returned to the husbandman who will work it. The earth belongs to the living, and the surplus belongs to the laborer.[33]

With this theme in mind, and remembering the archetypes of Beulah and Hesperia, we can get a better idea of why the impregnation of the shadowy female begins the poem. The colonists have seized the land, not only the continent as a political entity but the farmland in it which supports nine-tenths of them. The word "colonist" comes from *colonus,* "farmer." The shadowy wilderness will now be open to them, whereas the British had made difficulties about settling the trans-Appalachian regions. The "furrows of the whip" on the backs of the colonists will become the "furrows by thy lightnings rent," the fire of the plough "bright in the furrow," as Virgil has it (*Georgics* 1.46), and the fire of generative and "generous" seed. The revolution is a reclamation of the usurped land by those who deserve her.[34]

We are brought once more to the Book of Revelation, to which so much of *America,* not to say America, is indebted. I am not thinking so much of the wedding of Christ with his bride the Church of the faithful, though that derives from the Beulah tradition; the shadowy female remains terrestrial and natural, and not man's ultimate dwelling place. It is the final harvest and vintage of Revelation that informs the imagery of *America,* as it does "The Battle Hymn of the Republic," America's true national anthem. Here it is still springtime—the tender corn has just begun to appear—but America has claimed the right to its own harvest. At the end of *Milton,* dated 1804, despite all the defeats and perversions of revolution in Europe, the hero Los prepares "To go forth to the Great Harvest & Vintage of the Nations" (43:1). The Nations are to be "gathered" into a United Nations, through great spiritual warfare, as the thirteen colonies were gathered into the United States.

Notes

1. Blake's early *Poetical Sketches,* notably "To Summer" and "To the Muses," continue the theme of the westering of the *poetic* spirit that he found in Gray's *Progress of Poesy.* According to Gray, freedom and poetry thrive together. See Geoffrey

Hartman, "Blake and the Progress of Poesy," in *Beyond Formalism* (New Haven, Conn.: Yale Univ. Press, 1970). There was a theory that the American Indians are descendants, like the Romans, of escaped Trojans; see Henry Steele Commager, *The Empire of Reason* (Garden City, N.Y.: Doubleday Anchor, 1977), pp. 75–76, 84, on Lafitau. Bishop Berkeley's famous line, "Westward the course of empire takes its way," referred to America, and by the 1770s, the notion that the seat of empire was passing to the New World was current on both sides of the Atlantic. There was also a biblical westering theory, according to which the ten Lost Tribes made it to America. Leslie Tannenbaum cites this tradition as it bears on chapter 13 of the apocryphal Second Esdras, a chapter that may have left its mark on Blake's *America*; see *Biblical Tradition in Blake's Early Prophecies* (Princeton, N.J.: Princeton Univ. Press, 1982), pp. 136–38. All Blake quotations are from the fifth edition, revised, of David V. Erdman, *The Complete Poetry and Prose of William Blake* (Berkeley: Univ. of California Press, 1982), abbreviated E below. "Erdman" refers to the third edition of his *Blake: Prophet against Empire* (Princeton, N.J.: Princeton Univ. Press, 1977). *Illuminated* refers to Erdman's *The Illuminated Blake* (New York: Doubleday Anchor, 1974).

2. I owe some of what follows to Aileen Ward's good discussion of "revolution" in "The Forging of Orc: Blake and the Idea of Revolution," *Triquarterly* 23/24 (Winter/Spring 1972): 204–27; to Raymond Williams, *Keywords* (New York: Oxford, 1976); and to Hannah Arendt, *On Revolution* (1963; rpt. New York: Penguin, 1977), pp. 41–47.

3. Cited by T. Malcolm Knox, "A Plea for Hegel," in Warren E. Steinkraus, ed., *New Studies in Hegel's Philosophy* (New York: Holt, Rinehart, 1971), p. 2.

4. Jean Daniélou, *Primitive Christian Symbols* (London: Burns and Oates, 1964), pp. 113 ff.

5. This is the King James translation of Ephesians 6.12. On page 3 of *The Four Zoas*, Blake writes out the entire verse in Greek, as if to remind us that these places are very high indeed, *epouraniois*, "in the heavens."

6. Arendt, p. 42. See also Gerhard Kittel and Gerhard Friedrich, eds., *Theological Dictionary of the New Testament*, trans. Geoffrey W. Bromley (Grand Rapids, Mich.: Eerdmans, 1964–74). On *apocatastasis* in Blake, see Michael Ferber, *The Social Vision of William Blake* (Princeton, N.J.: Princeton Univ. Press, 1985), chap. 8.

7. Five thousand years is the period the King of France finds meaningful (*FR* 8, 70), whereas Burgundy, perhaps because he is the "ancientest" noble, speaks of six thousand (90). The latter figure Blake uses elsewhere to encompass all of human history (e.g., *M* 42:15), but he sometimes prefers seven thousand (*FZ* I, 9:10), or, most oddly, eight thousand five hundred (*J* 48:36, 83:52).

8. It is fourteen years between Rousseau's *Social Contract* (1762), which announced that man is in chains, and the Declaration of Independence (1776), which, as *America* beautifully restates, pronounced him free (Erdman, pp. 258–59). It is the age of puberty, and Orc is ready for his first sexual embrace (Erdman, p. 261, and others). As Orc is clearly an analogue of Prometheus, Blake might be recalling Prometheus's odd prophecy to Io, who is a bit like the shadowy female, that a child of hers "in the thirteenth generation" will release him from his chains (Aeschylus, *Prometheus Bound*, 1. 775). Orc also resembles Ares/Mars, who was once chained and confined to a brazen cauldron for thirteen months, according to Homer (*Iliad* 5.385–91). More germane are the "begats" of Matthew, three sets of fourteen sons: "and from the carrying away into Babylon unto Christ are fourteen generations" (1.17). Jacob labored for Rachel for fourteen years, though it was Leah who was "shadowy" on their nuptial night. If "sun" can mean "century," we may have a hint of the

Michael Ferber

fourteen centuries between the suppression of the last Orc (as *Europe* asserts) and the discovery of America.

9. MacPherson's "Ossian" may be Blake's precedent.

10. I am developing suggestions by Northrop Frye in *Fearful Symmetry* (Princeton, N.J.: Princeton Univ. Press, 1947), p. 209.

11. A remnant of another romance may be lodged in the lines about Atlantis (10:5–10). The "stolen bride" of Ariston (the aristocracy) may be the shadowy female, who must live in a primeval forest like pre-colonial America. Now Orc steals her back.

12. I shall drop the quotation marks around "Preludium" and "Prophecy."

13. Oothoon seems to quote the first two verses of this chapter in *Visions of the Daughters of Albion* (hereafter *VDA*) 1:13. Several lines of *Europe*, as Michael Tolley notes, echo other passages of the Song; see "*Europe:* 'to those ychain'd in sleep'," in Erdman and Grant, *Blake's Visionary Forms Dramatic* (Princeton, N.J.: Princeton Univ. Press, 1970). See also Tannenbaum, p. 147.

14. It is almost as if she represents the *pia mater*, the "soft mother" of the brain. Her helmet would then be either her skull or the *dura mater*, which puts a hard roof over the brain that "once open to the heavens and elevated on the human neck," as a later passage in *Europe* has it.

15. Tannenbaum likens the shadowy female to a fallen form of Milton's feminine Holy Spirit, the Uranian Muse derived in part from the figure of Wisdom in the Book of Proverbs and Ecclesiasticus. Wisdom describes herself as a tree, and Blake may be echoing her in *Europe* 1:8. See Tannenbaum, pp. 161–63.

16. It may have struck Blake that the New World was discovered by a man whose family name means "dove," to say nothing of his Christian name. We do know that Blake read the American Joel Barlow's *Vision of Columbus* (1787) and drew some ideas from it; see Erdman, p. 23. A passage at I Corinthians 2:10 may also be pertinent: "the Spirit searcheth all things, yea, the deep things of God."

17. In *The Four Zoas* version of this scene comes this line: "So Orc rolld round his clouds upon the deeps of dark Urthona" (*FZ* VIIb, 91b:10). Metonymical similes are distinctively biblical. See Robert Alter, *The Art of Biblical Poetry* (New York: Basic Books, 1985), p. 42.

18. The other three beasts are the primates of their orders and betoken air, earth, and water (the whale is *orca* in Latin), leaving fire for the serpent. Erdman (p. 259) associates them with Peruvian and Mexican emblems; but that is to localize them too precisely, and we are left wondering about serpents in Canada.

19. This imagery is clearer in *The Four Zoas* version: "As when the Earthquake rouzes from his den his shoulder huge / Appear above the crumb[l]ing Mountain. Silence waits around him / A moment then astounding horror belches from the Center" (VIIb, 91b:6–8). Volcanoes have long been symbols of popular insurrections. Mount Etna erupted in 1763 and again in 1792, perhaps while Blake was at work on *America*.

20. Virgil, *The Pastoral Poems*, trans. E. V. Rieu (Harmondsworth, Eng.: Penguin, 1949).

21. Dan. 3.25–27, 2.32–33, 10.6; Rev. 2.18, 1.15.

22. See Clarke Garrett, *Respectable Folly* (Baltimore: Johns Hopkins Univ. Press, 1975), pp. 136–37, and Jack Fruchtman, Jr., "Politics and the Apocalypse: The Republic and the Millennium in Late-Eighteenth-Century English Political Thought," *Studies in Eighteenth-Century Culture* 10 (1980): 153–64.

23. Henry Collins, ed. (Baltimore: Penguin, 1969), p. 290.

24. In his early *King Edward the Third*, Blake gives us his version of the tradition of the "New Troy" in Britain. A minstrel sings: "O sons of Trojan Brutus, cloath'd in war, . . . Your ancestors . . . landed in firm array upon the rocks / Of Albion"; Brutus prophesied, "Our sons shall rule the empire of the sea" (428–29). As early as 1779, Blake made a small pen-and-watercolor version of "The Landing of Brutus in England" (Butlin cat. 51). Blake included it in a list of subjects from English history (E 672) in the year he engraved *America*, 1793.

25. Erdman, *Illuminated*, p. 137.

26. Minna Doskow, "William Blake's *America:* The Story of a Revolution Betrayed," *Blake Studies* 8(2)(1979): 167–86. This interesting article, whose title alludes to Trotsky, makes the most of the negative possibilities of the work, which it finds mainly in the designs. That is its main problem, for most of the designs, beginning with the frontispiece, admit of "contrary" readings. If mine seem too optimistic, the reader should try this article as an antidote.

27. See Michael Ferber, "Mars and the Planets Three in *America*," *Blake: An Illustrated Quarterly* 59 (15:3) (1981–82): 136–37.

28. Paine brings out the importance of the *appearing* of truth (and of republicanism) in a passage that may have influenced Blake: "But such is the irresistible nature of truth, that all it asks, and all it wants, is the liberty of appearing. The sun needs no inscription to distinguish him from darkness; and no sooner did the American governments display themselves to the world, than despotism felt a shock, and man began to contemplate redress" (*Rights of Man*, Part II (1792), in Collins, ed., p. 181). See also Ronald Paulson, *Representations of Revolution 1789–1820*) (New Haven, Conn.: Yale Univ. Press, 1983), p. 89 n. 2.

29. Widely quoted. See R. R. Palmer, *The Age of the Democratic Revolution*, I (Princeton, N.J.: Princeton Univ. Press, 1959), pp. 249–50.

30. Erdman, chapter 11, is a valuable discussion of the "fatness of the earth" and the plague sent by Albion's Angel.

31. "Generous" and its derivatives occur four times in these twelve lines, as if Boston's Angel has discovered a wonderful new word. And wonderful it is. In Blake it ranges in meaning from "liberal," even in the political sense (the Duke of Orleans is "generous as mountains" in *FR* 175) to "generative" or "fertile" (the unfallen Urizen has a "lap full of seed" and "hand full of generous fire" in *Ahania* 5:29–30). It is almost an anagram of "energies," as Boston's Angel seems to sense in 11:9. And it may carry a hint of the sense of the Latin *generosus*, "well-born" or "noble," and thus snub the pseudo-nobility of the blood who are depriving the husbandmen of their produce.

32. Erdman, p. 248.

33. Blake must have noticed that Washington and the king of England had the same name, the name of the guardian saint of England. "George" means "earth-worker" in Greek, i.e., "ploughman" or "farmer" (as Virgil's *Georgics* reminds us). Only Washington, from Blake's point of view, was a real farmer (the American Cincinnatus); George III was a parasite, though he was called "Farmer George."

34. Blake is silent about the American Indians. For another discussion of the meaning of the rape, which sets it in the context of a father-son struggle, see Stephen C. Behrendt, " 'This Accursed Family': Blake's *America* and the American Revolution," *Eighteenth Century* 27 (1) (1986): 26–51.

Wordsworth, Wellington, and Myth

Eric C. Walker

> One of the two words erased from the title was "Bonaparte"; and just under his own name Beethoven wrote with a lead pencil in large letters, nearly obliterated but still legible, "Composed on Bonaparte."
>
> —Thayer's *Life of Beethoven*

> In the present age (emphatically the age of personality!) there are more than ordinary motives for withholding all encouragement from this mania of busying ourselves with the names of others.
>
> —Coleridge, *The Friend*

After William Wordsworth received an honorary degree at Oxford in 1839, the family liked to tell the story that the university had greeted only the duke of Wellington with greater acclamation.[1] Because Wordsworth and Wellington were almost exact contemporaries, and because the figures of warrior and poet often represent twin selves in Wordsworth's poetry, Wellington's place in that body of writing deserves more attention than it has received, especially considering the abundant studies of Napoleon's shadow in Wordsworth's poetry. Although other military figures such as Nelson and Michel Beaupuy also occupy the poet's imagination at important moments, the myth of the happy warrior that emerges from Wordsworth's entire career is tethered most directly to the human in the historical figures who faced each other at Waterloo.

Roland Barthes has remarked that the program of myth is to convert history into nature.[2] The scene of that transformation is often the proper name, the historically arbitrary linguistic unit empowered as myth with natural forces of necessity and inevitability. Warriors' names as mythological vehicles function unconventionally in Wordsworth's writing, for his habit is to withhold or withdraw warriors' names at just those moments when they might conventionally achieve the status of myth. I have argued elsewhere that these elisions and erasures of the warrior's name throughout Wordsworth's poetry together constitute an antonomastic rhetoric, a rhetoric of substitute naming.[3] Viewed as a tool of myth, Wordsworth's antonomastic rhetoric appears to be a demythologizing process, a reluctance to transform the historical name. The happy warrior remains unnamed in Wordsworth's verse; to put this demythologizing feature another way, we can say that Wordsworth creates for the warrior a paradoxical myth of anonymity. The unnamed warrior in "Character of the Happy Warrior" achieves anonymous mythological status chiefly because his bright promise is splendidly fulfilled; Wordsworth's human warriors, on the other hand, more often than not remain unnamed—and thus only intermittently intrude upon the happy warrior's nameless myth—because they repeat a dark pattern of failed promise.

Wellington's name appears only once in Wordsworth's poetry, in the title of an 1840 sonnet; the body of the sonnet first approaches and then finally withholds the proper name. Even more remarkable is the absence of Wellington's name in the Waterloo poetry Wordsworth published in the spring of 1816. On this occasion my aim is to examine a number of texts that help gloss Wordsworth's antonomastic strategies with Wellington's name. I will explore the initial location of Wordsworth's disappointment with Wellington in the prose tract *The Convention of Cintra*, published in 1809; I will then illustrate the mythologizing conventions Wordsworth skirts in the 1816 Waterloo poems by inspecting Wellington's figure in the journalist John Scott's prose *Paris Revisited*, which Wordsworth was reading while he wrote his Waterloo verses. Finally, I will compare Wordsworth's antonomastic practice in the 1840 Wellington sonnet with two other poetic representations of Wellington: Tennyson's salute in his "Ode on the Death of the Duke of Wellington," and Byron's attack in the opening of canto IX of *Don Juan*. In spite of what received notions of Wordsworth's apostasy might lead readers to expect, the poet's use of Wellington's name throughout his career resembles far less Tennyson's panegyric than Byron's own brand of demythologizing opposition.

Wellington's name first appears in Wordsworth's writing in letters of late September 1808, which express his dismay at the course of recent military action in the Peninsula: "We are all here cut to the heart by the conduct of Sir Hew and his Brother Knight in Portugal—for myself, I have not suffered so much upon any public occasion these many years"; two days later, to a different correspondent: "We are here all in a rage about the Convention in Portugal; if Sir Hew were to shew his face among us, or that other doughty Knight, Sir Arthur, the very Boys would hiss them out of the Vale."[4] During the next year, this warm contempt was translated into the arguments of Wordsworth's longest prose work, *Concerning the Relations of Great Britain, Spain, and Portugal, to Each Other, and to the Common Enemy, at this Crisis; and Specifically as Affected by the Convention of Cintra,* published in the spring of 1809.[5] Wellington, who was then Sir Arthur Wellesley, normally is named in exactly that style in *Cintra,* instead of the indignantly clipped, epistolary "Sir Arthur." Wordsworth focuses on Wellington's conduct in an early section of the argument, after introductory remarks on national characters and before his distressed review of the convention's articles. This prose discussion of the warrior's character reaffirms the principles declared in "Character of the Happy Warrior," published two years previously, where Wordsworth inscribes the convention—more often than not thwarted by himself—that the poet's office is to celebrate the heroic name of the happy warrior.[6] In addition to supplying evidence of the moral grounds upon which Wordsworth withholds Wellington's name after Waterloo, *The Convention of Cintra* also manifests the range of Wordsworth's characteristic rhetorical preoccupations with the warrior's name.

Fittingly, Wordsworth's first indictment of Wellington is that the general egregiously misnamed his opponent, Junot, in the treaty documents:

> Having occasion to speak of the French General, he has found no name by which to designate him but that of DUC D'ABRANTES—words necessarily implying, that Bonaparte, who had taken upon himself to confer upon General Junot this Portugueze title with Portugueze domains to support it, was lawful Sovereign of that Country, and that consequently the Portugueze Nation were rebels, and the British Army, and he himself at the head of it, aiders and abettors of that rebellion. (251)

Quickly admitting that Wellington could not have consciously intended such a backward state of affairs, Wordsworth then declares the actual failing this evidence suggests:

> It would be absurd to suppose, that Sir Arthur Wellesley, at the time when he used these words, was aware of the meaning really involved

in them: let them be deemed an oversight. But the capability of such an oversight affords too strong suspicion of a deadness to the moral interests of the cause in which he was engaged, and of such a want of sympathy with the just feelings of his injured Ally as could exist only in a mind narrowed by exclusive and overweening attention to the *military* character, led astray by vanity, or hardened by general habits of contemptuousness. (251)

Wordsworth's criticism is that Wellington's actions, however successful, do not rest upon what later in the essay he will argue is sound "principle"; as he puts this idea in "Character of the Happy Warrior," the warrior's conduct must always "on a right foundation rest."[7] In the spring of 1809, disheartened by the general's "flagrant proofs of unworthiness," Wordsworth in a letter to Coleridge is skeptical that Wellington on his return to the Peninsula can redeem himself, although he might achieve popular acclaim: "I have no doubt that one victory gained by Sir A. W. would blot out all remembrance of his former transactions, and yet what would ten victories avail if the moral spirit continues the same?"[8] Anticipating here the celebration of Wellington after Waterloo, Wordsworth also registers the grounds of his unwillingness on that later occasion to bless a warrior's fame for the sake of victory alone.

Wordsworth's case against Wellington in *Cintra* includes at least three varieties of antonomastic practice: the choice of office as telling epithet; a roster of heroic names as ideal counterpart; and, ultimately, the suppression of the proper name, a proleptic instance of an essential structure in the Waterloo poems seven years later.

In the midst of his attack on Wellington, Wordsworth pauses to consider the character of the military hero in the abstract, and he argues that these heroes exhibit different combinations of three qualities, "talents, genius, or principle" (256); it is soon clear that the presence or absence of "principle" is what chiefly interests Wordsworth. Throughout Wordsworth's poetry, unprincipled military heroes tend to be denominated "conquerors"; principled heroes, on the other hand, are often named "deliverers." Wordsworth begins to engage these antithetical epithets in the commentary surrounding Wellington in *Cintra*; he supplies examples of unprincipled heroes, for instance, in whom "the moral character be greatly perverted; as in those personages, who are so conspicuous in history, conquerors and usurpers, the Alexanders, the Caesars, and Cromwell" (256). As we shall see, the epithet "conqueror" is Wellington's ultimate name in the 1840 sonnet occasioned by Haydon's painting; for the moment, in addition to noting the pejorative sense of "conqueror" in *Cintra*, it is important to witness Wordsworth explicitly denying Wellington the office of deliverer. The general's conduct has convinced the poet that

> he must appear utterly unworthy of the station in which he has been placed. He had been sent as a deliverer—as an assertor and avenger of the rights of human nature. But these words [the misnaming of Junot] would carry with them every where the conviction, that Portugal and Spain, yea, all which was good in England, or iniquitous in France or in Frenchmen, was forgotten, and his head full only of himself. (251)

By misnaming his "conquered antagonist," Wellington has supplied grounds for naming himself, not a deliverer, but a conqueror alone.

The epithet "deliverer" figures prominently in the roster of ideal names Wordsworth supplies as a bright substitute for the darkened names of Wellington and his fellow generals. After naming unprincipled conquerors, Wordsworth turns to the idea of the happy warrior "in whom talents, genius, and principle are united" (256), and supplies these examples: "Such men, in ancient times, were Phocion, Epaminondas, and Philopoemen; and such a man was Sir Philip Sidney, of whom it has been said, that he first taught this country *the majesty of honest dealing*. With these may be named, the honour of our own age, Washington, the deliverer of the American Continent; with these, though in many things unlike, Lord Nelson, whom we have lately lost."[9] (256–57). Three times elsewhere in the essay, Wordsworth names heroes—especially Sidney—as deliverers. First, immediately prior to the attack on Wellington, Spanish warriors appear: "The names of Pelayo and The Cid are the watch-words of the address to the people of Leon; and they are told that to these two deliverers of their country . . . Spain owes the glory and happiness which she has *so long* enjoyed" (244). The nadir of the essay is a lament for England in which Sidney appears among a roster of deliverers: "O sorrow and shame for our country; for the grass which is upon her fields, and the dust which is in her graves;—for her good men who now look upon the day;—and her long train of deliverers and defenders, her Alfred, her Sidneys, and her Milton; whose voice yet speaketh for our reproach; and whose actions survive in memory to confound us, or to redeem!" (288). Then, near the end of the essay, Wordsworth invokes the "spiritual community binding together the living and the dead," and "among the most illustrious of that fraternity" he names "the elder Sidney—a deliverer and defender, whose name I have before uttered with reverence" (339). Wellington and his fellow

Peninsular generals, on the other hand, have delivered only in a darkly ironic sense: "they had changed all things into their contraries. . . . Whom had they delivered but the Tyrant in captivity?" (252).

The generals' conduct at Cintra was sufficiently questionable—and public outcry so great—that they were recalled to Britain to face a Board of Inquiry. Wellington was cleared of any wrongdoing; indeed, both houses of Parliament passed motions to thank him by name, simultaneously defeating motions to add the name of General Burrard.[10] Wordsworth refers to this public sanction of Wellington's name in the only other *Cintra* passage in which he directly attacks the general. In this later long paragraph, anticipating the structures of the Waterloo poems, Wordsworth withholds the proper name, in pointed contrast to government celebrations:

> Did we not (if, from this comprehensive feeling of sorrow, I may for a moment descend to particulars)—did we not send forth a general, one whom, since his return, Court, and Parliament, and Army, have been at strife with each other which shall most caress and applaud—a general, who, in defending the armistice which he himself signed, said in open court that he deemed that the French army was *entitled* to such terms. (300–301)

In addition to the misnaming of Junot, this defense of the French army's rights is Wordsworth's other major criticism directed specifically at Wellington. As he challenges the argument, Wordsworth substitutes a series of epithets for Wellington's proper name: "Of the MAN, and of the understanding and heart of the man—of the CITIZEN, who could think and feel after this manner in such circumstances, it is needless to speak; but to the GENERAL I will say, This is most pitiable pedantry" (301). Unspoken here, the antithetical names of "conqueror" or "deliverer" stand just beyond "general" in this series; before conferring the first of these epithets alone in the 1840 sonnet, Wordsworth after Waterloo continues, in the manner of this later section of *Cintra*, to withhold Wellington's increasingly celebrated name.

Because the virtue "magnanimity" is a key feature of Wordsworth's post-Waterloo debate about Wellington's name, it is useful, before turning to the Waterloo poems, to note the place of magnanimity in the *Cintra* tract. In three instances surrounding the attack on the generals' conduct, Wordsworth introduces magnanimity as a principle not of individual action but of corporate, national conduct. The purpose of the *Cintra* arguments is to recall the people to "those heights of magnanimity to which as a nation we were raised, when [Spain and Portugal] first represented to us their wrongs and entreated our assistance" (248). Wordsworth's indignation in large part stems from his conviction that this worthy national initiative has been betrayed: the generals representing the nation have "reversed every thing" when instead "we ought to have risen above ourselves, and if possible to have been foremost in the strife of honour and magnanimity" (252–53). The unnamed deliverer who is missing at Cintra, on the other hand, would be "he, who is the most watchful of the honour of his country, most determined to preserve her fair name at all hazards" and who "will have offered an example of magnanimity. . . . Nations will thus be taught to respect each other, and mutually to abstain from injuries" (259). This distinction between the nation and the individuals who fallibly serve its interests (represented here, we might notice, in a nominal figure, "her fair name") is maintained in the Waterloo poems, where the magnanimous conduct Wordsworth blesses by naming belongs not to Wellington but to the nation.[11] Wordsworth redirects the conventional myth of the warrior hero into a variety of channels, some familiar, some less familiar, and all of which are not regularly viewed together: his most radical and well-known substitution—the growth of an unnamed poet's mind for the epic hero—appears in the life's work accompanied by new myths of nationhood and, for the warriors of his own time, paradoxical myths of anonymity.

In August 1815, two months after Waterloo, a remarkable celebration occurred on the summit of Skiddaw. The company included, in addition to Wordsworth and Southey, various members of the Wordsworth and Southey households, the younger James Boswell, and, in the words of Southey—who left this account of the festivities—"our three maid-servants, some of our neighbors, some adventurous lakers, and Messrs. Rag, Tag, and Bobtail." The all-day excursion ended spectacularly:

> We roasted beef and boiled plum-puddings there; sung "God save the king" round the most furious body of flaming tar-barrels that I ever saw; drank a huge wooden bowl of punch; fired cannon at every health with three times three, and rolled large blazing balls of tow and turpentine down the steep side of the mountain. The effect was grand beyond imagination. We formed a huge circle round the most intense light, and behind us was an immeasurable arch of the most intense darkness, for our bonfire fairly put out the moon.[12]

Composed the following winter after a tour of the battlefield, Southey's laureate performance on Waterloo, *The Poet's Pilgrimage to Waterloo*, adopts Skiddaw as the central organizing image; invoked in topographical specificity to open the poem, the peak is transfigured at the end into a mount of vision upon which Southey locates and recalls the August celebrations: "And in our triumph taught the startled night / To ring with Wellington's victorious name."[13]

Wordsworth may have shouted Wellington's name on Skiddaw in August 1815, but such a blessing is conspicuously absent from his own body of Waterloo poetry, most of which was composed in the winter months of early 1816 and published in May of that year in a small volume of thirteen poems, *Thanksgiving Ode, January 18, 1816, with Other Short Pieces, Chiefly Referring to Recent Public Events*. Before turning to Wordsworth's suppression of the warrior's name in these texts, we can best witness the naming conventions he circumvents in a prose work, John Scott's *Paris Revisited*, which Wordsworth was reading as he composed his Waterloo poems.

In the winter of 1816, Wordsworth began corresponding with Scott, who was then editing the London paper *The Champion* and later—before his death by duel—was the founding editor of *The London Magazine*.[14] Like Southey and Walter Scott, John Scott had visited Waterloo within months of the June 1815 battle and soon published *Paris Revisited, in 1815, By Way of Brussels: including a Walk Over the Field of Battle at Waterloo*.[15] In February 1816 Wordsworth acknowledged receipt of the volume: "Your *Paris Revisited* has been in constant use since I received it—a very welcome sight it was." In another letter to Scott three days later, several relevant facts are evident: Scott has asked Wordsworth to read some of his own verses on Waterloo, which other letters make clear feature Wellington as hero, and Wordsworth himself has begun to address the Allied victory in verse:

> Most readily would I undertake the office which you propose to me, but for a reason which I am sure you will think sufficient for my declining it for a short while at least.—I am myself engaged with an attempt to express in Verse some feelings connected with these very subjects, and till that engagement is over neither in justice to you nor to myself can I introduce into my own mind such a stream as I have no doubt your Poem will be felt to be.[16]

According to Scott's recent biographer, the Waterloo verses were never finished or published, so Scott's treatment of Wellington must be witnessed in the same form experienced by Wordsworth, the prose of *Paris Revisited*.

Wellington comes off very well in Scott's care. The Allied general first appears in the account when Scott takes up the vexed question whether Napoleon surprised Wellington:

> We have seen nothing in the Duke of Wellington's military character . . . to render it tolerable that . . . he should be charged with gross want of care. It is not pretended that he was not most sensibly alive to the responsibility of his situation at the late terrible crisis, both as it concerned his own fame, and his country's fortunes. All that he had achieved was to be as nothing, or to be doubled in value, according as he might now succeed or fail. (114)

Scott generously measures Wellington's "military character"; far from Wordsworth's disillusioned estimation, Wellington's character to Scott exhibits "unexampled justice, forbearance, and humanity, with the more common military qualities of courage and fierceness" (196–97). These traits, Scott argues, serve Wellington well during this crisis not only of national "fortunes" but also of individual "fame," the vehicle of which is the embattled name.

After a battle narrative, Scott warms to his panegyric purposes: Wellington's "long military career . . . had now terminated in the utmost of dignity and glory that the unrestrained imagination of ambition could ever have presented as attainable" (159). Approaching his highest pitch, Scott proposes that Wellington provided his soldiers

> a brilliant example of presence of mind, courage, and confidence. This he did, in a style that was never surpassed, and which equals the finest of those instances of coolness and heroism, that have been shewn by great commanders, and which have immortalized their names, and given to history its chief interest . . '. he entered the field with as thorough a spirit of devotion as ever animated a Grecian or Roman warrior. (184–85)

Scott locates Wellington the "warrior" among a class of "commanders," an occasion on which Wordsworth would have been likely to pass the judgment of "deliverer" or "conqueror"; in Scott's conception, the heroic actions of these "great commanders" inspire a mythic process that has "immortalized their names." Scott at last confers this supreme blessing: "By the help of our army, the Duke has reached the pinnacle of military honours, saved two kingdoms from a fate which his censurers described as not to be averted, and gained a victory which leaves him no rival to contend with, and England no enemy to fear" (188). Although Scott does not use the term "deliverer," his language clearly demonstrates that he places

Wellington in that sacred office: in addition to having "gained a victory" and having "reached the pinnacle of military honours," Wellington has "saved two kingdoms," an action that Wordsworth refuses to attribute to Wellington.

Wordsworth admired Scott's account of Waterloo and European politics, but he demurred on one key issue, a "personal question [that] is the only material point in your books in which I differ from you":

> I wish that I could think as favourably as you do of the Duke of Wellington. Since his first debut in Portugal I have watched his course as carefully as my opportunities allowed me to do; and notwithstanding the splendour of those actions at the head of which he has been placed, I am convinced that there is no magnanimity in his nature . . . depend upon it, the constitution of his mind is not generous, nor will he pass with posterity for a hero.

In another letter a few days later, Wordsworth, recalling Scott's intention to feature Wellington in verse, softens his criticism: "As to the Duke of Wellington, I am almost sorry that I touched upon the subject; especially since I have heard of your design. Poetically treated he may pass for a Hero; and on that account I less regret what I wrote to you. But to the searching eye of the Historian, and still more of the Biographer, he will, I apprehend, appear as a man below the circumstances in which he moved."[17] Wordsworth holds himself to a more exacting standard than he allows Scott, for Wellington does not "pass for a hero" in any conventional sense anywhere in his poetry. In a surprising reversal of the Aristotelian hierarchy of history and poetry that he had invoked in the "Preface" to *Lyrical Ballads*, Wordsworth the poet instead follows in his verse what he represents here as the more rigorous vision of "the searching eye of the Historian, and still more of the Biographer."[18]

The magnanimity Wordsworth denies Wellington appears as the chief cause of victory in the "Thanksgiving Ode," the major text in the 1816 volume of the same name. To open the third stanza, the poet considers the ultimate source of Allied success: "the vengeful sword? / Ah no, by dint of Magnanimity."[19] No named warriors are associated with this virtue in this stanza or indeed elsewhere in the "Thanksgiving Ode," in spite of conventional wishes to hear such names celebrated. In stanza three, the "One that mid the failing never failed" (named by a later editor, William Knight, as Wellington in a footnote) is unambiguously "Britain" in Wordsworth's text, the nation again serving as mythic surrogate for the unnamed warrior.[20] In the entire set of thirteen poems in the volume, there appears—in a footnote to one sonnet—the name of only a single soldier, John Sobieski, a late seventeenth-century Polish monarch. The notoriety of Wordsworth's boldest moment of theodician rhetoric—"Yea, Carnage is thy Daughter"—has obscured many unconventional features of his Waterloo poems, such as the following sharply contrasting, chastened sentiment that belongs to a Wordsworthian *via negativa*, what he calls an "abyss of weakness": "Say not that we have vanquished—but that we survive."[21] The most remarkable of the unconventional features is surely the nearly total absence of the warrior's name, in pointed contrast not only to John Scott's prose but also to verse performances such as Southey's *The Poet's Pilgrimage* or Walter Scott's even more popular *The Field of Waterloo*, where the penultimate stanza closes with Wellington's name.[22]

Following Waterloo, Wordsworth's most notable antonomastic figure for the unnamed warrior appears not in the *Thanksgiving Ode* volume but in the volume *The River Duddon . . . and Other Poems*, published four years later. In the poem "Dion," Wordsworth draws from classical history a mythic analogue for contemporary warriors.[23] Dion—a pupil of Plato who liberated Syracuse—clearly approaches the happy warrior's ideal, for he is named "the great Deliverer" in the third stanza; and when his assassination is reported in the final stanza, we are told that "in calm peace the appointed Victim slept, / As he had fallen in magnanimity." Although both of these key terms withheld from Wellington are attributed to Dion, the classical warrior does not break the pattern of failed promise, for his career too is "stained" (Dion himself participated in an assassination conspiracy), ending in "the ruins of thy glorious name." By substituting Dion's name for Wellington and other warriors, Wordsworth is able simultaneously to point to the mythic ideal of the happy warrior, the magnanimous deliverer, and to reemphasize the pattern of disappointed expectations that leads him on most occasions to withhold the warrior's name.

To conclude "Dion" the speaker announces a "moral": " 'Him, only him, the shield of Jove defends, / Whose means are fair and spotless as his ends.' " The unsullied mythic name potentially signifies the ideal "spotless" warrior; this humanly impossible standard had been presented in even more striking fashion in *The Convention of Cintra*, where Wordsworth argues that the lamentable condition of Europe demands that "the Christian exhortation for the individual is here the precept for nations: 'Be ye therefore per-

fect; even as your Father, which is in Heaven, is perfect' " (340).
Through the last decade of his career, Wordsworth continues to
deny Wellington the mythic status conferred upon the unblem-
ished, unnamed, perfect happy warrior.

After Southey published the second volume of his *History of the
Peninsular War* in 1827, Wordsworth wrote to him, "I have read it
with great delight. . . . I did not notice a single sentiment or opinion that I could have wished away but one—where you support the
notion that, if the Duke of Wellington had not lived and commanded, Buonaparte must have continued the master of Europe."[24]
This refusal to join the conventional Tory praise of Wellington duplicates Wordsworth's single reservation about John Scott's book
nearly a dozen years earlier. In 1840 Wordsworth's estimation of
Wellington appears in his correspondence one last time, in a letter
to Henry Reed, his American editor:

> I am much pleased by what you say in your letter of the 18th of May
> last, upon the tract of the Convention of Cintra, & I think myself with
> some interest upon its being reprinted hereafter, along with my other
> writings. But the respect, which in common with all the rest of the
> rational parts of the world, I bear for the Duke of Wellington, will pre-
> vent my reprinting the Pamphlet during his life-time. It has not been
> in my power to read the Volumes of his Despatches which I hear so
> highly spoken of, but I am convinced that nothing they contain could
> alter my opinion of the injurious tendency of that, or any other Con-
> vention, conducted upon such principles.[25]

Although Wordsworth's contempt at the time of Cintra has now
been tempered to a generous "respect," he nevertheless quietly reaffirms here his consistently skeptical judgment of Wellington. The
letter to Reed also contained a draft of a recently composed sonnet
published in the following text two years later, titled "On a Portrait
of the Duke of Wellington Upon the Field of Waterloo, by
Haydon":[26]

> By Art's bold privilege Warrior and War-horse stand
> On ground yet strewn with their last battle's wreck;
> Let the Steed glory while his Master's hand
> Lies fixed for ages on his conscious neck;
> But by the Chieftan's look, though at his side
> Hangs that day's treasured sword, how firm a check
> Is given to triumph and all human pride!

Yon trophied Mound shrinks to a shadowy speck
In his calm presence! Him the mighty deed
Elates not, brought far nearer the grave's rest,
As shows that time-worn face, for he such seed
Has sown as yields, we trust, the fruit of fame
In Heaven; hence no one blushes for thy name,
Conqueror, 'mid some sad thoughts, divinely blest!

Although the title and certain sentiments represent the more generous attitude of the later Wordsworth, the sonnet as a whole once
again denies Wellington the mythic name. In the body of the poem,
the subject is named by a series of four epithets—Warrior, Master,
Chieftan, Conqueror—that as an antonomastic set withhold the human blessing of the proper name.[27] The last two verses make it very
clear that what is fundamentally at issue between warrior and poet
is in fact the name itself (in early drafts the phrase "thy name" was
italicized); Wordsworth ends his naming of Wellington not with the
redemptive epithet of Deliverer but with the far more problematic
Conqueror.

A dozen years after Wordsworth's sonnet, Wellington's celebrated name figures prominently in Tennyson's "Ode on the Death
of the Duke of Wellington."[28] The fifth stanza, for example, ends
with an invocation:

O civic muse, to such a name,
To such a name for ages long,
To such a name,
Preserve a broad approach of fame,
And ever-echoing avenues of song.

Stanzas six and eight conclude with a refrain of "honour, honour,
honour, honour to him, / Eternal honour to his name." Although
Tennyson also never includes the proper name except in the title,
the epithets he uses—"the Great Duke," "the last great Englishman," "the great World-victor's victor"—clearly participate in a cultural process of mythic fame that depends upon the celebrated
name, a process that Wordsworth's last epithet, "Conqueror," quietly but firmly subverts.

Much closer in effect to Wordsworth's demythologizing procedures, Byron's most notable attack on Wellington opens canto IX of
Don Juan with a focus on the subject's name:[29]

Oh, Wellington! (or "Vilainton"—for Fame
Sounds the heroic syllables both ways;
France could not even conquer your great name,

But punned it down to this facetious phrase—
Beating or beaten she will laugh the same)—
You have obtained great pensions and much praise;
Glory like yours should any dare gainsay,
Humanity would rise, and thunder "Nay!"

Byron's rhetoric of naming in the ten stanzas devoted to Wellington duplicates Wordsworth's antonomastic strategies in *The Convention of Cintra*. As Wordsworth withholds the epithet "deliverer," so Byron denies Wellington conventionally honorific epithets: "Called 'Savior of the Nations'—not yet saved; / And Europe's Liberator—still enslaved." Byron then places two heroic names in ideal contrast to Wellington, two names that Wordsworth had also used in a single passage in *Cintra*:

Great men have always scorned great recompenses:
Epaminondas saved his Thebes, and died,
Not leaving even his funeral expenses:
George Washington had thanks and nought beside,
Except the all-cloudless Glory (which few men's is)
To free his country.

Indeed, the one naming strategy in *Cintra* that Byron does not take up is Wordsworth's tendency—especially in the latter stages of the essay—to suppress the proper name, a procedure that, again, essentially informs the Waterloo poems. Byron, in contrast, trumpets the proper name to open the canto, in spite of his intention to devalue its currency. Gerald Newman has recently argued that, if we pay better attention to the social development of nationalist ideology, we will need to reverse the received ideological antithesis between the first and second generations of Romantic poets; similarly, the onomastic procedures of Wordsworth and Byron demonstrate that, contrary to conventional expectations, the older poet himself demythologizes—perhaps more effectively than the younger—one of the chief Tory heroes of the age.[30]

Antonomasia is a powerful tool of myth. Wellington's own case supplies ironic evidence of this process, for the primary example of antonomasia in the *Oxford English Dictionary* is "the Iron Duke," a mythic substitute that came into currency only after Wellington's death.[31] Wordsworth uses antonomastic figures to opposite, demythologizing ends, to elide or erase Wellington's name. Although he felt a deep sympathy for military life, Wordsworth responded to contemporary warriors such as Wellington not with the names that propel myths but with a myth of no name.

113

Eric C. Walker

Notes

1. For the Oxford anecdote, see, for example, *The Letters of William and Dorothy Wordsworth, The Later Years, Part III, 1835–1839*, ed. Ernest de Selincourt, rev. Alan G. Hill (Oxford: Clarendon Press, 1982), 722. The first epigraph is from *Thayer's Life of Beethoven*, rev. and ed. Elliot Forbes (Princeton, N.J.: Princeton University Press, 1967). I, 349. The second epigraph is from *The Friend*, ed. Barbara E. Rooke, in *The Collected Works of Samuel Taylor Coleridge*, Vol. 4 (Princeton, N.J.: Princeton University Press, 1969) Pt. 1, 358.

2. Roland Barthes, *Mythologies*, trans. Annette Lavers (New York: Hill and Wang, 1972), 129, 142, 151.

3. "Wordsworth, Warriors, and Naming," *Studies in Romanticism* (forthcoming).

4. *The Letters of William and Dorothy Wordsworth, The Middle Years, Part I, 1806–1811*, ed. Ernest de Selincourt, rev. Mary Moorman (Oxford: Clarendon Press, 1969), 267, 269. The editors identify the "Brother Knight" in the first passage as Sir Henry Burrard, but the second passage composed two days later—which is not annotated—suggests to my mind that "Sir Arthur" in the second is the "Brother Knight" in the first.

5. *The Prose Works of William Wordsworth*, ed. W. J. B. Owen and Jane W. Smyser, 3 vol. (Oxford: Clarendon Press, 1974), I, 193–415. Subsequent references to this edition are by page number in the text.

6. *"Poems, in Two Volumes," and Other Poems, 1800–1807*, ed. Jared Curtis (Ithaca: Cornell University Press, 1983), 84–86, especially verses 77–80.

7. *"Poems, in Two Volumes,"* 85, verse 32.

8. *Letters: Middle Years, Part I*, 333.

9. Wordsworth had named Nelson as an ideal in a note to "Character of the Happy Warrior" when it was published in 1807, but the note never again appeared with the poem in Wordsworth's lifetime; a sense of Wordsworth's growing disillusionment with Nelson is present here in the phrase "though in many things unlike." I discuss the place of Nelson's name in Wordsworth's poetry in "Wordsworth, Warriors, and Naming" (see note 3).

10. *Prose Works,* I, 395. As *Cintra* was going to press, Wordsworth became anxious that some of his comments on Wellington might be cause for libel action and sought advice on revisions; see *Letters: Middle Years, Part I*, 302, 327–44.

11. For a recent account of Wordsworth and nationalism, see Gerald Newman, *The Rise of English Nationalism; A Cultural History 1740–1830* (New York: St. Martin's, 1987). For another new perspective on poets and public figures, see Leo Braudy, *The Frenzy of Renown, Fame and Its History* (New York: Oxford University Press, 1986).

12. *The Life and Correspondence of Robert Southey*, ed. Charles C. Southey (New York: Harper and Brothers, 1851), 318.

13. *The Poet's Pilgrimage to Waterloo* (London, 1816); "Proem"; "Part the Second. The Vision," Section IV, stanza xxvi.

14. Patrick O'Leary, *Regency Editor: Life of John Scott* (Aberdeen: Aberdeen University Press, 1983).

15. 2d ed. (London, 1816). Subsequent references to this edition are by page number in the text.

16. *The Letters of William and Dorothy Wordsworth; The Middle Years, Part II, 1812–1820*, ed. Ernest de Selincourt, rev. Mary Moorman and Alan G. Hill (Oxford: Clarendon Press, 1970), 280, 282.

17. *Letters, Middle Years, Part II*, 280, 283.

18. From the "Preface" to *Lyrical Ballads:* "The obstacles which stand in the way of the fidelity of the Biographer and Historian, and of their consequent utility, are incalculably greater than those which are to be encountered by the Poet who comprehends the dignity of his art. . . . There is no object standing between the Poet and the image of things; between this, and the Biographer and Historian, there are a thousand"; *Prose Works*, I, 139.

19. *The Poetical Works of William Wordsworth*, ed. Ernest de Selincourt and Helen Darbishire, 5 vol. (Oxford: Clarendon Press, 1940–49; rev. ed., 1952–59), III, 157. Subsequent references to Wordsworth's *Poetical Works* are to this edition.

20. *The Poetical Works of William Wordsworth*, ed. William Knight, 8 vol. (London: Macmillan, 1896), VI, 80.

21. *Poetical Works*, III, 155, 158. Wordsworth wrote to Southey that the brief stanza about the "abyss of weakness" was "the passage which I most suspect of being misunderstood"; *Letters: Middle Years, Part II*, 325. James Chandler has recently examined Wordsworth himself as the subject of myth—the myth of the Renegade—after 1815; see " 'Wordsworth' after Waterloo," in *The Age of William Wordsworth*, ed. Kenneth R. Johnston and Gene W. Ruoff (New Brunswick: Rutgers University Press, 1987), 84–111.

22. *The Poetical Works of Sir Walter Scott* ed. J. L. Robertson (London: Oxford University Press, 1913), 619, stanza 22. Carl Woodring compares the Waterloo verses of Southey, Scott, and Byron in "Three Poets on Waterloo," *Wordsworth Circle* 18 (1987): 54–57.

23. *Poetical Works*, II, 272–78; in the *River Duddon* volume (1820), "Dion" appears on pp. 125–32. Barbara T. Gates comments on connections between *Cintra* and "Dion" in "Wordsworth's Lessons from the Past," *Wordsworth Circle* 7 (1976): 133–41.

24. *The Letters of William and Dorothy Wordsworth, The Later Years, Part I, 1821–1928*, ed. Ernest de Selincourt, rev. Alan G. Hill (Oxford: Clarendon Press, 1978), 517.

25. *Wordsworth & Reed; the Poet's Correspondence With His American Editor: 1836–1850*, ed. Leslie N. Broughton (Ithaca: Cornell University Press, 1933), 36.

26. *Poetical Works*, III, 53.

27. For an account of the poem's textual history, see Bishop C. Hunt, Jr., "Wordsworth, Haydon, and the 'Wellington' Sonnet," *Princeton University Library Chronicle*, 36 (1975): 111–32.

28. *The Poems of Tennyson*, ed. Christopher Ricks, 2d. ed., 3 vol. (London: Longman, 1987), II, 480–92.

29. Lord Byron, *The Complete Poetical Works*, ed. Jerome J. McGann, Vol. V: *Don Juan* (Oxford: Clarendon Press, 1986), 409–11.

30. Newman, *The Rise of English Nationalism*, 240–44.

31. Elizabeth Longford, *Wellington: Pillar of State* (New York: Harper & Row, 1972), 415–17.

Representing Robespierre

Brooke Hopkins

> We know it to be true of any seed or growing thing, whether plant or animal, that if it fails to find its proper nourishment or climate or soil, then the more vigorous it is, the more it will lack the qualities it should possess. Evil is a worse enemy to the good than to the indifferent; so it is natural that bad conditions of nurture should be particularly uncongenial to the finest nature and that it should come off worse under them than natures of an insignificant order . . . if their early training is bad, the most gifted turn out the worst. Great crimes and unalloyed wickedness are the outcome of a nature full of generous promise, ruined by bad upbringing; no great harm, or great good either, will ever come of a slight or feeble disposition.
>
> —Plato, The Republic, VI, 491 (Cornford translation)

What role does Robespierre play in the myth of the "growth of a poet's mind" that Wordsworth tells in The Prelude? The Prelude is a poem about power. Power for Wordsworth, as for other writers of his era, could be either imaginative, the power of the mind to mold or reshape the world, or destructive, "the shaping spirit of Ruin," as Coleridge wrote in the Biographia, the power "to destroy the wisdom of ages in order to substitute the fancies of a day."[1] The Prelude tells the story of the development of the first sort of power, the power to reshape. But it continually reminds its readers that that power is intimately related to, sometimes even inseparable from, the second, the power to unmake the world. It continually reminds them, in other words, that the two powers share the same source, a kind of primary energy "far hidden from the reach of words."[2] The role of Robespierre in The Prelude's mythology of power, then, is to embody the second sort, the power to destroy, the power to unmake. It is for this reason that Robespierre is associated throughout book 10 with Milton's Satan, the ultimate destroyer, the ultimate unmaker. Robespierre, in other words, represents Wordsworth's alter ego in *The Prelude*, his other side, the power to destroy that is so intimately connected with the power to create, the power to destroy that the poem seems finally to assert is what makes genuine creation possible.

The issues raised by Wordsworth's representation of the figure of Robespierre in *The Prelude* obviously have implications beyond the scope of that poem or even of the period in which it was composed. The problem of the relationship between power and genius has a long history in Western thought, a history that may be said to begin with Plato's own representation of the figure of Alcibiades in the *Symposium* (and the implicit contrast between that figure and the figure of Socrates). Dante's dramatic encounter with Ulysses in canto 26 of the *Inferno* offers another version of it: the poet's encounter with the "heroic" side of himself, with power and vision divorced from love. And of course there is Milton's own Satan, a figure quite clearly designed to represent the destructive potential of genius, what Coleridge calls "COMMANDING GENIUS" and of which he writes in *The Stateman's Manual*:

> This is the character which Milton has so philosophically as well as sublimely embodied in the Satan of his Paradise Lost. Alas! too often has it been embodied in *real* life! Too often has it given a dark and savage grandeur to the historic page! And wherever it has appeared, under whatever circumstances of time and country, the same ingredients have gone to its composition, and it has been identified by the same attributes. Hope in which there is no Chearfulness; Steadfastness within and immoveable Resolve, with outward Restlesness and whirling Activity; Violence and Guile; Temerity with Cunning; and, as the result of all, Interminableness of Object with perfect Indifference of Means.[3]

Wordsworth, of course, was not alone among his contemporaries in his fascination with the figure of Robespierre, in his use of that figure to explore the intimate relationship between the power to destroy and the power to create, and in his association of Robespierre with Milton's Satan. The latter phenomenon is already present in Coleridge's dramatic fragment *The Fall of Robespierre*, which was composed shortly after the French leader's execution in July 1794. There Robespierre is described in terms that recall Milton's account of Satan's qualities in book 1 of *Paradise Lost*:

> Sudden in action, fertile in resource,
> And rising awful 'mid impending ruins;
> In splendour gloomy, as the midnight meteor,
> That fearless thwarts the elemental war.[4]

117

It recently has been demonstrated how Coleridge continued to explore Robespierre's significance in his political lectures, culminating in a passage in his *Lecture on the Slave Trade* that at once celebrates the power of the "Imagination" (in terms, by the way, that look forward to Wordsworth's celebration of its power in book 6 of *The Prelude*) and condemns the "horrible . . . misapplication" of that power during the Reign of Terror.[5] The implication is that the same "power" can be used for good or ill, to create or to destroy. Meanwhile, of course, Wordsworth was exploring similar themes in *The Borderers*, through the character of Rivers and the relationship between Rivers and Mortimer. "Power is much more easily manifested in destroying than in creating," Wordsworth writes in his prefatory essay; "a child, Rousseau has observed, will tear in pieces fifty toys before he will think of making one."[6] Power is life to him / And breath and being," one of the band remarks of Rivers, "where he cannot govern / He will destroy."[7] And destroy he does, in Wordsworth's most explicit condemnation of the separation of hand and heart in revolutionary politics. As has frequently been pointed out, Rivers's betrayal of Mortimer into murdering Baron Herbert represents what Wordsworth believed to be his own self-betrayal during the revolutionary period, the terrible "misapplication" of his own power and energy toward destructive ends. Only Mortimer's capacity to repent, his desire to make reparation, give some reason for hope.

When we arrive at *The Prelude*, however, we have reached genuine psycho-history. What the French Revolution books explore is the border between external events and persons and the interior, the psychic life of their hero, the way the two interpenetrate and interact, the psychological processes of splitting and identification. As Wordsworth himself puts it with reference to Louvet's ill-fated charge that Robespierre was aiming at supreme power in France:

> but these are things
> Of which I speak only as they were storm
> Or sunshine to my individual mind.

(X, 103–5)

"Storm / Or sunshine" are natural images that correspond to inner states. Wordsworth's inner state at the time was, as he describes it, more like the former than the latter, more like the tempest that was so frequently used to figure the political weather of the times.[8] But it is his account of his fantasy of how he might single-handedly turn back the Jacobin tide and thus change the course of history that is

118

the most revealing in this context. What it reveals is how, even in opposition, he unconsciously identified with the solitary and courageous Robespierre, who had risen "in hardihood, and dared" (X, 93) his accuser. Wordsworth imagines a corresponding role for himself, "obscure" (X, 130) as he was: that no less than "the gift of tongues might fall" (X, 121) to aid him in the salvation of France. But the liberators with whom he goes on to identify himself are revealing (albeit, within the context of eighteenth-century rhetoric and iconography, fairly conventional) ones. Harmodius and Aristogiton both perished in the project of ridding Athens of tyranny,[9] and Brutus, who participated in the assassination of Julius Caesar, took on (in Shakespeare's version, at any rate) many of Caesar's characteristics after his death, in an attempt to disguise the bloody implications of his deed. This kind of bonding by identification is revealed most powerfully in the following passage:

> Well might my wishes be intense, my thoughts
> Strong and perturbed, not doubting at the time—
> Creed which ten shameful years have not annulled—
> But that the virtue of one paramount mind
> Would have abashed those impious crests, have quelled
> Outrage and bloody power, and in despite
> Of what the people were through ignorance
> And immaturity, and in the teeth
> Of desperate opposition from without,
> Have cleared a passage for just government,
> And left a solid birthright to the state,
> Redeemed according to example given
> By ancient lawgivers.

> (X, 176–88)

This had been precisely Robespierre's project as well, to raise a new state based upon examples of ancient virtue, "the public virtue which worked so many wonders in Greece and Rome and which ought to produce even more astonishing things in republican France—that virtue which is nothing other than the love of the nation and its laws."[10] The rhetoric of redemption embedded in the passage had been Robespierre's as well. But this brings us back to Robespierre himself, Wordsworth's alter ego in book 10, and to the question of power.

Power, according to *The Prelude*, originates in childhood. In fact, it seems to have been one of Wordsworth's original intentions in beginning the poem to recover a power, the power of mind to reshape—and even in some instances to deny—the very existence of the external world. "Of genius, power, / Creation, and divinity it-self, / I have been speaking," Wordsworth summarizes the "heroic argument" of the first two and part of the third books of his poem (III, 171-73, 182). Yet, as Ross Woodman has argued, Wordsworth's decision to continue his story to include his experience of the revo-lution "forced him radically to modify his [earlier] 'heroic argument' and view in a very different light the 'genuine prowess' proper to it. The failure of the French revolution forced him to abandon 'heroic argument' even as Milton was forced by the failure of the English revolution."[11] Perhaps the clearest evidence of this abandonment is Wordsworth's comparison of those responsible for carrying out the Reign of Terror, most notably Robespierre, with a child who, "not content" simply to watch the vanes of a windmill "spin in his eyesight,"

> with the plaything at arm's length . . . sets
> His front against the blast, and runs amain
> To make it whirl the faster.
>
> (X, 342–45)

The figure works on several levels: as a reminder that the guillotine itself, whose blade resembles the vanes of a windmill in its flashing motion, functions as a kind of large toy in the hands of those who operate it; that the same thing that fascinates the child, the whirl of the blades (cf. Coleridge's "outward Restlessness and whirling Ac-tivity"), fascinates the executioner and even the bureaucrat behind the executioner, the speed and efficiency of his machine; and that the latter, the executioner and the bureaucrat, are simply extensions of the former, the child. Even more significant than the psycholog-ical implications of the figure, however (and they are enormous), is the identification it forces the reader to draw between the child with the windmill and the child of the earlier books of *The Prelude*, the child, for instance, of the "ravens'-nest" spot or the boat-stealing episode, not to speak of the child of *Nutting*,[12] and the potentially destructive power shared by each. In fact, one could almost say that Wordsworth and Robespierre are united in the figure of this child, that at this moment in the poem they are revealed to be *doubles* of one another, with equal capacities for creation or destruction.

This identification is made quite explicit throughout the French Revolution books as Wordsworth reconstructs his own attitude to-ward violence during the revolutionary period. For instance, his ra-tionalization of the September massacres upon his return to Paris in October 1792, is dramatized in the following manner:

Lamentable crimes,
'Tis true, had gone before this hour—the work
Of massacre, in which the senseless sword
Was prayed to as a judge—but these were past,
Earth free of them for ever (as was thought),
Ephemeral monsters, to be seen but once,
Things that could only shew themselves and die.

(X, 31–37)

The impact of this passage depends almost entirely upon one's ability to appreciate its irony, the distance Wordsworth creates between the poet and the reader on the one hand, who *know* what those crimes were a prelude to, and the poet's previous self, who saw them as "ephemeral monsters . . . things that could only shew themselves and die." Somehow, the passage hints, such blind certainty as is implied in the adverb "only" here, implicates one in the events that follow. If such blindness is not an actual cause, it is at the very least something that gives certain diseases, certain "ephemera" (literally "things of a day"), the opportunity to grow. Besides, Robespierre himself viewed the massacres in much the same fashion, condoned them, but as something that would pass.[13] Or, to take another example of the identification Wordsworth draws between himself and Robespierre, this time from the second half of book 10. It is the passage in which he describes himself as "an active partisan" (X, 736), as having convinced himself

That throwing off oppression must be work
As well of licence as of liberty;
And above all (for this was more than all),
Not caring if the wind did now and then
Blow keen upon an eminence that gave
Prospect so large into futurity—

(X, 746–51)

Here, Wordsworth is virtually paraphrasing—in a wholly different context of course—the defense of revolutionary violence he had made in *A Letter to the Bishop of Llandaff* shortly after the execution of Louis XVI. That defense, it should be noted, parallels many of the speeches made in the French National Convention during the debate over the king's fate, some of which Wordsworth would have attended during the fall and early winter of 1792, including, perhaps even especially, those of Robespierre. Beneath the extraordinary reticence of the phrasing, the message is quite clear: the end, the creation of "a race of men . . . truly free,"[14] more than justifies the means, the use of violence to attain that end. In response to the

121

bishop's expression of horror at the violence done to "the faithful adherents of a fallen monarch," Wordsworth replies with energy:

> What! have you so little knowledge of the nature of man as to be ignorant, that a time of revolution is not the season of true Liberty. Alas! the obstinacy & perversion of men is such that she is too often obliged to borrow the very arms of despotism to overthrow him, and in order to reign in peace must establish herself by violence. She deplores such stern necessity, but the safety of the people, her supreme law, is her consolation.[15]

Many of the same arguments would be made by Robespierre the following year in his famous speech justifying a policy of terror, arguments that "the government of revolution is the despotism of liberty against tyranny," that violence was necessary in order to assure the safety of the people.[16] It might be recalled that the administrative body that carried out that policy was named, somewhat euphemistically, the Committee of Public Safety (cf. Wordsworth's "the safety of the people"). Finally, the last lines of the passage echo Coleridge's celebration of imaginative power in his *Lecture on the Slave Trade*. It is that power, Coleridge had written, "that stimulates to the attainment of real excellence by the contemplation of splendid Possibilities . . . and fixing our eye on the glittering Summits that rise one above the other in Alpine endlessness still urges us up the ascent of Being, amusing the ruggedness of the road with the beauty and grandeur of the ever-widening Prospect. Such and so noble are the ends for which this restless faculty was given us—but horrible has been its misapplication."[17] This seems to be precisely *The Prelude*'s point as well, only there Wordsworth is using his *own* experience to illustrate it. The line that separated his actions from Robespierre's was perhaps merely a matter of the circumstances in which they found themselves. He too might have been capable of similar "misapplication" of his powers had he found himself in Robespierre's position.

Far and away the most explicit admission on Wordsworth's part of his identification with Robespierre and his attraction to the kind of power Robespierre wielded, however, is to be found in a passage just preceding the episode in which he learns of the French leader's death. The passage is not an easy one to sort out, concealing as much as it reveals, revealing through its strategies of concealment Wordsworth's complex state of mind at the time of the Terror. It begins by reflecting upon the "change" brought about by his new dedication to the cause of mankind, how much more difficult it was than the love of nature (X, 381–400). "But," he goes on, "as the ancient prophets were enflamed" (X, 401) in times of difficulty, when the people fell away from the true path,

> So did some portion of that spirit fall
> On me to uphold me through those evil times,
> And in their rage and dog-day heat I found
> Something to glory in, as just and fit,
> And in the order of sublimest laws.
> And even if that were not, amid the awe
> Of unintelligible chastisement
> I felt a kind of sympathy with power—
> Motions raised up within me, nevertheless,
> Which had relationship to highest things.
>
> (X, 409–18)

The passage is vintage Wordsworth, even in—perhaps even because of—its "disturbing" implications.[18] As he does in "Tintern Abbey," Wordsworth peels back the layers of defense (writing "and even if that were not," i.e., and even if what I have just said about how I viewed the terrible events from a prophetic standpoint, as a manifestation of God's judgment, were not the case) to reveal what he genuinely "felt" at the time, "a kind of sympathy with power," and by implication, an identification with those who wielded it, not the least the context reminds us, with Robespierre himself. Yes, "the implications of the passage are . . . disturbing," that Wordsworth might have viewed the Terror as in some sense the inevitable outcome of past crimes, that he might actually have sympathized with those who carried it out as somehow justified in their mission of purification. But that is precisely what gives *The Prelude* the power *it* has, its ability to get its readers to acknowledge such facts: that power must be linked to love in acts of creation, otherwise the possibilities of its "misapplication" increase enormously.

What has been said above should allow us to read Wordsworth's account of how he first heard the news of Robespierre's death with new insight. What was it that drove him to make what on the surface, at any rate, appears to be the somewhat exaggerated claim to Coleridge that,

> few happier moments have been mine
> Through my whole life than that when first I heard
> That this foul tribe of Moloch was o'erthrown,
> And their chief regent levelled with the dust?
>
> (X, 466–69)

At least part of it must be that Robespierre's murder appeared to mean that the satanic part of himself had been murdered as well,

123

the part of Wordsworth that had actually acted out his own destructive, parricidal drives on the stage of history. Hence, the crucial, italicized emphasis Wordsworth gives to the traveler's reply, "That, *Robespierre was dead*" (X, 535), which appears, at any rate, to complete the cycle announced initially by the only other comparable use of italics in the 1805 version of the poem, "the voices of the hawkers. . . . Bawling, *Denunciation of the crimes / Of Maximilian Robespierre*" (X, 86–88) at the opening of book 10. It is almost as if by his use of italics Wordsworth was attempting to contain Robespierre within his own text, to make sure, through incantation, of a sort, as well as closure *("Robespierre was dead")* that the destructive part of himself that Robespierre represented would never rise from the grave again, or at the very least, attempting to embody the possibilities for genuine freedom Robespierre's death held for him at the time. Those possibilities, however, are completely belied by what follows, Wordsworth's account of the "hymn of triumph" he sang "on those open sands" to celebrate the "eternal justice" of Robespierre's murder (X, 540–43). " 'Come now, ye golden times,' " captures the utopian spirit of the day:

> "as the morning comes
> Out of the bosom of the night, come ye.
> Thus far our trust is verified: behold,
> They who with clumsy desperation brought
> Rivers of blood, and preached that nothing else
> Could cleanse the Augean stable, by the might
> Of their own helper have been swept away.
> Their madness is declared and visible;
> Elsewhere will safety now be sought, and earth
> March firmly towards righteousness and peace."
>
> (X, 542–52)

The rhetoric of this passage (and set off from the rest of the poem by quotation marks, that is obviously all it is, rhetoric in the negative sense of that word), has an unmistakably Robespierreian ring to it, as if one could produce an earthly paradise simply through the sound of one's voice. The irony is, of course, that that voice continues to echo Robespierre's own, in it evocation of "golden times," its celebration of purification through violence, its use of euphemisms like "safety," and in the general militancy of its vision of the future: "and earth / March firmly towards righteousness and peace." As Robespierre himself had put it only seven months before: "Let us, in sealing our work with our blood, see at least the early dawn of universal bliss—that is our ambition, that is our goal."[19]

Robespierre remains alive in *The Prelude,* therefore, even after his death, in the figure of the poem's hero, the future poet himself—a connection, I believe, that the poem continually *requires* its readers to make. The reader's awareness of Robespierre's continuing presence is surely the aim of Wordsworth's well-known and obviously quite deliberate quotation in the second part of book 10 from Rivers's defense of parricide in *The Borderers,* a play that is, as David Erdman has amply demonstrated, profoundly concerned with the nature and consequences of revolutionary—even more specifically, regicidal—terror.[20] What is noteworthy about that quotation, however—"the light of circumstances, flashed / Upon an independent intellect" (X, 828–29)—is that it appears at the end of a passage in which Wordsworth satirizes the attraction Godwin's thought had for him during the period after his rejection of revolutionary violence as a way of transforming society. The shift of context has—at least until quite recently—forced critics into reading *The Borderers* from a Godwinian perspective. That shift should work in the opposite direction as well, to force them to acknowledge how much of Rivers, how much of Robespierre, was still alive in the young Godwinian. But this connection is made perfectly clear in the confession that follows. "We dissect / The senseless body, and why not the mind?" Rivers had asked himself in *The Borderers.*[21] "I took the knife in hand," Wordsworth confesses in a similar vein in *The Prelude,*

> And, stopping not at parts less sensitive,
> Endeavoured with my best of skill to probe
> The living body of society
> Even to the heart. I pushed without remorse
> My speculations forward, yea, set foot
> On Nature's holiest places.

> (X, 872–78)

This is the penultimate image of violent destructiveness in the entire poem. (Rather characteristically, it is considerably toned down in the 1850 version.) But precisely what does the figure represent? It represents Wordsworth as an anatomist. It represents his cold-blooded dissection of social customs, a dissection he had exposed elsewhere with the collective confession: "—We murder to dissect" ("The Tables Turned," 28). "The guillotine has become a surgeon's knife," Nicholas Roe acutely observes, "and the surgeon is Wordsworth himself performing an operation of vivisection upon the 'living body of society,' as Robespierre had sought to purge the internal enemies of France and 'seal our work with our blood.' "[22]

125

But it represents more than that, as the figure is extended from probing, to pushing "without remorse," to setting "foot / On Nature's holiest places," what the Norton editors describe as "the heart (or mind, or soul) of the individual human being."[23] It represents a sacrilege, in other words. The terror has become an interior one, one in which it is no longer possible to distinguish the victim from the victimizer, the destroyer from the person being destroyed. Othello-like, Wordsworth destroys himself even as he probes "the living body" with his thoughts, even as he pushes "without remorse" his "speculations forward" into "the place / The holiest that I knew of—my own soul" (X, 379–80).[24] It is only at this point in the poem, after the crisis of "despair" (X, 900), a crisis in which he "lost / All feeling of conviction" (X, 897–98, emphasis added), that it can be said with any real conviction, "that, *Robespierre was dead,*" that he had finally destroyed himself.

Wordsworth, then, represents Robespierre in *The Prelude* not just as a figure who commanded the stage at a certain moment in the history of Western Europe (as, say, Byron might have done); but (closer to Blake's or Shelley's method of representation) as an exemplar of a certain kind of power with which the poem's hero himself, and everything the poem's hero represents, had deep sympathy. He is represented as part of the psyche of the poem's hero, the destructive—ultimately, the self-destructive—part of his psyche. But, the poem's account of the poet's growth goes, there were other parts to that psyche as well, exemplified by other figures in the poem's mythology, not the least that of Wordsworth's own sister, Dorothy, whose role in the poem is to represent another power, the power of gentleness and love. So it is not surprising that the two figures are brought together at the end, in Wordsworth's tribute to his sister, to the part of himself she represents or helped to foster. The passage, which begins "Child of my parents, sister of my soul" (XIII, 211), is well known and need not be quoted in full. But in typical Wordsworthian fashion, at the end of a series of relative clauses that pay tribute to Dorothy's influence (the structure goes, "For, spite of . . . and spite of . . . I . . . "), it contains this strange, self-critical reference to Milton, or rather to Milton's Satan:

> I too exclusively esteemed that love,
> And sought that beauty, which as Milton sings
> Hath terror in it.
>
> (XIII, 224–26)

126

It is not surprising that editors and commentators have found some difficulty in coming to terms with the reference. For one thing, of course, it is not Milton who "sings" this in book 9 of *Paradise Lost*, or at least not directly. It is Satan, as he watches Eve before the fall:

> She fair, divinely fair, fit Love for Gods,
> Not terrible, though terror be in Love
> And beauty.[25]

What Satan is referring to, of course, is the power of love and beauty to overwhelm the soul: their sublimity, which is not the sort of love and beauty Eve represents. Hers is more down-to-earth. Wordsworth's allusion, then, accomplishes two things: it identifies his past self with Robespierre through the figure of Milton's Satan, with whom Robespierre has been associated throughout the poem; and it serves to remind readers once more, and for the last time, of the consequence of satanic power, of the terror that results when power is divorced from love.

All this, however, is contained in a passage that celebrates Dorothy's influence. The revision of *Paradise Lost* is crucial here. It is as if, to follow the parallels through to their logical conclusion, Satan had been won over by Eve, as if Eve had been able to draw Satan, so to speak, back down to earth, to the appreciation of a love and beauty *free* of terror.[26]

> Thou didst soften down
> This over-sternness; but for thee, sweet friend,
> My soul, too reckless of mild grace, had been
> Far longer what by Nature it was framed—
> Longer retained its countenance severe—
> A rock with torrents roaring, with the clouds
> Familiar, and a favorite of the stars.
>
> (XIII, 226–32)

This last image, "a favorite of the stars," should remind us of the frequent "prospects" we have encountered in our discussion, prospects associated with power divorced from love. It should also remind us of the kind of power Satan promises Eve, that "ye shall be as Gods" (*PL*, IX, 708). *The Prelude* never denies the importance of such power. Indeed, the poem continually reminds its readers that it owes its very existence to the visionary impulse, to the impulse associated with Robespierre. No less, however, does it remind them of the importance of another power, a power associated with Dorothy, the power to recognize the place we live in as the paradise we have been searching for all along. The power of terror and the power of love, "these two attributes / Are sister horns" (XII, 3–4) throughout the entire poem. And it remains a question to the end which is the most powerful. But for a poem the chief concern of which is the fate of power itself, that is perhaps not inappropriate. At least its readers are aware of the alternatives.

Notes

1. Samuel Taylor Coleridge, *Biographia Literaria*, ed. James Engell and W. Jackson Bate, *The Collected Works of Samuel Taylor Coleridge*, vol. 7 (Princeton: Princeton University Press, 1983), 33.

2. William Wordsworth, *The Prelude, 1799, 1805, 1850*, ed. Jonathan Wordsworth, M. H. Abrams, and Stephan Gill (New York: Norton, 1979), 1805 version, Book III, 185. 1805 version hereafter cited by book and line in the text.

3. Samuel Taylor Coleridge, *Lay Sermons*, ed. R. J. White, *The Collected Works of Samuel Taylor Coleridge*, vol. 6 (London: Routledge & Kegan Paul, 1972), 65–66.

4. *The Complete Poetical Works of Samuel Taylor Coleridge*, 2 vols. ed. E. H. Coleridge (Oxford: Oxford University Press, 1912), II, 496.

5. Samuel Taylor Coleridge, *Lectures 1795: On Politics and Religion*, ed. Lewis Patton and Peter Mann, *The Collected Works of Samuel Taylor Coleridge* (Princeton, N.J.: Princeton University Press, 1971), 235–36, cited in Nicholas Roe, "Imagining Robespierre," *Coleridge's Imagination: Essays in Memory of Peter Laver*, ed. Richard Gravil, Lucy Newlyn, and Nicholas Roe (Cambridge: Cambridge University Press), 172.

6. William Wordsworth, *The Borderers*, ed. Robert Osborn (Ithaca: Cornell University Press, 1982), 2.

7. William Wordsworth, *The Borderers*, Early Version, 204.

8. For the storm imagery that was so prevalent in the writing of the period, see Ronald Paulson, *Representations of Revolution (1789–1820)* (New Haven: Yale University Press, 1983), chs. 2–3.

9. Cf. Collins's (mistaken) allusion to Alcaeus's celebration of their heroism in his *Ode to Liberty*, Thomas Gray and William Collins, *Poetical Works*, ed. Roger Lonsdale (Oxford: Oxford University Press, 1985), 148–49.

10. Maximilien Robespierre,"On the Principles of Moral Policy that ought to Guide the National Convention" (given 5 February 1794), in *The Ninth of Thermador: The Fall of Robespierre*, ed. Richard Bienvenu (New York: Oxford University Press, 1968), 34.

11. Ross Woodman, "Milton's Satan in Wordsworth's 'Vale of Soul-making,' " *Studies in Romanticism*, 23 (Spring 1984), 17.

12. Which Wordsworth later claimed had been written originally for *The Prelude*.

13. J. M. Thompson, *Robespierre*, 2 vols. (New York: Howard Fertig, 1968), I, 275.

14. William Wordsworth, "A Letter to the Bishop of Llandaff," *The Prose Works of William Wordsworth*, ed. W. J. B. Owen and Jane Worthington Smyser, 3 vols. (Oxford: Clarendon Press, 1974), I, 34.

15. William Wordsworth, *The Prose Works*, I, 33.

16. Robespierre, "On the Principles of Moral Policy," in *The Ninth of Thermador*, 37.

17. S. T. Coleridge, *Lectures 1795: On Politics and Religion*, 235–36.

18. Nicholas Roe, "Imagining Robespierre," 176.

19. Robespierre, "On the Principles of Moral Policy," in *The Ninth of Thermador*, 34.

20. David Erdman, "Wordsworth as Heartsworth; or, Was Regicide the Prophetic Ground of Those 'Moral Questions'?" in *The Evidence of the Imagination: Studies of Interactions between Life and Art in English Romantic Literature*, ed. Donald H. Reiman, Michael C. Jaye, and Betty T. Bennett (New York: New York University Press, 1978), 12–41.

21. William Wordsworth, *The Borderers*, Early Version, 184.

22. Nicholas Roe, "Imagining Robespierre," 175.

23. William Wordsworth, *The Prelude, 1799, 1805, 1850*, 406, n.4.

24. This is a classic example of what Stanley Cavell has described as the tragedy at the heart of skepticism, "the attempt to convert the human condition, the condition of humanity, into an intellectual difficulty, a riddle," *The Claim of Reason* (New York: Oxford University Press, 1979), 493. Naturally, Cavell takes Shakespeare's *Othello* as the best example of such tragedy. Cf. Wordsworth's allusion to Othello's "I'll have some proof" (III, iii, 392) in his account of his crisis:

> now believing,
> Now disbelieving, endlessly perplexed
> With impulse, motive, right and wrong, the ground
> Of moral obligation—what the rule,
> And what the sanction—till, demanding proof,
> And seeking it in every thing.
>
> (X, 892–97)

25. John Milton, *Complete Poems and Major Prose*, ed. Merritt Y. Hughes (New York: Odyssey Press, 1957), Book IX, 489–91.

26. This only makes genuine sense if, along with Winnicott, we acknowledge such gender as containing "male" and "female" elements, the primary component for each being the "capacity to be," D. W. Winnicott, *Playing and Reality* (New York: Basic Books, 1971), 79–85.

"Bright Star, Sweet Unrest": Image and Consolation in Wordsworth, Shelley, and Keats

Nicholas Roe

For Wordsworth the French Revolution was lived experience in 1790 and in 1791–92. It was also an event that he immediately mythologized, as a "lovely birth" in *Descriptive Sketches* (1792); as "a convulsion from which is to spring a fairer order of things" in *A Letter to the Bishop of Llandaff* (1793); and as the "march" of "Heroes of Truth" in his first version of *Salisbury Plain* (1793). In the years immediately after, Wordsworth's mythical treatment of the revolution grew increasingly personal in orientation, as he discovered his own greatest subject to be himself. One can read *The Borderers* as a dramatized abstraction of Wordsworth's own revolutionary involvement and, later, books 6, 9, 10, and 11 of *The Prelude* present a selective and stylized version of the same experience as a stage in the "growth of a poet's mind."

The Prelude integrates the French Revolution with the development of Wordsworth's imagination, and in so doing it offers an ideal account of the revolution as personal mythology. Wordsworth's principal poetic model in writing *The Prelude* was, of course, *Paradise Lost*, and Milton's experience in the English Revolution of the seventeenth century was the single most significant precedent for Wordsworth's construction of his own revolutionary past in *The Prelude:* Milton offered Wordsworth a prototype for his own ideal self-image as a republican revolutionary who at a period of "dereliction and dismay" had turned political defeat to poetic and philosophical gain. This essay will explore Wordsworth's use of Milton in his self-mythologizing, as a response to the failure of the French Revolution and the reform movement in Britain. It will do so by illuminating a comparably mythic status for Wordsworth in the poems of Shelley and Keats. For Shelley, Wordsworth was a political apostate who had deserted the revolutionary cause of his youth. For Keats, Wordsworth's development from republican to Tory was a troubling focus for Keats's own ambition and insecurity as a poet.

Tom Keats and "Lord Wordsworth"

I begin with a few lines from Keats's *Ode to a Nightingale:*

Oh, for a beaker full of the warm South . . .
That I might drink, and leave the world unseen,
And with thee fade away into the forest dim—

Fade far away, dissolve, and quite forget
What thou among the leaves hast never known,
The weariness, the fever, and the fret
Here, where men sit and hear each other groan;
Where palsy shakes a few, sad, last gray hairs,
Where youth grows pale, and spectre-thin, and dies;
Where but to think is to be full of sorrow
And leaden-eyed despairs;
Where Beauty cannot keep her lustrous eyes,
Or new Love pine at them beyond to-morrow.

Away! away!

(15, 19–31)[1]

Keats's lines toll out the elegiac burden of his greatest poetry—the paradox of beauty and suffering, the irony of love and mortality—and the poem as a whole enacts a resolving dissolution of self: to "leave the world"; "fade away"; "Fade far away"; "dissolve"; "forget"; "Away! away!" The poem descends into the "embalmed darkness" of reverie to contemplate the final release of "easeful death": "Now more than ever seems it rich to die, / To cease upon the midnight with no pain" (55–56).

131

Keats's younger brother Tom is usually invoked as the spectral youth of the *Nightingale Ode*, wasted away and destroyed by tuberculosis. But Keats's line refers to "youth" in general—"Where youth grows pale"—not "a youth" in particular. This serves as a reminder that Keats's preoccupations in the *Nightingale Ode* transcend his own personal horizons, and most obviously so where Keats is entering into a dialogue with his predecessor and contemporary Wordsworth. Keats's line "Where youth grows pale, and spectre thin, and dies" is an echo of a passage in Wordsworth's *Excursion:*

> a thought arose
> Of Life continuous, Being unimpaired;
> That hath been, is, and where it was and is
> There shall endure,—existence unexposed
> To the blind walk of mortal accident;
> From diminution safe and weakening age;
> While man grows old, and dwindles, and decays;
> And countless generations of mankind
> Depart; and leave no vestige where they trod.
>
> (IV, 754–62)

In his *Nightingale Ode*, Keats outbids Wordsworth by imagining youth as a pale, spectral existence—like the Ancient Mariner's death-in-life—prior to Wordsworth's "weakening age" that ultimately leaves "no vestige" behind. This passage from *The Excursion* recurred to Keats in his invocation to the nightingale as a consoling emblem of "Life continuous, Being unimpaired": "Thou wast not born for death, immortal bird! / No hungry generations tread thee down" (61–62). Keats's communion with the nightingale's song is an ecstatic life-in-death—"Now more than ever seems it rich to die, / To cease upon the midnight with no pain" (55–56)—and it resembles Wordsworth's "blessed mood" in *Tintern Abbey,*

> In which the burthen of the mystery,
> In which the heavy and the weary weight
> Of all this unintelligible world
> Is lighten'd:—that serene and blessed mood,
> In which the affections gently lead us on,
> Until, the breath of this corporeal frame,
> And even the motion of our human blood
> Almost suspended, we are laid asleep
> In body, and become a living soul.
>
> (38–47)[2]

Wordsworth and Keats both compensate mortality by imagining a sweet arrest of soul that Harold Bloom likens to the "highest state of the imagination which Blake called Eden."[3] But it is in fact Hamlet, not Blake, who ultimately presides over *Tintern Abbey* and the *Nightingale Ode*, and specifically Hamlet's meditation on human suffering in act three, scene one:

> To die, to sleep—
> No more, and by a sleep to say we end
> The heartache and the thousand natural shocks
> That flesh is heir to—'tis a consummation
> Devoutly to be wished. To die, to sleep.
>
> (3.i.62–66)[4]

Tintern Abbey and the *Nightingale Ode* enact Hamlet's wishful consummation of mortality, respectively, as a "serene and blessed mood" and as an "easeful death." For both Wordsworth and Keats, such a contemplated release is but momentary and vulnerable; each returns—again like Hamlet—to "this mortal coil," the "sole self," "this unintelligible world." I want now to move on to explore the wider implications of this imaginative identity of *Tintern Abbey* and the *Nightingale Ode*.

Wordsworth's awareness of human vicissitude and frailty was bought at the cost of revolutionary failure in France during the 1790s. His most immediate memorial of that experience is not the personal archaeology in *The Prelude*; it is *Tintern Abbey*, a poem that profoundly affected Keats and that was written in July 1798—a little more than twenty years before Keats began work on his Odes.[5] In *Tintern Abbey* Wordsworth offers his own moments of visionary insight and the power of his memory as compensation for his awareness of personal loss, erosion, and change. The measure of that recognition is the period of "five years" that has passed since Wordsworth's first visit to Tintern in July 1793. Those five years had embraced his belief "That if France prospered good men would not long / Pay fruitless worship to humanity" (1805, X.222–23)[6]—but those five years had also disappointed the hopes of all "good men" by war, the Terror, and the imperial expansion of France under Napoleon. Wordsworth's poetry of human suffering, "The still, sad music of humanity" ("Tintern Abbey," 91), was uttered out of his experience of that defeat. By a collateral process of internalization, Wordsworth's moments of exalted introspection when "we are laid asleep / In body and become a living soul" ("Tintern Abbey," 45–46) represent the imaginative manifestation of the revolution that had formerly seemed to promise the regeneration of all mankind through political change in Paris, London, Europe, the world.

133

Given the revolutionary background of *Tintern Abbey*, how are we to read Keats's echoes of that poem—and those of *The Excursion*—in the *Nightingale Ode*? Keats's "weariness, the fever, and the fret" clearly recalls from *Tintern Abbey* "the fretful stir / Unprofitable, and the fever of the world (54–55). But does this echo supply nothing more than a Wordsworthian resonance to Keats's poem? I have already suggested that Wordsworth's "fretful stir / Unprofitable" is a gloss for the French Revolution up to July 1798, when he wrote *Tintern Abbey*. Keats's echo of this passage keys his *Nightingale Ode* to Wordsworth's poem but also—if one grants this reading of *Tintern Abbey*—to the revolutionary milieu of the 1790s. Like *Tintern Abbey*, Keats's *Nightingale Ode* is a belated commentary upon, and lament for, the French Revolution as a cause for all mankind. More particularly, the *Ode* is a elegy for the "revolutionary youth" of Wordsworth himself.

Keats was a political liberal and a friend of the reformist and journalist Leigh Hunt, who published Keats's earliest verse in his radical newspaper the *Examiner*. Keats, like Hunt, was well aware of Wordsworth's former sympathy with the French Revolution, and of his subsequent retreat into Toryism and Church of England orthodoxy. When Wordsworth published *The Excursion* in 1814, he dedicated his poem to the local Tory nobleman, the "illustrious Peer" William Lowther, earl of Lonsdale. Keats cannot have missed this dedication when he read the poem, and he would have understood the political opinions it implied. While visiting the Lake District in June 1818, he inquired about Wordsworth, only to discover that he was out election-campaigning for William Lowther against the Whig candidate Henry Brougham. "What think you of that," Keats wrote to his brother Tom: "Wordsworth versus Brougham!! Sad—sad—sad—and yet the family has been his friend always. What can we say?" Keats wavers toward accommodating Wordsworth's political demise as family friendship with the Lowthers, but then rallies with a splendidly sarcastic swipe at Wordsworth's Tory pretensions. "Lord Wordsworth," he tells Tom, "Lord Wordsworth, instead of being in retirement, has himself and his house full in the thick of fashionable visitors quite convenient to be pointed at all the summer long."[7] Having exposed Wordsworth as a political toady and exhibitionist, Keats says no more on the matter in his letter to Tom. But his uneasiness about Wordsworth lasted through the following winter, during which Tom Keats died on 1 December 1818, and it informs those lines from the *Nightingale Ode* that recall Wordsworth's *Excursion* and *Tintern Abbey*:

Fade far away, dissolve, and quite forget
What thou among the leaves hast never known
The weariness, the fever, and the fret
Here, where men sit and hear each other groan;
Where palsy shakes a few, sad, last gray hairs,
Where youth grows pale, and spectre-thin, and dies;
Where but to think is to be full of sorrow
And leaden-eyed despairs.

(21–28)

The lyrical self-dissolution of the *Nightingale Ode* is won against Keats's intimidating knowledge as a poet of Wordsworth's achievement in *Tintern Abbey*. But the allusive references to Wordsworth's poetry of human mutability in *The Excursion* and *Tintern Abbey* in this passage also work as reminders of "Lord Wordsworth" out on the campaign trail for William Lowther, and of Keats's vexed letter to Tom the previous summer. Keats's "youth grown pale, and spectre thin" may arguably refer to Tom Keats. But the Wordsworthian texture of the verse suggests that Keats subliminally identified Tom with Wordsworth, and specifically Wordsworth as a poet who had foresaken the republican idealism of his youth for the Tory status quo represented by his dedication to *The Excursion*. Keats's association of the two is compounded by his preoccupation with his own death and his wish for "posterity's award": that is, poetic immortality.

Poets Who "Cease to Be"

Keats's anxiety to be "among the English poets after [his] death" is a constant refrain in his poetry and letters. A characteristic expression is his early sonnet *On Seeing the Elgin Marbles*:

My spirit is too weak—mortality
Weighs heavily on me like unwilling sleep,
And each imagined pinnacle and steep
Of godlike hardship tells me I must die
Like a sick eagle looking at the sky.

(1–5)

Keats first visited the Elgin Marbles early in March 1817. The beauty of the sculptures astonished and inspired Keats, but also oppressed him with a sense of his inadequacy to achieve the "imagined pinnacles" of his own ambition. Keats's hopes and his insecurity gave issue to his conscious self-fashioning as a poet, for instance, in his

135

writing *Endymion* as a deliberate "trial of [his] Powers of Imagination."[8] He set this calculated determination against his awareness of Wordsworth's literary achievement and, behind him, that of the great English poets of the more distant past. In contrast, the measure of Keats's fears that he might fail as a writer was Wordsworth's contemporary political orthodoxy; this Keats perceived as an emblem of human vicissitude, and of his own fragile mortality. The poem to which one should look is Keats's sonnet "When I have fears that I may cease to be":

> When I have fears that I may cease to be
> Before my pen has gleaned my teeming brain,
> Before high-pilèd books, in charactery,
> Hold like rich garners the full ripened grain;
> When I behold, upon the night's starred face,
> Huge cloudy symbols of a high romance,
> And think that I may never live to trace
> Their shadows with the magic hand of chance;
> And when I feel, fair creature of an hour,
> That I shall never look upon thee more,
> Never have relish in the fairy power
> Of unreflecting love; then on the shore
> Of the wide world I stand alone and think
> Till love and fame to nothingness do sink.

Keats wrote his sonnet sometime between 22 and 31 January 1818. Like his earlier poem on the Elgin Marbles, it presents Keats's anxiety of unfulfillment "Before [his] pen has gleaned [his] teeming brain." The opening line may be an echo of Keats's best-loved Shakespearean play, *King Lear*, specifically Lear's banishment of Cordelia:

> By all the operation of the orbs
> From whom we do exist and cease to be,
> Here I disclaim all my paternal care . . .

(1.i.111–13)

Equally, Keats's despairing "feel" that he "shall never look upon thee more" takes one back to Lear grieving over Cordelia: "Thou'lt come no more / Never, never, never, never, never" (5.iii.283–84). We know that Keats had reread *King Lear* as recently as 22 January 1818, when he wrote his sonnet *On Sitting Down to Read King Lear Once Again*, so that these echoes are not farfetched. But two other important influences are also available, and both have an obvious relevance for Keats's ambitions and self-doubting as a poet.

Just over two months before Keats wrote "When I have fears," he borrowed a copy of Coleridge's *Sybilline Leaves* from his friend Charles Dilke. Keats's greatest biographer Walter Jackson Bate comments that Keats "seems to have caught very little from Coleridge at this point."[9] But it may well be that one of Coleridge's poems in particular would have drawn Keats's attention, for it is a remarkable shadowing of Keats's own thinking about life, mortality, and poetry:

Human Life,
On the Denial of Immortality

If dead, we cease to be; if total gloom
Swallow up life's brief flash for aye, we fare
As summer-gusts, of sudden birth and doom,
Whose sound and motion not alone declare,
But are their whole of being! If the breath
Be Life itself, and not its task and tent,
If even a soul like Milton's can know death;
O Man! thou vessel purposeless, unmeant,
Yet drone-hive strange of phantom purposes!
Surplus of Nature's dread activity,
Which, as she gazed on some nigh-finished vase,
Retreating slow, with meditative pause,
She formed with restless hands unconsciously.
Blank accident! nothing's anomaly!
If rootless thus, thus substanceless thy state,
Go, weigh thy dreams, and be thy hopes, thy fears,
The counter-weights!—Thy laughter and thy tears
Mean but themselves, each fittest to create
And to repay the other! Why rejoices
Thy heart with hollow joy for hollow good?
Why cowl thy face beneath the mourner's hood?
Why waste thy sighs, and thy lamenting voices,
Image of Image, Ghost of Ghostly Elf,
That such a thing as thou feel'st warm or cold?
Yet what and whence thy gain, if thou withhold
These costless shadows of thy shadowy self?
Be sad! be glad! be neither! seek, or shun!
Thou hast no reason why! Thou can'st have none;
Thy being's being is contradiction.[10]

Coleridge's poem holds a number of intriguing possibilities for Keats's subsequent writing. The "nigh-finish'd vase," for instance, is an uncanny forecast of the image and emblem in Keats's *Ode on a Grecian Urn*. But it is Coleridge's agony of ephemeral mortality that would have borne directly upon Keats in the winter of 1817–18:

If even a soul like Milton's can know death;
O Man! thou vessel purposeless, unmeant . . .
Go, weigh they dreams, and be thy hopes, thy fears,
The counter-weights!—Thy laughter and thy tears
Mean but themselves . . .

Keats's response to the "feel" of his own mortality appears at the conclusion of his sonnet:

And when I feel, fair creature of an hour,
That I shall never look upon thee more,
Never have relish in the fairy power
Of unreflecting love; then on the shore
Of the wide world I stand alone and think
Till love and fame to nothingness do sink.

(9–14)

Coleridge looks into the "total gloom" of death, but in hope to preserve Milton's soul from annihilation. Keats, on the other hand, clings to the "feel" of life even as he anticipates his own extinction. His "fears that [he] may cease to be" do not hang upon the problem of the soul's immortality but characteristically return to his anxiety of a life so foreshortened "that [he] may never live to trace" those "symbols of a high romance" in his own verse. Keats's sonnet possibly echoes Coleridge's fragment in *Sybilline Leaves.* But if the two poems are related in this way, the sonnet reduces Coleridge's metaphysical speculation to the perimeter of Keats's own dilemma as a hopeful, uncertain poet who "may never live" to fulfill his potential.

The second influential presence at work in Keats's sonnet links his fears that he may "cease to be"—and fail as a poet—with Wordsworth, and specifically to Wordsworth's political mutability, which I have suggested informs the *Nightingale Ode.* This second influence is Shelley, in his 1816 sonnet *To Wordsworth:*

Poet of Nature, thou hast wept to know
That things depart which never may return:
Childhood and youth, friendship and love's first glow,
Have fled like sweet dreams, leaving thee to mourn.
These common woes I feel. One loss is mine
Which thou too feel'st, yet I alone deplore.
Thou wert as a lone star, whose light did shine
On some frail bark in winter's midnight roar:
Thou hast like to a rock-built refuge stood
Above the blind and battling multitude:
In honoured poverty thy voice did weave
Songs consecrate to truth and liberty,—

Deserting these, thou leavest me to grieve,
Thus having been, that thou should'st cease to be.[11]

Shelley's sonnet is an elaboration of Mary Shelley's comment on *The Excursion* in her Journal. On 14 September 1814, she writes "Shelley . . . brings home Wordsworths Excursion, of which we read a part,"—and she comments, "—much disapointed—He is a slave."[12] Shelley published his sonnet with *Alastor* in 1816, and Keats most likely read it at Leigh Hunt's house during or shortly after Shelley's stay there in December 1816. For Keats, Shelley's poem would have served to underline the political orthodoxy represented by Wordsworth's dedication to *The Excursion;* it bears directly upon Keats's developing attitude to Wordsworth's Toryism and, most obviously, upon the sonnet he was to write a little over a year later: "When I have fears."

If we read Shelley's and Keats's sonnets alongside each other, Wordsworth's extinction as the republican poet of "honoured poverty . . . truth and liberty" in Shelley's poem is the initiation of Keats's own meditation upon poetic ambition and mortality: "When I have fears that I may cease to be." Wordsworth's political demise consequently emerges as a reminder of Keats's own mortal identity as a poet, much as Wordsworth had invoked Burns and Chatterton as emblems of his own disquiet in *Resolution and Independence:*

I thought of Chatterton, the marvellous Boy,
The sleepless Soul that perish'd in its pride;
Of Him who walk'd in glory and in joy
Behind his plough, upon the mountain-side:
By our own spirits are we deified;
We Poets in our youth begin in gladness;
But thereof comes in the end despondency and madness.

(43–49)[13]

In the deaths of Burns and Chatterton, Wordsworth projected his anxieties about Coleridge as well as his own insecurities as a poet. For Keats, however, it was Wordsworth's political apostasy in particular that was a register of the mortal instability he feared in himself. And for both Shelley and Keats, the measure of Wordsworth's eclipse "as a lone star, whose light *did* shine" was Milton's unchanging luster as poet and republican hero.

Milton and Wordsworth as "Lone Stars"

Shelley's lament for Wordsworth's radicalism is construed through Wordsworth's own invocations to Milton as an English patriot in his "Sonnets Dedicated to Liberty." Wordsworth first published this group of sonnets in his *Poems in Two Volumes*, which appeared in 1807, and Shelley and Keats certainly read them in this or a subsequent edition. Wordsworth wrote a number of the sonnets when revisiting France during the Peace of Amiens, in August 1802. The immediate reason for Wordsworth's trip was to see his former lover Annette Vallon and to tell her of his intended marriage to Mary Hutchinson. The occasion would inevitably have reminded Wordsworth of his previous stay in France in 1792, from where he had returned to London to attack the British government in his pamphlet *Letter to the Bishop of Llandaff*, which he subtitled "by a Republican." Now, in August 1802, France had undergone a transformation to become an imperial military power under Napoleon, and presented a melancholy contrast with his memories of revolutionary and republican France: "then," Wordsworth writes in one of his sonnets,

> Then this Way,
> Which I am pacing now, was like the May
> With festivals of new-born Liberty:
> A homeless sound of joy was in the Sky;
> The antiquated Earth, as one might say,
> Beat like the heart of Man: songs, garlands, play,
> Banners, and happy faces, far and nigh!
> And now, sole register that these things were,
> Two solitary greetings have I heard,
> *'Good morrow, Citizen!'* a hollow word,
> As if a dead Man spake it!
>
> ("To a Friend," 2–12)

Wordsworth's "festivals of new-born Liberty" celebrated the first anniversary of the Revolution on 14 July 1790, by coincidence the first day of his visit to France that summer. But like the pastoral "festival" of a "sweet May-morning" in *Ode* "Intimations," the "songs, garlands, play / Banners and happy faces" of revolutionary France participated in a joyful, homeless vulnerability. The opening four verses of the *Ode* were written in March 1802, and are a memorial of a lost vision,

> The earth, and every common sight,
> To me did seem
> Apparell'd in celestial light   (2–4)

Wordsworth's sonnet, written some five months after he began the *Ode*, is a lament for a time when revolutionary France had seemed

140

to embody that "glory and dream" in the political renovation of humankind. In each case Wordsworth's childhood, and the Fête de la Fédération, are interpreted by a myth of banished innocence. By August 1802 France had already subdued the ancient republics of Switzerland and Venice, and for some time had presented an immediate threat to Britain. It was this development, above all, that conditioned Wordsworth's political realignment from a citizen of the French Republic in 1792 to English patriot and Commonwealthman in 1802. It is Milton whom Wordsworth calls upon to inspire the English at this period of national crisis:

London, 1802

Milton! thou should'st be living at this hour:
England hath need of thee: she is a fen
Of stagnant waters: altar, sword, and pen,
Fireside, the heroic wealth of hall and bower,
Have forfeited their ancient English dower
Of inward happiness. We are selfish men;
Oh! raise us up, return to us again;
And give us manners, virtue, freedom, power.
Thy soul was like a Star and dwelt apart:
Thou hadst a voice whose sound was like the sea;
Pure as the naked heavens, majestic, free,
So didst thou travel on life's common way,
In chearful godliness; and yet thy heart
The lowliest duties on itself did lay.

Wordsworth invokes Milton as a militant inspiration to England, a redeemer whose second coming will "raise us up" and restore the "virtue, freedom, power" of England at the time of the Commonwealth in the seventeenth century. Wordsworth had originally hailed Milton's constancy as republican and poet in his revised version of *An Evening Walk*, written in May or June 1794. And in this instance, too, he had returned to Milton as a saving inspiration at a time of political crisis. In May 1794 the leading members of the British reform movement in the Corresponding and Constitutional Societies had been arrested and imprisoned to await a charge of high treason. Treason was, of course, a capital crime; and to Wordsworth, Coleridge, and many other friends of liberty at the time, it appeared that the prime minister, William Pitt, was attempting to establish his own system of violent terrorism after the model presented by Robespierre and the Committee of Public Safety in Paris.[14] At this moment of opposition and intimidation, Words-

141

worth recalled Milton at work on *Paradise Lost*, isolated and in hiding after the Restoration of the monarchy:

> So Virtue, fallen on times to gloom consigned,
> Makes round her path the light she cannot find,
> And by her own internal lamp fulfills,
> And asks no other star what Virtue wills,
> Acknowledging, though round her Danger lurk,
> And Fear, no night in which she cannot work;
> In dangerous night so Milton worked alone,
> Cheared by a secret lustre all his own,
> That with the deepening darkness clearer shone.
>
> (680–88)[15]

Wordsworth is thinking of the moment in May 1660 when, as Milton's biographer William Hayley said, "the anxious friends of Milton, who thought the literary champion of the parliament might be exposed to revenge from the triumphant royalists, hurried him into concealment."[16] In that "time to gloom consigned," the "star" becomes an image of Milton's inner radiance, his imagination. It is also a symbol for the celestial muse Urania, whom Milton invokes at the start of *Paradise Lost* book 7, simultaneously the inspiration of his poetry and the guarantee of his safety "though fallen on evil days." And it is, of course, Milton's divine constancy in isolation that Wordsworth celebrates in his 1802 sonnet: "Thy soul was like a Star and dwelt apart."

Milton's star-like virtue was an ideal to which Wordsworth himself aspired as a poet, in the version of *An Evening Walk* written during the "evil days" of repression in 1794 and subsequently in the verses written early in 1800 as a "Prospectus" to his planned philosophical poem *The Recluse*. In his "Prospectus" Wordsworth had anticipated his calling as a prophetic poet,

> that my song may live, and be
> Even as light hung up in heaven to chear
> The world in times to come.
>
> (61–63)[17]

As the poet of *The Recluse*, Wordsworth would "chear the world" in the aftermath of the French Revolution, following the example of Milton, who in *Paradise Lost* had sought to intercede for "the ways of God" and thereby to explain the failure of his own, English, revolution. Wordsworth never completed *The Recluse*, but he did publish his magnificent "Prospectus" verses as a "Preface" to *The Excursion* in 1814—directly underneath his obsequious dedication to

142

the "illustrious Peer" William Lowther. This published text of the "Prospectus" incorporates the image of the star,

> that my Song
> With star-like virtue in its place may shine,
> Shedding benignant influence, and secure,
> Itself, from all malevolent effect . . .

(88–91)

—and in so doing it implicitly identifies Wordsworth with Milton. But there is already a decline from the selfless generosity of Wordsworth's earlier poem—"that my song may live . . . to chear / The world"—a decline toward the token gesture of "benignant influence" and a priority of self-security that is at odds with the sublime disinterest of Milton working alone in "dangerous night."

In his sonnet "To Wordsworth," Shelley imagined Wordsworth's revolutionary self as "a lone star, whose light did shine," attributing to him a luminous constancy that Wordsworth himself associated with Milton. Following publication of *The Excursion*, Shelley's poem is also a lament for Wordsworth's descent from the glorious independence of Milton's "star-like virtue," and it ironically measures the Tory "slave" of 1814 against the Miltonic aspirations with which Wordsworth had once contemplated his poetic calling. Shelley's sonnet weighs the poet of *The Excursion* against the poet of *Paradise Lost*, and finds Wordsworth wanting. More damagingly, it balances the "Sonnets to Liberty" and "Prospectus" to the *The Recluse* against the dedication to William Lowther, and finds that the poet of *The Excursion* has "ceased to be."

"Bright Star, Sweet Unrest"

For Wordsworth as for Shelley, the star is a radiant emblem of imagination as the translated expression of political ideals. For Wordsworth and Shelley, too, the star was explicitly associated with Milton's political constancy, the lack of which Shelley "alone deplored" in Wordsworth. I want now to return to Keats, and offer a reading of one of his best-known sonnets that will draw upon the political and literary context that I've been exploring so far:

> Bright star! Would I were steadfast as thou art—
> Not in lone splendour hung aloft the night
> And watching, with eternal lids apart,
> Like nature's patient, sleepless eremite,
> The moving waters at their priestlike task

Of pure ablution round earth's human shores
Or gazing on the new soft-fallen mask
Of snow upon the mountains and the moors;
No—yet still steadfast, still unchangeable,
Pillowed upon my fair love's ripening breast,
To feel for ever its soft fall and swell,
Still, still to hear her tender-taken breath,
And so live ever—or else swoon to death.

Keats's "Bright star" sonnet is frequently read as a love poem to Fanny Brawne, alongside other lyrics to her such as "The day is gone"; "To Fanny"; "I cry your mercy, pity, love"; and "Ode to Fanny." But as John Barnard recently pointed out, these "poems [to Fanny Brawne] are painful to read because they are private and desperately confused." "Only the 'Bright star' sonnet," he goes on "is in control of its emotions."[18] That control derives from the imaginative priority of the poem as one more effort to reconcile Keats's central themes of poetry and mortality; the permanence of art and the transience of life. This ballasts Keats's private feeling for Fanny, and generalizes the poem beyond personal intimacy to address the great presiders of Keats's art: Milton and Wordsworth.

A number of Keats scholars, among them Christopher Ricks, have linked the "Bright star" sonnet with Keats's letter to Fanny of 25 July 1819, particularly Keats's closing words:

> I am distracted with a thousand thoughts. I will imagine you Venus to night and pray, pray, pray to your star like a Hethen.
> Your's ever, fair Star,
> John Keats

However, as John Barnard again points out, in this letter "Fanny is . . . imagined as the evening star, Venus, and in the sonnet Keats is thinking of the North Star."[19] And indeed, the sonnet does open as a prayer to be "constant as the northern star," but then withdraws from that remote, inhuman changelessness to admit the sensual intimacy of the lovers. Keats's symbolic wish is in fact that his "Bright star" might simultaneously represent a polar constancy as well as the westering presence of Venus, the lover's evening star. This potential reconciliation takes one back to Keats's letter to Tom in June 1818, where he describes his response on seeing Lake Windermere for the first time. "There are many disfigurements to this Lake," he writes, "—not in the way of land or water. No; the two views we have had of it are of the most noble tenderness—they can never fade away—they make one forget the divisions of life; age, youth, poverty and riches; and refine one's sensual vision into a sort of north star which can never cease to be open lidded and stedfast."

The point here is not that the "Bright star" sonnet echoes the letter word for word, "north star . . . open lidded . . . stedfast"; "Bright star . . . steadfast . . . eternal lids apart." Keats's letter to Tom describes an imaginative process by which apprehended beauty—or "sensual vision"—is refined into a permanent ideal that Keats likens to the "north star." For Keats such an abiding constancy assuages the mortal "divisions of life." Not only is this the wishful state of Keats's sonnet—"Awake for ever in a sweet unrest"—it is the distinctive ideal of all Keats's greatest poetry: the eternal yearning of lovers in the *Grecian Urn;* the ecstatic ceaseless ceasing of the *Nightingale Ode;* the patient prolonging of the moment in *To Autumn,* such that the season's passing is infinitely delayed, while "by a cyder-press, with patient look, / Thou watchest the last oozings hours by hours" (21–22). Keats's desire to "refine . . . sensual vision into a sort of north star" is the imaginative pole to which all of these great poems move. In the letter to Tom, though, it is an immediate consolation for "the divisions of life" and for what he terms "the many disfigurements to [the] Lake." The source of this "disfigurement" is rather surprising. Keats's letter goes on: "The disfigurement I mean is the miasma of London. I do suppose it contaminated with bucks and soldiers, and women of fashion— and hat-band ignorance. The border inhabitants are quite out of keeping with the romance about them, from a continual intercourse with London rank and fashion. But why should I grumble? They let me have a prime glass of soda water—O they are as good as their neighbors." Yet this conceited tirade against London tourists—of whom Keats was one himself—is actually a distraction from the focal point of "disfigurement" Keats has in mind, and which immediately follows: "But Lord Wordsworth, instead of being in retirement, has himself and his house full in the thick of fashionable visitors quite convenient to be pointed at all the summer long." Keats's desire to resolve the "divisions of life" into permanence finds its ultimate cause in Wordsworth's forsaken retirement; his political orthodoxy; his fashionable popularity. And Keats's "north star which can never cease to be open lidded and stedfast" represents a constancy that finds its deepest significance in Keats's disappointed recoil from a Wordsworthian mutability: "Sad—sad— sad . . . What can we say?"

Keats's "Bright star" sonnet is a love poem for Fanny Brawne that also draws upon this more distant but enduring disenchantment with Wordsworth. In that "Lord Wordsworth's" orthodoxy was the final station in his own experience of revolutionary defeat, Keats's sonnet is a late approach to consolation for that failure and an attempt to compensate for the Miltonic task that Wordsworth had set himself in the "Prospectus" to *The Recluse,* and apparently failed to carry through. One can substantiate this larger point by returning to the first poem in Wordsworth's "Sonnets Dedicated to Liberty":

Composed by the
Sea-Side, near Calais,
August, 1802

Fair Star of Evening, Splendor of the West,
Star of my Country! on the horizon's brink
Thou hangest, stooping, as might seem, to sink
On England's bosom; yet well pleas'd to rest,
Meanwhile, and be to her a glorious crest
Conspicuous to the Nations. Thou, I think,
Should'st be my Country's emblem; and should'st wink,
Bright Star! with laughter on her banners, drest
In thy fresh beauty. There! that dusky spot
Beneath thee, it is England; there it lies.
Blessings be on you both! one hope, one lot,
One life, one glory! I, with many a fear
For my dear Country, many heartfelt sighs,
Among Men who do not love her linger here.

This sonnet was written at Calais during Wordsworth's visit in August 1802. It presents the translation of Wordsworth's political allegiance from France to England and—at another level—the shift in his affections from Annette Vallon to his future wife Mary. Hence the "Fair Star of Evening" is Venus, the lover's evening star about to "sink" in its evening splendor "On England's bosom." But as if to rescue the star from a wholly erotic declination and preserve it as a national "emblem" of England, Wordsworth has it "well pleas'd to rest, / Meanwhile," apparently stationary over "[his] Country."

Wordsworth's "Fair Star" is an image of arrested incipience calculated to strike Keats, "stooping . . . yet well pleas'd to rest." It provides a symbolic reconciliation of the sonnet's political and personal themes, an ideal poise that Keats believed Wordsworth had failed to sustain. Keats's "Bright star" sonnet retains the star as an emblem of steadfastness, "watching, with eternal lids apart, / Like nature's patient, sleepless eremite"—but rejects its "lone splendour" in isolation for the erotic fulfillment that Wordsworth's sonnet had deferred,

> No—yet still steadfast, still unchangeable,
> Pillowed by my fair love's ripening breast,
> To feel for ever its soft fall and swell,
> Awake for ever in a sweet unrest.

For Wordsworth the star was associated with a Miltonic constancy that he had celebrated in *An Evening Walk* in 1794, and sought to emulate in *The Recluse* as projected in the "Prospectus." For Shelley the "lone star" had represented Wordsworth's former dedication to republican ideals, an eminence that he had lost in later years. But Keats's wish for "steadfastness" as a poet is conditional only upon "earth's human shores"; his "Bright star" sonnet admits human vulnerability and redeems it in the tender union of the lovers. In so doing the upheaval of revolution, "the weariness, the fever, and the fret," is moderated by the "sweet unrest" of their lovemaking. And the disappointed idealism of Wordsworth, Shelley, and of Keats himself finds a last, fully human consolation.

Notes

This essay is a revised version of a lecture presented at the School of English, Leeds University, in December 1987. I am grateful for a number of suggestions made on that occasion, which have been incorporated here.

1. Unless indicated otherwise, quotations from the poetry of Keats and Wordsworth will be from the following editions: *The Poems of John Keats*, ed. M. Allott (London: Longman, 1972); *Wordsworth's Poetical Works* ed. E. de Selincourt and H. Darbishire, 5 vols. (Oxford: Clarendon Press, 1940–49).

2 *Tintern Abbey* is quoted from *Lyrical Ballads*, ed. R. L. Brett and A. R. Jones (London: Methuen, 1965).

3. Harold Bloom, *The Visionary Company*, rev. ed. (Ithaca: Cornell University Press, 1971), 408.

4. Quotations from Shakespeare's plays are from *The Complete Works*, ed. S. Wells and G. Taylor (Oxford: Clarendon Press, 1986).

5. For the political context of *Tintern Abbey*, see the "Epilogue" in N. Roe, *Wordsworth and Coleridge: The Radical Years* (Oxford: Clarendon Press, 1988), 268–75.

6. William Wordsworth, *The Prelude 1799, 1805, 1850*, ed. J. Wordsworth, M. H. Abrams, and S. Gill (New York: Norton, 1979).

7. All quotations from Keats's letters are from *Letters of John Keats*, ed. R. Gittings (Oxford: Oxford University Press, 1970). Wordsworth's relation to the Lowthers had, of course, been strained for many years because of Sir James Lowther's refusal

to pay his debts in settlement of Wordsworth's father's estate. After the death of Sir James on 24 May 1802, the debt was settled by his cousin Sir William Lowther early in 1803.

8. Letter to Benjamin Bailey, 8 October 1817.

9. W. Jackson Bate, *John Keats* (Cambridge, Mass.,: Harvard University Press, 1963), 238.

10. Quoted from *The Complete Poetical Works of Samuel Taylor Coleridge*, ed. E. H. Coleridge, 2 vols. (Oxford: Clarendon Press, 1912), I. 425–26.

11. Quoted from *Shelley's Poetry and Prose*, ed. D. Reiman and S. Powers (New York: Norton, 1977).

12. *The Journals of Mary Shelley 1814–1844*, ed. P. R. Feldman and D. Scott-Kilvert, 2 vols. (Oxford: Clarendon Press, 1987), I. 25.

13. Quoted from William Wordsworth, *Poems in Two Volumes, and Other Poems*, ed. J. Curtis (Ithaca: Cornell University Press, 1983). Subsequent quotations from Wordsworth's "Sonnets Dedicated to Liberty," *Ode* "Intimations," and *Resolution and Independence* are also drawn from this edition.

14. See *Wordsworth and Coleridge: The Radical Years*, 200–206.

15. Quoted from the "Expanded Version" of *An Evening Walk* dated to 1794 in William Wordsworth, *An Evening Walk*, ed. J. Averill (Ithaca: Cornell University Press, 1984).

16. W. Hayley, *The Life of Milton, in three parts, to which are added, Conjectures on the Origin of Paradise Lost*, 2d ed. (London: Cadell and Davies, 1796), 145.

17. Quoted from the text of the "Prospectus" in J. Wordsworth, *The Borders of Vision* (Oxford: Clarendon Press, 1982), 388–90.

18. J. Barnard, *John Keats* (Cambridge: Cambridge University Press, 1987), 127.

19. See C. Ricks, *Keats and Embarrassment* (Oxford: Clarendon Press, 1974), 114, and John Keats, *Complete Poems*, ed. J. Barnard, 2d ed. (Harmondsworth: Penguin, 1977), 684.

History as Character:
Byron and the Myth of Napoleon
Christina M. Root

In canto 3 of *Childe Harold's Pilgrimage,* Byron visits the fields of Waterloo and contemplates the character of Napoleon. In a series of stanzas in which sympathy vies with condemnation, Byron explores the reason for Napoleon's failure, describing a man of extraordinary public strengths undone by private weaknesses; Napoleon's genius for command and his skill in manipulating kingdoms and men were matched by a crippling inability to discipline or understand himself. Byron's analysis culminates in the judgment that Napoleon's failings stemmed not simply from his egotism and ambition but, more fundamentally, from predispositions in his nature over which he could have had little control. The source of his restless energy lay in a fever shared by all "the madmen who have made men mad / By their contagion" whether they were "Conquerors and Kings, Founders of sects and systems . . . Sophists, Bards [or] Statesmen":[1]

> Quiet to quick bosoms is a Hell
> And *there* hath been thy bane; there is a fire
> And motion of the Soul which will not dwell

In its own narrow being, but aspire
Beyond the fitting medium of desire;
And, but once kindled, quenchless evermore,
Preys upon high adventure, nor can tire
Of aught but rest; a fever at the core,
Fatal to him who bears, to all who ever bore.

(42:370–78)

By including Bards among the "unquiet things" likely to suffer from this fever, Byron makes explicit for the first time a connection his audience long would have taken for granted. Here he acknowledges that he understands Napoleon because he too is a man "extreme in all things" possessed of a "Spirit antithetically mixed" (36:320; 317).

Modern readers have tended to focus only on what the passage tells us about Byron himself. Although he does, in part, use Napoleon as a "device for self-analysis," as Jerome McGann maintains,[2] a crucial effect of the intimacy of the passage is to stress the depth of the identification between the two men and to explore the nature of their shared qualities.

Why Byron should wish to confirm and enlarge upon the popular notion that he and Napoleon were at heart very similar men is not a question that can be answered simply. Most critics have cautiously characterized Byron's attitude toward Napoleon as ambivalent or, more simply, vacillating, and have agreed with Carl Woodring that "no one of [Byron's] many references to Napoleon can be properly interpreted in isolation from the rest."[3] Byron's recorded comments on Napoleon range from condemnation to affectionate praise, but consistent throughout his judgments and observations of Napoleon is a deep personal interest in, and engagement with, the man. As in the passage quoted from *Childe Harold's Pilgrimage*, Byron most often expresses his sense of identification through his sympathy for, and understanding of, the forces propelling him "beyond the fitting medium of desire."

This personal approach does not mean that Byron's interest in Napoleon was apolitical. In fact, Byron was following his usual practice: merging the private, personal sphere with the public and political describes his method of exploring most political issues.[4] Byron rarely attempted to keep the two spheres separate and seemed most preoccupied with the borders between them. What Byron only reluctantly accepted was the fact that, in his case, at least, poetry provided the best medium through which to take political stands.

Byron cherished plans for a political career of his own, plans he acted on intermittently throughout his life. Initially, however, the overwhelming response to his poetry distracted him from his purpose. In *Detached Thoughts* he remembers that "just after my first speech in Parliament my poem *Childe Harold* was published—and nobody ever thought about my *prose* afterwards, nor indeed did I."[5] The public had found what it wanted in Byron the poet rather than in Byron the Whig reformer. As he himself proved several times, a poem could cause a far greater stir than a speech on the same subject in Parliament.[6]

These very real distractions notwithstanding, it is also the case that pamphlets and speeches were not congenial media for Byron. Though arguably the most politically engaged of the Romantic poets, and certainly the most ambivalent among them about poetry as a vocation, Byron left no prose record of his political projects and beliefs, and relied almost entirely on his verse to convey the range of his ideas. Byron preferred to merge the political and the personal in poetry that explored the psyche of a political figure. His audience preferred to believe that those portraits were of Byron himself. Though he claimed to be irked by the public's assuming that his poems described his own character and exploits, he fostered the confusion, blurring distinction especially between himself and Napoleon.

For example, in 1816, after the breakup of his marriage to Annabella Milbanke, when public opinion turned against him, Byron exiled himself from England. If his social defeat recalled Waterloo, it was at least in part because Byron, for his theatrical departure, commissioned a replica of the coach that had been confiscated from Napoleon at Jemappes and put on public display in London. Like Napoleon for his journey to St. Helena's, Byron took with him a biographer and personal physician. The eccentricity of these flamboyant gestures has led more than one critic to conclude that Byron was "mimicking Napoleon in adversity."[7] He succeeded in suggesting an equivalence between Napoleon's military and his own personal catastrophe.[8]

The public took Byron up on his analogy: after Waterloo he wrote several lyrics seeing the end of the war through the eyes of Napoleon and his loyal soldiers. Originally published anonymously in the daily press, they were soon pirated and issued under the title *Poems on his Domestic Circumstances*. The enormous popularity of this edition demonstrated the public's eagerness to buy the connection between Napoleon and Byron as revealing secrets about Byron himself.

Beginning with the *Turkish Tales*, the poetry describing what came popularly to be known as the "Byronic hero" emphasized the same character traits as the poetry literally about Napoleon: a dazzling ability to command and "to make even the mightiest deeds [of others] appear his own."[9] Though not explicitly topical, within the context of wartime British politics, these portraits were radical. Not only did they seem to celebrate the kind of character possessed by England's archenemy, but they represented generally the power of an individual to subvert or at least disrupt the reigning order. These figures could be used by people trying to foment rebellion among the discontented populace. Carl Woodring describes the *Tales* this way: "In the continuum of Byron's lifelong study of ambition, the *Tales* stress daring and domination. The protagonists, variously outlawed and alienated, represent the temptation to force and violence. The *Tales* are to this extent antidemocratic. But they are unmistakably antiroyalist, and their effect was to make every young reader feel superior to kings. Without having to preach it, they stimulate rebellion against staid arrangements of society."[10] Perhaps William Hone, the man responsible for the pirated *Poems on his Domestic Circumstances*, hoped Byron's verses would have that effect. A notorious radical, he published a wide range of political parodies and seditious pamphlets (sometimes from jail), including another famous pirated work: Southey's disavowed Jacobinical *Wat Tyler*.[11]

Byron's poetry was used in this political way in the trial of Jeremiah Brandreth, the radical "Nottingham Captain" found guilty of treason in the Pentridge uprising (1817). The defense attempted to explain the actions of the men indicted with Brandreth by arguing that they had "yielded to the overpowering force of their extraordinary leader."[12] The power of this radical leader could best be understood, the defense maintained, as the embodiment of Byron's Corsair—a man able to mesmerize his men with his "commanding art." To illustrate this point, the defense read out fifty lines of the poem in court.

However gratuitous the comparisons between himself and Napoleon may initially appear, then, it is clear that they could be made to serve a purpose not only by those appropriating Byron's work but by Byron himself. The connection provided him with a kind of larger-than-life stature and a politically radical stance. From that position his more serious investigations into what Napoleon represented politically and historically were guaranteed a popular audience. As we shall see, two tales, *The Corsair* and its sequel *Lara*, begin Byron's study of the Napoleonic type, their exotically subversive but ambivalent portraits laying the foundation for the more philosophical, mythic approach of *Manfred*.

Napoleon himself most convincingly raised the issues of character and destiny: he combined the continually improvising qualities of a great general, whose victories are the fruit of brilliant strategy, with the qualities of a man above circumstance, who is propelled through a series of events that remain in themselves less important than the destiny guiding him: a life patterned by fate rather than forged by will.

Byron explores the effect of that sense of destiny on the Napoleonic type's feeling of responsibility for his actions. Is the commanding genius, to borrow Coleridge's term, sincerely moved by the needs of the people he leads, or is he simply driven by the desire to rule? Given a predisposition to seek power, how able is the Napoleonic type to transform that impulse into selfless actions? Byron examines the times of crisis that test the moral fiber of his heroes, that moment, which seemed to him inevitable, when the myth and the life part ways, and the hero, contrary to all expectations, outlives his own defeat. How he behaved under these adverse circumstances provided insights Byron considered crucial to understanding the relationship between the world historical individual's personal character and his public mission. It had been Napoleon's fate not once but twice. He abdicated the throne first in 1814 when the Allies marched through Paris and again after his defeat at Waterloo.

Byron began *The Corsair* on 18 December 1813 and published it in February of the following year, writing during a time when Napoleon faced certain defeat. His armies had been destroyed at Leipzig by the Allies that October in one of the largest and bloodiest battles in two decades of war. Only weeks before Leipzig, Wellington had finally succeeded in pushing the French northward to the Pyrenees and had crossed into France himself. Though the end was clearly in sight, how Napoleon would respond to defeat and meet the fall of his empire remained to be seen. *The Corsair* is, in a sense, Byron's preabdication vision of an imagined outcome for a Napoleonic leader.[13]

Byron's remarks in his journal several weeks before embarking on *The Corsair* help provide a context for his politics at the time and are particularly significant for understanding the mythic terms in which he saw Napoleon:

> If I had any views in this country, they would probably be parliamentary. But I have no ambition; at least, if any, it would be "aut Caesar aut nihil" . . . Past events have unnerved me; and all I can now do is make life an amusement, and look on, while others play. After all—even the highest game of crowns and sceptres, what is it? *Vide* Napoleon's last twelvemonth. It has completely upset my system of fatalism. I thought, if crushed, he would have fallen, . . . and not have been pared away to gradual insignificance;—that all this was not a mere *jeu* of the gods, but a prelude to greater changes and mightier events. But men never advance beyond a certain point;—and here we are, retrograding to the dull, stupid old system,—balance of Europe—poising straws upon king's noses instead of wringing them off! Give me a republic, or a despotism of one, rather than the mixed government of one, two, three. . . . The Asiatics are not qualified to be republicans, but they have the liberty of demolishing despots, which is the next thing to it. To be the first man—not the Dictator—not the Sylla, but the Washington or the Aristides—the leader in talent and truth—is next to Divinity! . . . I shall never be anything, or rather always be nothing. The most I can hope is, that some will say, "He might, perhaps, if he would." (*BLJ*, 3:217–18)

It is possible here to see how closely Byron connected his own political plans with Napoleon's career. Sharing Napoleon's grand expectations—"*aut Caesar aut nihil*"—and horrified by Napoleon's fate, Byron abdicates his own career virtually before embarking on it. Napoleon's recent defeats raise the troubling possibility that he may be less historically significant than Byron had assumed, contributing to the disappointing judgment that "men never advance beyond a certain point," rather than disproving it, as Byron had hoped he would. The Eastern setting of *The Corsair* may suggest, in the context of these remarks, that Byron scaled down his expectations of what a Napoleon was capable of: like the Asiatics he could disrupt the old order, but he could not envision a new society.[14]

Byron's decision at the end of this passage to remain simply an observer while at the same time keeping alive the hope that others will perceive in him a potential for action reflects the depth of his fear of the defeats with which glorious careers seemed inevitably to end, and the ambivalence that fear engendered. *The Corsair*, in keeping with this cautious mood, offers a sympathetic account of the reasons a Napoleonic type might fail but also suggests what might still be possible through him despite that failure.

Like Napoleon, Conrad is a "king scatterer."[15] He and his band of pirates attack the palace of a slothful Persian lord, and though the raid fails, their rescuing the seraglio of slaves awakens in the women a desire for freedom and fundamentally upsets the pacha's authority. Conrad, who saved the women out of a sense of chivalry, is appalled by the passionate energy his act unleashes in Gulnare, the favorite of the pacha. Her freedom is a new kind of fact and beyond his experience. Conrad's sense of honor dictates that he resist Gulnare's attempts to free him when he in turn is captured, and he remains to the end baffled by the effects of his actions. In Conrad's mind death is the only alternative to victory: living on under these new circumstances would mean adjusting to a world that has outstripped his vision. When death is denied him, he disappears, a broken man.

In Conrad's story, Byron offers a positive rendering of his hero's being "pared away to gradual insignificance." Though a sympathetic account of such a paring away involves our seeing the hero as much more limited than Byron may have wished or imagined Napoleon to be, it does not diminish his importance as a historical force. Conrad acts as a catalyst for the progress of freedom without understanding the events he naïvely initiates. Though Conrad possesses the titanic individualism and charisma of the Napoleonic type, his ultimate significance lies in the role he plays rather than in his personality. That personality may be necessary to galvanize change but is not in itself part of what is new.

The view suggested by The Corsair expresses some of the disappointment evident in Byron's journal entry, but Byron has not yet given up on the possibility that the Napoleonic type has a historically significant role to play, even if it is only to act for a time as a conduit for forces beyond his control. Lara, the hero of the poem Byron considered a sequel to The Corsair, reflects the bitter disillusionment he felt once Napoleon actually abdicated, a disillusionment expressed most vividly in the "Ode to Napoleon Buonaparte." Lara encounters a situation similar to Conrad's and, like him, initiates a chain of events that have devastating consequences; but he, unlike his predecessor, is indifferent both to the suffering of his men and to the dilemmas his actions pose. Lara, a feudal lord, prepares to avenge an insult to his honor by rallying his slaves around him, feeding them well, and freeing them at a moment calculated to guarantee their loyalty and ferocity in fighting for him. Far from being baffled by a slave's desire for liberty, Lara controls and directs that desire to his own purposes. His motives are entirely cynical: "What cared he for the freedom of the crowd? / He raised the humble but to bend the proud" (2:4,251–52). Like Conrad, Lara unleashes something new into the world, but it dies almost as soon as it is born. The freed slaves' inchoate ideal of liberty devolves very quickly, under the pressure of battle, into "blind confusion," "lust for booty and thirst of hate." Very soon "it is too late to check the wasting brand, / And desolation reaped the famished land" (2:5,278–79).

The poem's emphasis on Lara's loneliness and private (unexplained) sorrow, as in Conrad's case, goes a long way toward making him a sympathetic figure; nevertheless, what emerges most clearly is Lara's want of sympathy and the selfishness of his using his power to avenge a personal wrong. He is "haughty still and loth himself to blame" for the desolation he has made of his life:

> He called on Nature's self to share the shame . . .
> Till he at last confounded good and ill,
> And half mistook for fate the acts of will.
> Too high for common selfishness, he could
> At times resign his own for others' good,
> But not in pity, not because he ought,
> But in some strange perversity of thought,
> That swayed him outward with a secret pride
> To do what few or none would do beside;
> And this same impulse would, in tempting time,
> Mislead his spirit equally to crime;
> So much he soared beyond or sunk beneath,
> The men with whom he felt condemned to breathe,
> And longed by good or ill to separate
> Himself from all who shared his mortal state.
>
> (1:18,331–48)

This picture of a "man extreme in all things" and of "a spirit antithetically mixed" anticipates very nearly Byron's description of Napoleon in Childe Harold's Pilgrimage. Like Napoleon, Lara possesses a character over which he has only partial control. The "strange perversity of thought" that leads him to attempt things beyond the scope of an ordinary man "mislead[s] his spirit equally to crime." Lara does not possess the kind of moral sense that could shape anarchic impulses into virtuous actions, but in this portrait, the Napoleonic type's greatest wrong lies in his abdicating responsibility. The astute and calculated mistake of considering his own acts synonymous with larger forces of destiny allows him to take advantage of his slaves' incipient desire to be free.

In this angry poem, the Napoleonic type is, in the end, antithetical to, rather than a precipitating cause of, or even an accidental participant in, progressive forces of change. The "magic of his mind" that allows him to hold sway over others will always by its nature work against any needs but his own. That Lara fights bravely and dies stoically demonstrates little more than that he has nothing left to lose.

Between the anger of *Lara* and the sympathy of *Manfred* fell the shadows of Waterloo, the breakup of Byron's marriage, and his own and Napoleon's exile. Because he felt that fatal flaws in his own character had doomed his marriage and career in London society, Byron was now more interested than ever in understanding rather than judging the character he felt he and Napoleon shared. He wished to explore fully the experience of aftermath—of living on as "the relic of some higher material being wrecked in a former world" (*BLJ* 9:46).[16] *Manfred* represents an investigation into the nature of the Byronic hero[17] that is simultaneously deeper and more open-ended than Byron's previous treatments of the type. Here he struggles to understand the nature of the self-destructive character, not as it impinges on the lives of others, but as it reveals itself upon introspection. In dramatizing the Byronic hero's remorse, Byron shows him directly confronting the dilemma of his destiny's being "simultaneously in his hands and out of his control"[18] and also the issue of how much responsibility he must take for what he has done. The mythic qualities of the drama underline Byron's deepening engagement with the issues of destiny and freedom raised by his hero's "commanding art." Manfred is literally larger than life. The supernatural setting also makes possible the shift in focus from the hero's effect on society to his nature. Manfred battles spirits rather than armies of men.

To understand how Byron's thinking shifted between the anger expressed in *Lara* and the intensely sympathetic exploration of character and destiny in *Manfred*, it is useful to trace the changes in his attitude toward Napoleon through the One Hundred Days and Waterloo. In the midst of his bewilderment and disappointment over Napoleon's defeat and abdication, Byron held out hope that "his little pagod [would] play them some trick still," and allow Byron to believe that the abdication had not been evidence of weakness but was instead a strategy, consciously devised to prepare the way for a return to power. When Napoleon lived up to that hope by escaping from Elba, Byron was so relieved and pleased that he forgave "the rogue for utterly falsifying every line of [his] ode." In reversing his fortunes, Napoleon proved once again that he was above them.

Nevertheless, Byron recognized the possibility of crediting too much to character when he acknowledged how fortuitous the particular chain of events of Napoleon's escape had been. In a letter to Thomas Moore (27 March 1815), he says:

> Making every allowance for talent and the most consummate daring, there is after all a good deal of luck or destiny. He might have been stopped by our frigates—or wrecked in the Gulf of Lyons, which is particularly tempestuous—or a thousand things. But he is certainly fortune's favorite. . . . It is impossible not to be dazzled and overwhelmed by his character and career. . . . Nothing ever so disappointed me as his abdication, and nothing could have reconciled me to him but some such revival as his recent exploit; though no one could have anticipated such a complete and brilliant renovation. (BLJ 4:282)

Byron's awareness that only an extraordinary coincidence of events, circumstances, and personality could have allowed Napoleon to resume power increased rather than diminished his belief that Napoleon was the master of his fate. After Waterloo, Byron despaired most over the fact that Napoleon failed to live up to the image of a man above circumstance that he and his career had created.[19]

One of Byron's greatest fears, to return to his reflections of 1814, was that "men never advance beyond a certain point," and Europe's "retrograding to the dull stupid old system" after Napoleon's fall served only to confirm that fear. If the titanic individual had a decisive role to play, Byron felt, it was to harness the forces of historical change to work through his biography so that his actions were not "a mere *jeu* of the gods but a prelude to greater changes and mightier events." When a man like Napoleon lapsed into scrambling to survive at all costs, he not only betrayed Byron's faith in him as a hero but also betrayed the causes his name had been synonymous with—giving the lie to the direction history had been headed in through him. Byron had counted on Napoleon, whatever his shortcomings, to break through the cyclical round of historical repetition to create something new. Despite these expectations, however, throughout this period of disappointment and reappraisal,

Byron struggled toward a more realistic understanding of the world-historical individual.

In *Manfred*, Byron explores the possibilities for heroism after all action is past and the Byronic hero has fallen shamefully from destiny into mere biography. Byron is looking for ways that his hero may play "some trick still" and shows him achieving a considerable dignity in proving himself unafraid to die. But Byron is also questioning the whole notion that someone might be a world-historical individual by exploring the vexed issues of control and responsibility. The man through whom historical forces furthering the progress of freedom work and the man driven by private demons may equally be absolved of responsibility for what happens through them. Byron continually questioned his own motives for involving himself in political movements and was particularly concerned with how private energies could be harnessed to public causes; in *Manfred* he dramatizes the experience of the Byronic hero precisely to ask what kinds of transformations of self he is capable of and how much control over his destiny he actually has. Rather than answering the questions it raises, *Manfred* complicates them, rendering questions of control and responsibility fundamentally unresolvable. Both Manfred and various spirits claim power over his actions, and none of their claims is explicitly contradicted. Through conflicting descriptions of the shape of Manfred's life and the forces compelling him, a complex picture of the relation between a titanic individual and his destiny emerges.

The play's mythic context allows Byron to examine Manfred's defeat in the light of the great fallen heroes, Prometheus, Faust, and Satan. Not only do comparisons to these figures bestow significance upon his own hero, they also provide a way of understanding that significance.[20] In the Romantic period, Prometheus especially was freighted with considerable symbolic power. As Stuart Curran has discovered, Prometheus had been neglected throughout the eighteenth century, but by the 1790s had become "a profoundly political icon, . . . an avatar of revolution against specific oppressions: civil, racial, sexual, and religious. He stands for a humanity bound to an undeserved state and no longer acquiescent in its degradation, a humanity with the will to be free and the power to dictate the terms of that freedom."[21]

Two years before writing *Manfred*, in his "Ode to Napoleon Buonaparte," Byron had momentarily comforted himself on the occasion of the emperor's first abdication with the thought that Napoleon might emerge from his defeat a Promethean figure, and asked: "Like the thief of fire from heaven wilt thou withstand the shock? / And share with him the unforgiven / His vulture and his rock!" At that point, Byron rejected the possibility, concluding that, unlike Napoleon, Prometheus "in his fall preserved his pride, / And, if a mortal, had as proudly died!" (136–44). By the time he came to write *Manfred*, Byron was again willing to explore similarities between the two figures, though not ready to equate them or to see Napoleon as the agent who had freed mankind and propelled human history forward. In fact, except insofar as he is undeniably a mythic being himself, Manfred is not more easily categorized in this way than as a man. He comes tantalizingly close to, but never merges with, not only Prometheus but Faust and a Miltonic Satan, suggesting by the similarities the crucial ways in which he differs from them. Like Faust, Manfred embarked on a quest for knowledge and power, but unlike him he does not sell his soul; like Milton's Satan he rose too far and lives out the punishment of his fall, but unlike him he inhabits an unordered universe of uncertain hierarchies. Like Prometheus, Manfred bears his destiny's reversal stoically but, unlike him, has brought nothing new into the world through his self-sacrifice. Manfred hovers somewhere among these mythic heroes, not conforming to any of the patterns they set out. The poem thereby emphasizes the essential ambiguity of Manfred's own heroic plot.

Initially, the mystery of "that fatal hour" in which Manfred precipitated the death of his lover, Astarte, and his own present sufferings appears to be the central issue of the play. His particular crime dwindles in significance, however, as it becomes clear that a fundamental aspect of his nature is to exceed whatever bounds have been set on it. Given his personality, some form of sinning was inevitable. Instead, the more important issue becomes how much control and freedom Manfred had in the face of such a strong predisposition to transgress.

With the first invocation to the spirits, Manfred demonstrates that the strongest source of power is not "written charm" or sign but the "tyrant spell, / Which had its birthplace in a star condemned, / The burning wreck of a demolished world, / A wandering hell in the eternal Space" (I, i, 43–46). The "strong curse upon [his] soul" from which Manfred draws his power sounds very like the seventh spirit's description of the destiny that rules his life:

Space bosomed not a lovelier star.
The Hour arrived—and it became

160

A wandering mass of shapeless flame,
A pathless Comet, and a curse,
A menace to the Universe.

(I, i, 115–19)

But the spirit insists that Manfred's power is only borrowed, and
that its obedience to him is not exacted but bestowed by a higher
power. Manfred's continued ability to command—that signal characteristic of the Byronic hero—and even to command that very
spirit who claims to be joining the weaker spirits on a whim, renders ambiguous the notion put forward in both speeches: that Manfred's destiny, and hence his life, has gone out of control. The
image of a "pathless comet" careening through space, cutting a
swath of destruction, contradicts the vision of the spirit, who curses
Manfred simply by drawing on his own poison. Accusing him of
"unfathomed gulfs of guile" and hypocrisy, as well as of deriving
delight from other's pain, she says, "In proving every poison
known / I found the strongest was thine own." (I, i. 240–41) Manfred is able to use the image that implies no control to command,
but the picture of him that implies he is in full control can, paradoxically, be used as an instrument to curse him successfully.

Manfred's own assessment of his character points to a conflict
between high and low in his make-up that would seem to tend
more toward paralysis than action:

We, who name ourselves [the world's] sovereigns, we
Half dust, half deity, alike unfit
To sink or soar, with our mixed essence make
A conflict of its elements, and breathe
The breath of degradation and of pride,
Contending with low wants and lofty will,
Till our Mortality predominates,
And men are—what they name not to themselves
And trust not to each other.

(I. ii, 39–46)

The events this kind of character causes result from warring desires
within the self rather than from specific intentions.

In addition to the deepening ambiguities about what kind of
man he is, throughout his conversations with various spirits,
witches, destinies, and men, Manfred continually shifts his explanation of the origins of his troubles. To the Chamois Hunter, he
says his crime was to love where love was forbidden (reminding us
of Byron's description of Prometheus, whose "God like crime was

161

to be kind"); to the Witch of the Alps, Manfred emphasizes his Faustian quest for hidden knowledge that somehow involved and destroyed his lover. To the Abbot he sounds most like Milton's Satan:

> I have had those early visions,
> And noble aspirations in my youth,
> To make my own the mind of other men,
> The enlightener of nations; and to rise
> I knew not whither—it might be to fall;
> But fall even as the mountain-cataract,
> Which, having leapt from its more dazzling height,
> Even in the foaming strength of its abyss . . .
> Lies low but mighty still.—But this is past,
> My thoughts mistook themselves. . . .
> I could not tame my nature down; for he
> Must serve who fain would sway.

(III, i, 104–17)

These self-analyses all share a recognition of a propensity to go too far, but differ in their assessment of his original intentions. In the last speech, Manfred reveals that if to do good and to rise "I knew not whither" were for a time synonymous, it was coincidental that they were. "He must serve who fain would sway," and for that, Manfred says, "I could not tame my nature down." His noble aspirations had too much in them of a desire to hold sway: they were the transitory expression of a constant will to power.

Though how much control Manfred possessed to avert the seemingly inevitable catastrophe his destiny projected is left unresolved, there is no doubt about his remorse. With self-knowledge comes a new kind of power: the ability to make "his torture tributary to his will" (II, iv, 160). His nobility consists not only in his aristocratic bearing and his larger-than-life suffering but in his acceptance that all is indeed over for him. The strength gained from that recognition allows him to reject all counsel and defy a spirit who summons him to die. There is a kind of triumph in willing his own death, and in his insistence that it is easy to do, as is revealed in his last words to the Abbot: "Old man!" he says, "'tis not so difficult to die." When Murray left this line out of the first edition, Byron wrote him an angry letter saying he had "destroyed the whole effect and moral of the poem" (*BLJ* 5:257). The end of Manfred implies that the metaphysical question of the titanic individual's control over his destiny is insoluble, but, although he is never entirely in control, he is never without a choice. Though catastrophe may be inevitable, cowardice never is, and a belief in dignity gives its own shape and purpose to a life. However abject one's present condition, heroism is always possible through an act of self-knowledge and self-sacrifice.

Manfred is meant to be exactly contemporaneous with the One Hundred Days, as the play's references to Napoleon make clear. The spirits appear directly from "repairing shattered thrones, marrying fools, restoring dynasties." One voice sings:

> The Captive Usurper
> Hurled down from the throne,
> Lay buried in torpor,
> Forgotten and lone;
> I broke through his slumbers,
> I shivered his chain,
> I leagued him with numbers—
> He's tyrant again!
> With the blood of a million he'll answer my care,
> With a nation's destruction—his flight and despair.
>
> (II, iii, 16–25)

This is the voice of Napoleon's destiny who sets the fallen emperor's story up as the mirror of Manfred's own. Manfred's destiny is much more complex than his star would allow; very soon Manfred will defy not only this spirit's power but its master's as well. The same choice, Byron would have us believe, was open to Napoleon. Manfred's triumph is inextricably bound to his defeat. The dignity he achieves derives from his understanding and embracing the end to which his character has led him. Byron's sympathetic imagining of a way for Napoleon to respond to his final exile on St. Helena does not include the possibility of a daring escape or any "complete and brilliant renovation." As in *Childe Harold's Pilgrimage*, Canto III, however well Napoleon's "soul . . . brooked the turning tide," the enormous energy he possessed spent itself without enabling the creation of a new society.

In the years following Napoleon's defeat and exile, Byron continued to puzzle over the possibilities that had been open to the emperor and to feel that "never had mortal man such opportunity . . . or abused it more" (*DJ* 9:4). But he no longer focused so exclusively on the issue of personality, shifting his concern, instead, to the social forces shaping the world the Napoleonic type attempts to rule. Marino Faliero and Lambro, Haidee's pirate father in *Don Juan*, the two characters in Byron's later work that most closely resemble Napoleon, are both diminished by this new attention to context. They become less compelling as their actions are rendered more comprehensible. *Manfred,* then, represents the culmination of an attitude toward the Napoleonic type that Byron came to regard as excessively romantic. The post-Napoleonic period raised new questions about how lasting change could come about and demanded a more skeptical and self-conscious approach to both poetry and politics. Byron found the voice to meet the challenge of the new era in *Don Juan.*

Notes

1. *The Complete Poetical Works of Lord Byron* ed. Paul Elmer More (Cambridge: Riverside Press, 1933), 43:379–82. All references to Byron's poetry are taken from this edition and are cited by line number in the text.

2. This is the generally accepted view of Byron's use of historical figures in *Childe Harold's Pilgrimage;* I single out Jerome McGann only because he glosses the stanzas this way in his edition of Byron's poetry: *Byron* (Standard Author Series) (Oxford: Oxford Univ. Press, 1986), 1031.

3. Carl R. Woodring, *Politics in English Romantic Poetry* (Cambridge: Harvard Univ. Press, 1970), 176. See also James Hogg, "Byron's Vacillating Attitude towards Napoleon," in *Byron: Poetry and Politics,* ed. Erwin A. Sturzl and James Hogg (Salzburg: Institut für Anglistic und Amerikanistik, 1981), 380–427.

4. Karl Kroeber speaks of this quality in Byron in the following way: "The *ad hominem* character of [Byron's] rhetorical ferocity . . . is essential to the political efficacy of [his] art. . . . Byron is concerned with specific abuses and particular tyrants and their sycophants, not abstractions such as political scientists devise. This specificity endeared him to many diverse kinds of patriots, who would not have found him so appealing had he not been so abusively ad hominem in his own voice." *British Romantic Art* (Berkeley: Univ. of California Press, 1986), 217.

5. *Byron's Letters and Journals,* ed. Leslie A. Marchand, 12 vols. (Cambridge: Harvard Univ. Press, 1973–81), 9:16. Hereafter *BLJ,* and cited in the text.

6. Byron's maiden speech in the House of Lords denounced a bill that made "frame-breaking" a capital offense. His efforts on behalf of the Nottingham frame-knitters proved ineffectual, however, and the revisions to the bill he endorsed were defeated the next day in the Commons. Byron created far greater publicity for the knitters' cause by publishing an angry poem in the *Morning Chronicle* condemning the "Framers of the Frame Bill," who "when asked for a remedy, sent them a rope" (2 March 1812).

7. E. Tangye Lean, *The Napoleonists: a Study in Disaffection* (London: Oxford Univ. Press, 1970), 79. Ronald Paulson quotes this phrase of Lean's in *Representations of Revolution (1789–1820)* (New Haven: Yale Univ. Press, 1983), 168.

8. Byron's friend Thomas Medwin recalled that Byron "used to say there were three great men ruined in one year, Brummell, himself, and Napoleon!" *Medwin's Conversations with Lord Byron,* ed. E. J. Lovell (Princeton: Princeton Univ. Press, 1966), 72.

9. *The Corsair:* I:7,86.

10. *Politics in English Romantic Poetry,* 166.

11. For an excellent discussion of William Hone's use of Byron, see: Peter J. Manning, "The Hone-ing of Byron's *Corsair*," in *Textual Criticism and Literary Interpretation*, ed. Jerome McGann (Chicago: Univ. of Chicago Press, 1985), 107–26.

12. Quoted in David V. Erdman "Byron and Revolt in England," *Science and Society*, 11 (1947), 239, which contains a full discussion of the episode. See also Manning's "The Hone-ing of Byron's *Corsair*."

13. Perhaps because the poem was so identified with Napoleon's fate, Byron announced in the preface to *The Corsair* that it would be his last work for some years. However sincere that proclamation, it was precisely the shock of Napoleon's abdication that forced him almost instantly out of retirement to write first the angry "Ode to Napoleon Buonaparte" and then *Lara*.

14. That Byron believed Napoleon could be an effective liberator, whatever his personal shortcomings, is reflected in his comment, "The Greeks will, sooner or later, rise against them [the Turks]; but if they do not make haste, I hope Bonaparte will come and drive the useless rascals away." Recorded anonymously in "Recollections of Turkey," in *New Monthly Magazine* XVII (1826). Cited from E. J. Lovell, "His Very Self and Voice (New York: Macmillan, 1954), 31.

15. This is Carl Woodring's phrase. See *Politics in English Romantic Poetry*, 177.

16. Byron attributes this condition to *Man* in general, in *Detached Thoughts* (1821); but during the period under discussion he used almost the same terms to describe Manfred's state (I, i, 45); see below.

17. I am using the terms "Byronic hero" and "Napoleonic type" interchangeably here, though I am aware that the connotations of the former go beyond resemblances to Napoleon. For a detailed discussion of the sources of the Byronic hero, see Peter Thorslev, *The Byronic Hero, Types and Prototypes* (Minneapolis: Univ. of Minnesota Press, 1962).

18. Erdman, "Byron and Revolt in England," 237.

19. See, for instance, Byron's comments to James Hamilton Brown about Napoleon's fate, in Lovell, *His Very Self and Voice*, 428.

20. For particularly useful discussions of this point, see Thorslev, *The Byronic Hero*; and Paulson, *Representations of Revolution (1789–1820)*.

21. Stuart Curran, "Political Prometheus," *Studies in Romanticism*, 25 (1986), 455.

Old Myths for the New Age: Byron's Sardanapalus

Lynn Byrd

Byron is often relegated to the back seat in studies of Romantic myth and mythology, but such placement is unjust.[1] Like other Romantics he sought to make myth a creative tool. Byron's use of myth, in fact, closely resembles a system called mythopoesis, whose process Harry Slochower defines: "While mythology presents its stories as if they actually took place, mythopoesis transposes them to a symbolic meaning."[2] According to Slochower, mythology has a limited historical frame, but by putting the values of the past into symbolic form, writers can form a literature that has universal relevance: "The living myth would not restore the dead past, but would *redeem* its living heritage. The myth also contains *the tradition of re-creation*. . . . The culture hero in mythopoesis *chooses* his tradition, rejects the stultified in favor of the creative roots of the past."[3] The king in Byron's *Sardanapalus* is such a character. He mocks the prevailing religion in his country (and the ex-mortals his people worship) as worn-out ideology and creates a new myth through his style of life and mode of death. Furthermore, this theme, the new from the roots of the old, is picked up in the dra-

166

matic form itself. The play refers to, and builds upon, old myth and tales, but it also presents new versions of the sacrificial and phoenix motifs. The structure is almost recursive; the layers build upon, and comment on, each other. Myth is the means and the end. Myth and history form the foundation for the work, but the tragedy transcends not only its geographical setting but also its immediate time frame.

There are, of course, many purely mechanical elements of myth in the work. Byron chose the popularized Greek name for his hero rather than the original Assyrian title,[4] and one critic even believes that Byron included the Ionian Myrrha in the drama to justify his heavy reliance upon, and allusion to, Greek mythology.[5] Furthermore, Byron records Assyrian mythology accurately. His dramatic structure, with pivotal events marked by the sun's movement, follows primitive worship patterns. According to E. Stucken, "celestial revolutions were regarded by the Mesopotamians as the expression of the power, will, and intelligence of the deities."[6] These mythic elements, however, can easily appear casual and superficial until their structural integrity is recognized: Byron's tragedy is in fact about myth. It explores both the creation and the function of myth and includes a historical perspective on mythology. And finally, as Gerard remarked a century ago, the tragedy "traverses, explores, and displays through action many spheres of human emotion."[7] This exploration and explanation of humanity and the embodiment of human feeling joins Byron to both the mythic and the mythopoeic writers.

Sardanapalus is deceptively difficult. The mythographic tools needed for an archetypal analysis are already present in the drama. The character of the king, which confounded his subjects and has baffled Byron's critics, is revealed through his own actions. That Sardanapalus is the hero of the drama is, or should be, indisputable. Furthermore, that he is a noble character—inherently and actively—should raise little more question. A reader need not look past Byron's introduction to ascertain the king's role. Byron's insistence on adhering to the unities implies an Aristotelian model. Aristotle required a noble character in tragedy: a character who is admittedly imperfect, but whose error lies in his judgment, or "calculation," not in his "vice and depravity."[8]

Much of the bias against the king originates in the drama itself. One of the major stumbling blocks in interpreting Sardanapalus's character has been, and continues to be, the other dramatic figures and their attitudes toward their king. The dilemma is apparent from the opening scene. Salemenes' soliloquy describes a king who has seemingly failed his family, his citizens, and his heritage.[9] The prince's condemnation sounds almost like an opening Greek chorus, and his seeming support actually undermines the audience's sympathy for the king. Myrrha plays a similar role. She agrees that Sardanapalus's "throne" is imperiled (I, ii, 510–11). She too feels that it is the king's own fault, admitting that Sardanapalus should have kept a "show of war" to keep peace, and that he should have sought to be more "fear'd than loved" (I, ii, 579–81). She summarizes his mistakes: "A king of feasts, and flowers, and wine, and revel, / And love, and mirth was never king of glory" (I, ii, 589–90). She, like Salemenes, wants to help him, and she tells Sardanapalus that her love rightfully "claim[s] the privilege to save [him]" (I, ii, 552). She believes that she can arouse the heroic nature in him, and urges the king to look to both "the gods thy fathers" and "the annals of thine empire's founders" (I, ii, 591, 594) for guidance. The two traitors, Belesus and Arbaces, are also convinced that Sardanapalus has failed as king. They are so dissatisfied, however, that they would rather instigate a completely new regime than accept changes in his—or even in him. Both men consider their treasonous cause just. Belesus believes that the stars have proclaimed the overthrow (II, i, 6–11), and Arbaces believes that they are fighting to avenge all honorable men against the "fool" on the throne (II, i, 100–102).

Sardanapalus is thus threatened on all fronts. With supporter and usurper alike singing his sins, Sardanapalus has little chance of being heard or of convincing anyone that he is a good ruler. Everyone finds him failing, but no one realizes that Sardanapalus simply fails to compromise. He refuses to conform to other individuals' expectations. In their clamor for kingliness, the characters drown out the voice of the king. Their list of faults is long and varied, but the charges against Sardanapalus fall largely into two categories: lifestyle and leadership. Most of the characters complain about Sardanapalus's life of indolence and languor. He remains steadfastly unmoved by their disapproval, and in fact, seems even to relish his truancy, adding fuel to their fire. He calls his personality "easy" (I, ii, 108) and speaks of his time as "soft hours" (I, ii, 55). He refuses to forgo banquets for any reason (I, ii, 355–60) and is openly "indulgent" of his human "follies" (I, ii, 323–25). He is king, but he is blatantly disrespectful of majesty of "station" (I, ii, 495). He constantly entreats those around him to treat him as an individual rather than a figurehead. Often his rebukes are humorous. When

Salemenes over-zealously reprimands the king, for instance, Sardanapalus cautions the earnest prince, "Thou dost forget thee: make me not remember / I am a monarch" (I, ii, 98–99). Sardanapalus confides more seriously to Myrrha, however, that kings are cursed with titles (I, ii, 63). Furthermore, he admits that he has never really "prized" his title, he has just "suffer'd" it (I, ii, 489–92). Sometimes, he sighs, he even finds his position false and repressive, and he wants to "lay down the dull tiara, / And share a cottage on the Caucasus" (I, ii, 493–99).

Although he sometimes questions his suitability for the role or jests about his responsibility as king, Sardanapalus never doubts his right to reign. He once concedes rather ambiguously to Salemenes: "I am unfit / To be aught save a monarch" (I, ii, 410–11); but he cannot imagine even a "pretext" for revolt in his kingdom because, in his words: "I am the lawful king, descended from / A race of kings who knew no predecessors" (I, ii, 250–51). Sardanapalus's life is pleasurable but not purposeless. It is Salemenes who calls Sardanapalus's sensuality slothful (I, ii, 117) and claims that ease is worse than the "worst acts of one energetic master" (I, ii, 119). Salemenes' intolerance leads him to conclude that Sardanapalus has an "easy, far too easy, and idle nature" (I, ii, 109). But the king's life-style is intentional, not merely the product of laziness. Sardanapalus sees his life as a tool he can use to instruct his subjects. He wants to rule as monarch rather than master or "conqueror" (I, ii, 169), to "sway" as role model rather than "subdue" as despot (I, ii, 192–93).

Sardanapalus's refusal to play the part of the "tyrant" (I, ii, 112) is not merely a deviation from, but a complete break with, his ancestor's precedent, a refusal to conform that makes his rule harder for his subjects to accept. Although he never voices the thought, Salemenes' reproaches echo the adage of custom (it has always been done this way). The prince adulates even the memory of the "man-queen" Semiramis (I, ii, 43). Sardanapalus, on the other hand, describes her sacrilegiously as a "sort of semi-glorious human monster" (I, ii, 228). He refuses to honor his ancestors' memory, contending that his predecessors pursued glory, "tracking it through human ashes, / Making a grave with every footstep" (III, i, 15–16). He believes that their glory-quest was really a circuitous route to pleasure, and he maintains that his rule exemplifies a short-cut through a tragic reign of bloodshed. He has bypassed war and claimed the reward—"enjoyment" (III, i, 12–14). Logically pointing out that Semiramis could not hold all the kingdoms that she conquered (III, i, 6), the king refuses to follow her example: "But what wouldst have? the empire *has been* founded. / I cannot go on multiplying empires" (I, ii, 596–97). Past Assyrian rulers "kept [their subjects] to toil and combat; / And never changed their chains but for their armour" (I, ii, 381–82). Sardanapalus gives his "peace and pastime, and the license / To revel and to rail" (I, ii, 383–84). He prefers the banquet hall to the battlefield. He sees his "true realm" at feasts where the "faces" are as "Happy as fair!" (III, i, 2–3). Sardanapalus translates time to place when he exclaims, "Here sorrow cannot reach." (III, i, 3). In his enthusiasm the king asks his courtiers if such a life is not superior to anything his ancestors offered. Only Altada and Pania agree. Their vigorous assent upsets Myrrha, who labels their exuberance "impiety" (III, i, 5–31).

Closely connected to Sardanapalus's leisurely, banqueting lifestyle is the issue of his effeminacy. In fact, the charge clearly relates to his sensual nature rather than his sexual identity. Sardanapalus has, after all, had children by Zarina—and sons at that. He casually claims to have "proved" more than a thousand females' love (I, ii, 505); and whatever else she complains of, Myrrha casts no aspersions on Sardanapalus's virility. Whether the charge stems from his apparel—flowing robes and flower crowns—or his unusual fair appearance, or whether it is based upon his indolence and preference for banquets over battles, the stigma of effeminacy follows this last Assyrian king throughout the drama.

The issue is certainly important in the play, but when it is viewed within Byron's canon generally, it becomes even more interesting. The "she-king" (II, ii, 48) seems a contradiction to, or outright rebuttal of, the Byronic hero. Sardanapalus, however, cannot simply be dismissed as an "effeminate thing" (II, ii, 95). If not the typical Byronic hero, the 'she Sardanapalus" (II, ii, 404) is certainly not the stereotypic homosexual that such a term connotes today. Paul Elledge's use of the term ''bisexual" is not really an appropriate description either.[10] A look at what the word implied during Byron's time might clarify some of the confusion. As an intransitive verb, *effeminate* did mean "To become womanish; to grow weak, languish." The verb, however, could also be used transitively to denote ennervation. "Softness" and "weakness" are the two adjectives used most in the definitions.[11]

Such a description would certainly fit the traditional historical / literary figure upon which Byron based his work.[12] It fits Byron's Sardanapalus too. Superficially. Byron took the behavior of the historical king but changed his character. Byron's Sardanapalus is not debauched: he is sensual but not lascivious. Indeed, the king's eas-iness of person and ease of life-style are admirable in Byron's ac-count: they are virtues rather than vices. If this attitude appears to turn traditional values upside down and inside out, so, in fact, does Sardanapalus himself. All of the other major figures dismiss females as weak and fragile beings, but Sardanapalus recognizes that it is the female lion who fights ferociously. He also informs Myrrha that the desire for revenge is "feminine" and springs from fear. Angry women, he says, are "timidly vindictive" to a degree that he would not want to emulate (II, ii, 586–87). In a related vein, Salemenes believes that Bacchus became a god because of his martial ability, but Sardanapalus maintains that his glory comes from "the immor-tal grape" (I, ii, 209–21). Salemenes worships the conqueror-god, but Sardanapalus admires the one who "express'd the soul," and who invented something to "gladden" man's; Bacchus's marital success he dismisses as "victorious mischiefs." For Sardanapalus, Bacchus's wine is an "atonement" for the suffering that accompa-nied his military achievements (I, ii, 222–24).

Many critics have observed that Sardanapalus holds Bacchus up as a model. Arthur Kahn feels that Byron must have "recognized the appropriateness of associating the effeminate pleasure-loving god who had once been a great conqueror with the hedonistic As-syrian who was to emerge belatedly as a courageous warrior."[13] He thinks that Sardanapalus tries to "excuse his unmartial luxury by pointing to Bacchus as one whose glory derived more from peaceful than warlike accomplishments."[14] That is not so. Sardanapalus is not trying to excuse anything. He is sincere in his toast, just as he is sincere throughout the play. Furthermore, Sardanapalus is actually correct in his assumption: most accounts of Dionysus concen-trate on his wine-making and revelry; his heroic efforts are largely forgotten.

Bacchus is more than a model for Sardanapalus's life-style: he is a symbol of the very principle Sardanapalus attempts to live. Both characters debunk conformity and conventional restraint. The toast that Sardanapalus proposes is extremely important in understand-ing this idea. He toasts the human figure, rather than the deity, to suit Salemenes' prejudice; but he toasts "a true man, who did his utmost / In good or evil to surprise mankind" (I, ii, 232–41). The Greek god and the Assyrian king both avoid the traditional, the trite. Both are enigmas. J. E. Harrison calls Dionysos the "mystery-god."[15] Marcel Detienne records that "Dionysos has long borne the guise of foreigner," but "the reason lies in his affinity for what is foreign."[16] Detienne also notes that the Greek divinity could be "at once present within and without the city," and that he enjoyed a ritualistic game of sociability. The deity always wears "a mask that exposes but . . . conceals him, particularly when he seems to show his most familiar face."[17] Both figures personify the out-of-the-ordinary. Both are known, but unknown. Although Sardanapalus is very open and direct, he is constantly misunderstood. He knows his people neither appreciate nor understand him. He knows how they view him, and he knows how false their views are; but he seems not to mind. Only once does he exclaim in disbelief, "Were I the thing some think me" (II, ii, 284). The king often subtly reminds Salemenes that the prince takes for granted the easy nature to which he constantly objects. The ruler humors his brother-in-law: "Come, I'm indulgent, as thou knowest, patient / As thou hast often proved" (I, ii, 143–44). At one point, however, a vexed Sardanapalus finally tells Salemenes, "Ye knew nor me, nor monarchs, nor mankind" (I, ii, 264). A paradox of secrecy within obviousness develops, and this paradox, along with several others, plays a major part in structuring and resolving the story line.

In addition to their hospitable natures and their apartness from their peers, Dionysos and Sardanapalus share other characteristics. Wendy O'Flaherty records in *Women, Androgynes, and Other Mythical Beasts* that Dionysus, whom she once even labels a "transvestite," was ridiculed "for being so woman-like."[18] She explains that the god is "androgynous in appearance and function" because he is "the deity presiding over the liquid element and the procreative powers of the earth and nature."[19] Sardanapalus can readily be considered just such an androgynous and fertile figure. In his opening speech, Salemenes describes his king as "femininely garb'd" (I, i, 42). The first stage directions support Salemenes' opinion. Sardanapalus enters "effeminately dressed, his Head crowned with Flowers, and his Robe negligently flowing" (I, ii). Furthermore, he has a train of women and slaves following him—a typical Bacchian portrait. The king is also very fair; even in battle he allows his long, blond hair to show (III, i, 202–7).

The issue of androgyny in function is a more difficult matter. The androgyne is an important and fairly prevalent religious symbol. It is also an ancient one. Modern society tends to view androgyny in physical terms, but the idea is more complex. O'Flaherty notes that although androgyny is popularly viewed as a representation of sexual equality or equilibrium, the androgyne can, and more often does, signify imbalance—either favorable or unfavorable. The context does not even necessarily have to be sexual; androgynes can represent "a tension based on unequal distribution of power."[20] Androgynes can also be classified into aesthetic and moral categories. O'Flaherty explains that

> in some societies androgynes play positive social roles, affirming culturally acceptable values, while others are despised as symbols of an undesirable blurring of categories . . . androgynes may be regarded as "good," in the sense of symbolically successful, when the image presents a convincing fusion of the two polarities and as "bad" when the graft fails to "take" visually or philosophically—when it is a mere juxtaposition of opposites rather than a true fusion.[21]

This discussion opens several new avenues of analysis in *Sardanapalus*. First, "androgynous" is probably a more apt description than "homosexual" or "bisexual." Any undue effeminacy Sardanapalus assumes is superficial. The designation also helps clarify the Assyrian king's emulation of the Greek god Bacchus. Furthermore, Sardanapalus's eccentricities in dress and manner have a clear and consistent meaning when considered as indications of a symbolic androgyny—even androgyny representing an imbalance of power or a power struggle.

Several other hints in the drama imply that Sardanapalus's life is a struggle to fuse opposites and achieve balance (however painful the process for himself and the subjects). O'Flaherty reveals that androgyny may be the result of earlier incest.[22] When Sardanapalus describes his nightmare to Myrrha, he likens himself to an earlier son who slew Semiramis for that crime (IV, i, 156–58).[23] In addition, this former queen also has associations with androgyny: Salemenes refers to her as the "man-queen" (I, i, 43). Although most of the characters in the drama worship this past Assyrian ruler, their own descriptions reveal her violence, greed, and unnatural lust. Interestingly, these characteristics tie in with the mythical interpretation of androgynes. O'Flaherty reports that male androgynes have the most numerous occurrences in history and that they represent a positive moral force. Female androgynes have negative associations and usually hold a negative moral status.[24]

In light of this background, not only the character of the king but also the meaning of the drama become more accessible. Sardanapalus's feminine appearance indicates an androgynous nature within him and in the kingdom he rules and symbolizes. The balance of power is askew. Furthermore, the problem is compounded, not only by the political struggles but also by many of the characters' obtuseness. Sardanapalus must struggle against the traitors in his kingdom, but this battle, though the most obvious and concrete in the story, is the least significant. Like Sardanapalus's effeminacy, it is external, designed to symbolize deeper conflicts. Sardanapalus is fighting to restore and maintain a historical cycle, and he is struggling to achieve some sort of philosophical and spiritual compromise for man's duality. He is, then, androgynous in function as well as appearance. Caught between the temporal and the eternal, he and the rule he has established are hung between the past and the future of the mighty Assyrian line of kings.

The kingdom that Sardanapalus builds is thus one of careful contrivance and considered neglect. The thought underlying Sardanapalus's life and reign is not a simple "seize the day" philosophy, although that is how Salemenes misconstrues it. The moral that so offends the prince may be read as a *carpe diem* chorus, but it implies more. Sardanapalus explains that the verse he composed "contain[s] the history/Of all things human" (I, ii, 295–96). In view of the value he places on learning, life, and humanity, it is hard to imagine the king's intending the lines to be strictly carnal, although the verse does sound flippant.

> "Sardanapalus,
> The king, and son of Anacyndaraxes,
> In one day built Anchialus and Tarsus.
> Eat, drink, and love; the rest's not worth a fillip."
>
> (I, ii, 296–99)

If, however, the last line is regarded hierarchically, "all things human" are included: sustenance, fellowship, and spirituality are implicit in the command. In contrast to the reductionist interpretation of Salemenes, the moral actually suggests succor and nurture. It allows the fulfillment of human potential. Sardanapalus prefers his precept to the war and work edicts of his ancestors. He tells Selemenes, "enough / For me if I can make my subjects feel / The weight of human misery less" (I, ii, 309–11). Even when reflecting upon the end of his empire and his life, Sardanapalus reasons with himself in similar terms:

> Why, what is earth or empire of the earth?
> I have loved, and lived, and multiplied my image;
> To die is no less natural than those
> Acts of this clay!
>
> (I, ii, 446–49)

In this soliloquy, Sardanapalus reverses the hierarchy set up in his cities' inscription. He places love first, and he finally equates his life with his philosophy: "my life is love" (I, ii, 453).

Love is the basis for Sardanapalus's accepting and tolerant attitude toward humanity. His sentiments are evident when he defends his dislike of force to Salemenes:

> I hate all pain,
> Given or received; we have enough within us,
> The meanest vassal as the loftiest monarch
>
> (I, ii, 395–97)

These important words reveal Sardanapalus's essentially democratic attitude. He is concerned more with humanity's common condition, mortality, than with individual stations in life. Death ultimately governs all, but Sardanapalus's temporal government allows mankind dignity and self-control. The ruler metaphorically abdicates, making each individual a king. He sees life as a feast, one in which he too partakes, but as an equal. When Sardanapalus relates his nightmare to Myrrha, he describes his rule as a banquet:

> I dream'd myself
> Here—here—even where we are, guests as we were,
> Myself a host that deem'd himself but guest,
> Willing to equal all in social freedom.
>
> (IV, i, 78–81)

His behavior throughout the drama sets up and supports this analogy. Unfortunately, his people are uncomfortable at such a party. They cannot reply responsibly to their freedom. Unable to establish an individual sense of authority, they blame the crown for failing to supervise and direct.

Salemenes, speaking for the people, confronts the king with the kingdom's end. Ironically, he describes the wreck of two ideals. The people are disappointed by the king, but they also, in turn, have disappointed the king. They fail to fulfill their potential role in Sardanapalus's empire of peace. Like the Assyrian subjects, the mouthpiece prince is unable to see that the flaw is not in the theory but in mankind's inability to practice it. Impasse. Sardanapalus does see that the old way of war and conquest is no longer viable. He exclaims, "the empire has been founded. / I cannot go on multiplying empires" (I, ii, 596–97). Sardanapalus is disillusioned with both the principles and the practices of the former Assyrian rulers. Even apart from humanitarian interests, continued warfare is not practical for the country. Conquest feeds on itself. Ever increasing

Lynn Byrd

territory requires ever increasing protection and maintenance. Sardanapalus recognizes this and tries to break away from the consuming cycle. Sardanapalus's disillusionment leads him to propose a new paradisiacal reign.[25] His solution suits his androgynous role: there has been an imbalance in government, and his shock treatment is the only way to restore balance. As the experiment collapses around him, he poignantly points out to Myrrha what it might have been: an "era of sweet peace," "a green spot amidst desert centuries," a "paradise" and an "epoch of new pleasures." (IV, i, 511–18).

Even deeper than the conflict over Sardanapalus's political experiment is the familial conflict. The end of Sardanapalus's empire seems to end the reign of the "race of kings who knew no predecessors" (I, ii, 251). Salemenes depicts the whole conflict as an attempt to preserve "Nimrod's line" (I, ii, 133). Although he despises Sardanapalus at the outset of the drama, the prince does not want to see "thirteen hundred years / Of empire ending like a shepherd's tale" (I, i, 7–8). In his first conference with the king, Salemenes warns Sardanapalus of impending war. Salemenes threatens, "in another day / What is shall be the past of Belus' race" (I, ii, 331). The insurgents too see themselves as attacking Belus's race, rather than just the reigning monarch. On the night of the insurrection, Beleses worships the sun setting on the "furthest / Hour of Assyria's years" (II, i, 9–10). Arbaces predicts that the king's evening wine "will be the last / Quaff'd by the line of Nimrod" (II, i, 52–53). The soldier uses a chain analogy to describe this line of kings. He says the rebellion will "mend" the "weak" link, Sardanapalus (II, i, 54–55).

These statements depict the historical tension in the drama. Sardanapalus is not a man, or a ruler, overly concerned with kingdoms or with what they usually represent: territory and power. He has established an empire of peace and prosperity. Sardanapalus's realm breaks the mold of traditional rule—the very rule his predecessors imposed. In breaking the mold, Sardanapalus rejects ancestral precedents and violates decorum. He refuses to issue the edicts that his ancestors did, and he openly mocks his forefathers. He blasphemes the once-king, now-god Nimrod by toasting Bacchus's humanity out of Nimrod's chalice (I, ii, 206–41); and he labels Semiramis, his grandmother, a "sort of semi-glorious human monster" (I, ii, 228). Although he belittles his ancestors and scorns their rules, Sardanapalus cannot completely sever familial ties. On the contrary, he reveals a sense of family: he considers himself the

176

"lawful king" based on his birthright (I, ii, 250–51), and in the dedication for the cities Anchialus and Tarsus, Sardanapalus refers to himself not only as the "king" but also as the "son of Anacyndaraxes" (I, ii, 297).

Tension develops as Sardanapalus simultaneously identifies with and denies his family. In the scene with Myrrha, Sardanapalus refuses to fight for either past or future family (I, ii, 635–42), but he still affiliates himself with his ancestors. A dialogue between the king and Myrrha about the aftermath of a rebellion is revealing:

Myr.	If the worst come, I shall be where none weep,
	And that is better than the power to smile.
	And thou?
Sar.	I shall be king, as heretofore.
Myr.	Where?
Sar.	With Baal, Nimrod, and Semiramis,
	Sole in Assyria, or with them elsewhere.
	Fate made me what I am—may make me nothing—
	But either that or nothing must I be:
	I will not live degraded.

(I, ii, 669–76)

The king is secure on his throne and in his position, but much of his strong identity and individualism seem based on the very family ties he seeks to sever.

This tension, then, lies within the king. He knows he was born to rule (I, ii, 250), yet he feels a "falseness" in his position because it sets him apart from other men and separates him from those he loves (I, ii, 490–500). His inner conflict is apparent when he tells Salemenes, "Unhappily, I am unfit / To be aught save a monarch; else for me / The meanest Mede might be the king instead" (I, ii, 410–12). Sardanapalus is trapped. As king he must break the traditions and conventions that are stifling his kingdom, but as man he cannot break entirely with his family. Differentiating between family and family practices is a difficult task. Knight explains that Nimrod and Semiramis "represent all traditional values, and suggest the dark ingrained fear of ancestral authority whose weight so often masquerades as conscience."[26] Sardanapalus's heritage is undeniable, but neither the family itself nor its rule has much to commend it to a lover of peace and a believer in man.

Sardanapalus loves humanity. He presents a new, tolerant personality to his subjects. He is an individualist who stands out and apart from the mass of unenlightened men in his kingdom. These characteristics reflect his Dionysian personality. Innovative, even

Lynn Byrd

defiant, the king brings freshness and renewal to an aging empire. Even he, however, cannot completely escape his heritage. The new adventure in governance he undertakes is unavoidably tainted by his inheritance—name and position. His family has set a precedent rule that still governs the masses. If Sardanapalus chooses not to follow the precedents, his close friends and advisers are quick to remind him of his deviation.

The issue is intensified by the controversy in the kingdom. The battle precipitates Sardanapalus's confrontation with his heritage: he must resort to his family's means, if not their ends. As Elledge points out, Sardanapalus's identification with his ancestors increases during the first three acts. Elledge, however, believes that Sardanapalus fares unfavorably in this comparison. He maintains that "the king broods excessively upon the conquests of Semiramis and attempts to rationalize his own preservation of his peace."[27] Actually, the king is attempting to rationalize his use of force: he has been coerced into using violence. Before the actual outbreak of fighting, Sardanapalus says to Salemenes: "If I must shed blood, it shall be by force" (I, ii, 453). For him even defense is aggression. He does believe, however, in the empire he created—or rather, in the principles the empire epitomizes, and he goes to war to protect those principles and the people's freedom to practice them.

The dilemma is almost untenably ironic, which may account for some of Sardanapalus's flippancy and ambivalence. In the opening act, Salemenes asks, "Wouldst thou not take their lives who seek for thine?" (I, ii, 343). Sardanapalus responds, "That's a hard question, but I answer, Yes" (I, ii, 344). The ambivalent answer portrays Sardanapalus's inner turmoil. In the third act, however, Sardanapalus is again approached by Salemenes after the revolt has started. The prince sends Pania to entreat the king to show himself to his soldiers. Without any reflection or consideration, Sardanapalus calls for his armor. Myrrha asks doubtfully, "And wilt thou?" (III, i, 99). Sardanapalus responds, "Will I not?" (III, i, 99). The king rushes into battle and battles bravely, finally settling his followers' doubts about his ability.

The actions that set their minds at ease, however, have the opposite effect on the king himself. Wounded in the fighting, Sardanapalus returns to the palace and falls into a fitful sleep. His nightmare sums up the conflict and foreshadows the drama's end. In the nightmare Sardanapalus meets the ancestors whose precedents have been haunting his rule. In the dream sequence, the ideological confrontation between Sardanapalus and his predecessors is acted out, appropriately enough, in a banquet setting. The king-host is seated at the head of the table. Nimrod is on his left and Semiramis on his right. These two are flanked by more crowned figures—other Assyrian kings, including Sardanapalus's father. Nimrod is armed with a quiver of arrows, and Semiramis is holding two goblets, one filled with blood. Their presence terrifies and mesmerizes Sardanapalus, who finally finds the courage to laugh at the specters. Sardanapalus's laughter breaks the spell; but Nimrod still reaches for his hand, and Semiramis embraces him. His escape is amorphous. He can only describe it vaguely:

> I was dead, yet feeling—
> Buried, and raised again—consumed by worms,
> Purged by the flames, and wither'd in the air!

(IV, i, 159–61)

He admits that he can recall "nothing further of [his] thoughts" (IV, i, 162).

Even though he cannot remember, he speaks as he wakes up, and his words inform the entire dream cycle:

> Not so—although ye multiplied the stars,
> And gave them to me as a realm to share
> From you and with you! I would not so purchase
> The empire of eternity. Hence—hence—

(IV, i, 24–27)

The banquet was a family conclave. Sardanapalus sat before his predecessors, and they took one another's measure. The balance first tipped in favor of Nimrod and Semiramis: their presence so awed Sardanapalus that he seemed to "grow stone" like them; he says that he even felt a "horrid kind / of sympathy" bonding them together (IV, i, 122–23). This segment of the dream represents Sardanapalus's increasing identification with his ancestors: he had, of course, by this time actually engaged in war—the very thing his rule opposed. However, just as it seems the former rulers have overpowered Sardanapalus, he laughs and breaks the understanding between them, thus setting a limit to their influence. When Nimrod offers his hand, Sardanapalus takes it, but the grip is not secure. Significantly, Nimrod's hand melts away. The king also escapes Semiramis's violent embrace—through flames. The melting and purging images foreshadow the actual fire at the drama's end.

Awakening, Sardanapalus denounces his ancestors' methods and their idea of a fixed and eternal reign. Thus, Sardanapalus affirms his autonomy but also accepts the end of his rule. He ex-

179

Lynn Byrd

changes a sense of personal destiny for a sense of history, acknowledging that empires are not ends in themselves but, rather, parts of a historical progression. Consequently, he can later tell his wife to train their sons for the throne even if it is temporarily lost (IV, i, 270–83). He can also anticipate joining his ancestors when he dies (V, i, 422–32) without rejecting or compromising the principles of his own reign. Sardanapalus can even foresee the cycles of history. He tells the rebel messenger that he expects to see Belesus before the year is out. Sardanapalus prophesies that Belesus will "depart" from Babylon to meet him (V, i, 350–53).

Several image patterns support the theme of family conflict / historical progression in the drama. For example, throughout the drama, images of silk characterize the monarch. Myrrha refers to Sardanapalus's leisure as "silken dalliance" (I, ii, 627), and Altada describes the king's war helmet as a "silk tiara" (III, i, 205). The officer later even refers to the king as Baal's "silken son" (III, i, 314). Silk is, of course, a suitable fabric for royal garments, but the image has greater significance in the play. In either the positive or negative sense, the soft and refined material suits Sardanapalus's role and his nature. Furthermore, the silk images contribute to the weaving motif that runs through the drama.

After Sardanapalus spares Belesus and Arbaces, the priest exclaims, "I blush that we should owe our lives to such / A king of distaffs" (II, i, 343–44). The derogatory label is double-edged. First, it associates the king's rule with domestic work, spinning. Second, the label associates the king with femininity. As an adjective, "distaff" characterizes women in general or the female side of a family. Thus, this term is tied to Belesus's later label, the "she-Sardanapalus" (II, i, 404). Arbaces' "silkworm" epitaph for Sardanapalus effectively ties the silk and spinning motifs together. Although the soldier intends to be derogatory, his remark proves appropriate and complimentary. Like "distaff," "silkworm" has female connotations. Used contemptuously, it refers to one who wears a silken gown or dress.[28] It also connotes a creature that creates—out of itself—a valuable and beautiful commodity. Throughout the play Sardanapalus has been spinning costly threads of peace in an attempt to hold the kingdom together, yet the actions that save the kingdom cost its king's life.

Several characters use spinning / distaff images, giving the motif an added richness. When Sardanapalus goes to war, Myrrha likens the king to Hercules: the Greek hero had once disguised himself in "she-garb." Myrrha recalls Hercules' "wielding her

180

[Omphale's] vile distaff" (III, i, 218–24). In her analogy Myrrha unwittingly reveals Sardanapalus's strength. Like both Bacchus and Hercules, Sardanapalus is able to "surprise mankind" (I, ii, 241). Furthermore, Myrrha's choice of the verb "wield" strengthens the idea of the rod as a tool of rule and power.

Sardanapalus is actually the first to employ a weaving image in the play, and his application is positive. When Salemenes upholds Semiramis as a model ruler, Sardanapalus protests,

> she had better woven within her palace
> Some twenty garments, than with twenty guards
> Have fled to Bactria, leaving to the ravens,
> And wolves, and men—the fiercer of the three—
> Her myriads of fond subjects.

(I, ii, 181–85)

The image recurs when the two men discuss armor. Sardanapalus tells Salemenes, "And now I think on 't, 't is long since I've used them [the javelin and the sword], / Even in the chase" (I, ii, 366–67). The king scorns violence, but he admits that if it is unavoidable, he will fight to protect the kingdom:

> Oh! if it must be so, and these rash slaves
> Will not be ruled with less, I'll use the sword
> Till they shall wish it turn'd into a distaff.

(I, ii, 370–72)

Salemenes responds, "They say thy sceptre's turned to that already" (I, ii, 373). The king rejects the implication of ineffectuality, pointing out that the same was said of Hercules. Sardanapalus realizes that the people have simply adopted this label to belittle him (I, ii, 374–79). The issue's complexity, however, is revealed as Salemenes and Sardanapalus continue their discussion. The distaff rule idealistically opposes the sword regimes of the earlier Assyrian rulers who "kept [their people] to toil and combat; / And never changed their chains but for armour" (I, ii, 381–82). Throughout the drama tension builds as Sardanapalus wavers between the sword and the distaff. His soft silken rule battles his ancestors' harsh, metallic regimes.

Closely tied to the fabric / metal imagery is the blood-hunt motif that runs throughout the drama. The motifs actually converge when Arbaces uses a chain image to describe the line of Baal, with Sardanapalus as its weakest link (II, i, 54). Blood functions in the play in two related ways: it denotes war and violence and family or class position.[29] The "right of blood, derived from age to age" (III, i, 169)

Lynn Byrd

makes Sfero a shieldbearer and Sardanapalus king, and blood "blotted o'er" the annals of Assyria (I, ii, 548) as her founders and rulers built the empire with "blood and toil" (I, ii, 118). These two strains merge in the descriptions of Nimrod and Semiramis—"once bloody mortals . . . now bloodier idols" (IV, i, 30). In contrast their descendent Sardanapalus is "bloodless" (II, i, 434). He does not shed the blood of subjects or enemies (I, ii, 227; 402–3; 408–9). The tension between distaff and sword is again evident here. The "bloodless" (II, ii, 434) "she-Sardanapalus," (II, i, 404) who would be content among the spinning women in his palace of peace, opposes his ancestor, the militant "blood-loving" (I, ii, 238) "man-queen" (I, i, 43) Semiramis who led the Assyrians "to the solar shores of Ganges" (I, ii, 171–85) for glory—and slaughter.

The struggle between distaff and sword symbolizes Sardanapalus's struggle to deny his ancestors. Although Sardanapalus deviates from his family's traditional rule, the warrior-hunter haunts him. His unsuccessful struggle to escape his forefathers' influence climaxes in the nightmare scene. Significantly, of the two goblets which Semiramis holds, only one's contents—blood—is given. When she spills it, the blood forms a poisonous, "hideous river" around them (IV, i, 153). Sardanapalus's rejection of Semiramis and this nightmare river foreshadow not only his wife and sons' escape on the river (IV, i, 422) but also the palace-dwellers and Pania's escape to tell the tale of what they saw at parting (V, i, 257–74).

Sardanapalus's paradoxical life is mythic. Although a king, he is an object of scorn. Considered effeminate and weak at the outset of the play, his offer of love and peace rejected by his people, Sardanapalus dies having proved his valor and strength. In both a personal and a political context, his death does indeed become a "light to lesson ages" (V, i, 440–41). The king who drank to Bacchus's humanity humanizes his family's lineage. Upon their deaths his forefathers were simultaneously named gods and turned to stone. Sardanapalus was the first in Baal's line to be called a god as a man (III, i, 27). Instead of deifying the dead, Sardanapalus apotheosizes the living. Instead of fighting to hold his kingdom and his power, he relinquishes it in a phoenix-style death that symbolizes resurrection and continuation. His actions give Assyria, a kingdom of static ancestral worship, potential for change. Sardanapalus's last words to Pania reveal his awareness of his mythic role for Assyria. He tells Pania to pass the message on, to tell what he saw at parting (V, i, 395). The king's actions create a new myth from the old.

The poet, too, created a new myth from the old. The story of Sardanapalus was well-known in Byron's day. Byron reworked the familiar tale to create both a new figure and another story. This reworking becomes a mythopoeic production. On one level, the king, his kingdom, and his fate depict another historical struggle. On a metaphorical plane, *Sardanapalus* relates the demise of the Romantic construct itself. As the drama transcends its geographical setting and time-frame, Sardanapalus and his kingdom come to represent the "grand elementary principle of pleasure" that Wordsworth extolled in his Preface to *Lyrical Ballads*. Wordsworth not only had maintained that this pleasure comprises "the naked and native dignity of man," but also had considered it the force by which mankind "knows, and feels, and lives, and moves."[30] History records the problems Victorian society had with the concept, and Lionel Trilling notes the negative connotations the term bears in the contemporary society. Trilling maintains, however, that the pleasure the Romantics advocated was anything but carnal: it was divine. He interprets Wordsworthian pleasure as the quality that defines both nature and life, an emotion tending toward transcendence.[31]

This is in fact the pleasure principle that Sardanapalus symbolizes. The androgyne king becomes a symbol of cosmic completeness and wholeness. In the drama's opening scenes, he asks Salemenes, "I live in peace and pleasure: what man can / Do more?" (I, ii, 577–78). The question is rhetorical; its answer, "nothing." According to the Romantics, pleasure was the highest achievement, and man's fallen condition, a lack of it.[32] Since pleasure is the highest state of life, nothing can surpass it. Sardanapalus, unabashedly living pleasure, attains the sublime.

The king evinces another aspect of this Romantic pleasure. The dialogue at the final banquet reinforces Sardanapalus's emphasis on pleasure and reveals pleasure's relationship to power:

> *Alt.*   Mighty though
> They were, as all thy royal line have been,
> Yet none of those who went before have reach'd
> The acme of Sardanapalus, who
> Has placed his joy in peace—the sole true glory.
> *Sar.*   And pleasure, good Altada, to which glory
> is but the path. What is it that we seek?
> Enjoyment! We have cut the way short to it,
> And not gone tracking it through human ashes,
> Making a grave with every footstep.
>
> (III, i, 7–16)

Sardanapalus bypassed force for luxury. Trilling observes that plea-sure is often considered a sign of power. Richness and elaborateness are simply more subtle signs of power than overt force.[33] This point clarifies a behavioral change in Sardanapalus which superficially ap-pears to be a drastic shift from passive to active. His character did not change; he simply shifted his show of authority.

In the mythopoeic reading, Byron's drama moves dialectically between acceptance and rejection of the pleasure principle. Sardan-apalus presents the ideal; his kingdom rejects it. The subjects' rejec-tion of the king reveals their discomfort with such a construct. Their self-validation comes through thwarting his philosophy. Therefore, the rule of peace and pleasure fails politically in the drama and aes-thetically outside the play. Unable to woo the subjects to his teach-ings, and unwilling to compel them, Sardanapalus lets go. His actions fulfill the requirements of his kingdom and the expectations of an audience who "does not set great store by the principle of pleasure in its simple and primitive meaning" or who even holds "an antagonism to the principle"; Sardanapalus's sacrificial death represents what Trilling would term "the repudiation of pleasure in favor of the gratification which may be found in unpleasure."[34] As Sardanapalus mounts the death pyre with Myrrha, he claims that the fire will be

> a light
> To lesson ages, rebel nations, and
> Voluptuous princes.
>
> (VI, i, 440–42)

His statements could easily be read as a retraction of his life-style.[35] Not so. The king adds that although his descendants will be unable to "despise," and afraid to "imitate," his act, they may "avoid the life / Which led to such a consummation" (V, i, 447–49). His cryptic statement becomes not an apology but a warning for those who are to come.

Sardanapalus is about continuance. In a work built upon para-dox, a final irony emerges. As the king (within the drama) destroys evil—stasis—the poet destroys the instrument of good. On both levels continuity, accompanied by self-awareness and even fulfill-ment, is achieved. Sardanapalus recognizes that giving up his king-dom is all that will save it. The poet recognizes that the loss of the pleasure construct is inevitable; he promises continuity only through denial and reversal. The measure of hope contained within the historical story, then, is greater than the degree of hope afforded the construct itself: only its "dust" will be "borne abroad upon / The winds of heaven, and scatter'd into air" (V, i, 477–78).

Notes

1. In the preface to his seminal work *Natural Supernaturalism*, Abrams relates, "Byron I omit altogether; not because I think him a lesser poet than the others but because in his greatest work he speaks with an ironic countervoice and deliberately opens a satirical perspective on the basic stance of his Romantic contemporaries." M. H. Abrams, *Natural Supernaturalism* (New York: Norton, 1971), p. 13.

2. Harry Slochower, *Mythopoesis* (Detroit: Wayne State Univ. Press, 1970), p. 15.

3. Slochower, p. 15.

4. Hugo Winckler, *The History of Babylonia and Assyria*, trans. and ed. James Alexander Craig (New York: Scribner's Sons, 1907), pp. 281–83.

5. Arthur D. Kahn, "Seneca and *Sardanapalus*: Byron, the Don Quixote of Neo-Classicism," *SP*, 66 (July 1969), p. 664. John Genest's complaint that Byron should have called Ninus and Belesus by their Greek names since he was following Siculus's account may challenge Kahn's observation. John Genest, *Some Account of the English Stage, 1660–1830.* (Bath, 1832), II, pp. 135–36; cited in Margaret Howell, "Sardanapalus," *Byron Journal*, 2 (1974), p. 53.

6. E. Stucken, *Astralmythen* (Leipzig, 1896–1907); cited in Burton Feldman and Robert D. Richardson, *The Rise of Modern Mythology* (Bloomington: Indiana Univ. Press, 1972), p. xiv.

7. William Gerard, *Byron Re-studied in His Dramas* (London: White, 1886), p. 82.

8. Aristotle, "From Aristotle's Poetics," trans. Leon Golden; cited in *Twentieth Century Criticism*, eds. William J. Handy and Max Westbrook (New York: Free Press, 1974), pp. 128–29.

9. *Sardanapalus*, in *The Poetical Works of Byron*, Cambridge ed. and rev. Robert F. Gleckner, p. 550. All further references to this work will be noted in the text.

10. Paul Elledge, *Byron and the Dynamics of Metaphor* (Nashville: Vanderbilt Univ. Press, 1968) pp. 11, 119. G. Wilson Knight, in "Byron: The Poet," also considers Sardanapalus bisexual, but he explains the concept more fully; his statements describe a bisexual consciousness: "Our hero, poet-like, may be called bisexual, joining man's reason to woman's emotional depth, while repudiating the evil concomitants. Sardanapalus is to this extent rightly to be designated, as is Semiramis (1.i.43), a 'Man-Queen,' with no condemnation of effeminacy." *Poets of Action* (Methuen, 1967; rpt. Washington, D.C.: 1981), p. 226.

11. "Effeminate," *OED*.

12 *Byron's Letters and Journals*, ed. Leslie A. Marchand, 12 vols. (Cambridge, Mass.: Belknap Press, 1982), VIII, p. 26; 13 January 1821. The accounts of the actual king seem lost amid the various popularized and exaggerated versions. The figure that history recalls seems to be a mish-mash of several persons. Byron used two accounts for the drama. Diodorus Siculus and Mitford, who "rather vindicate[d]" the king. Siculus's *Bibliothecea Historicae* labels Sardanapalus the "last king of the Assyrians, who outdid all his predecessors in luxury and sluggishness."

13. Kahn, p. 665.

Lynn Byrd

14. Kahn, pp. 665–66. Both of Kahn's statements reveal an association between Bacchus and feminine pursuits / characteristics; both are also viewed negatively. W. F. Otto's study affirms this correlation. He points out that since women did dominate the Dionysian cult, much of the traditionally negative view of things Dionysian stems, in part, from the negative view of things feminine. Walter F. Otto, *Dionysus: Myth and Cult*, trans. Robert B. Palmer (Bloomington: Indiana Univ. Press, 1965), p. 126.

15. J. E. Harrison, "Introduction," *Themis* (Cambridge: Cambridge Univ. Press, 1927), p. xiii; cited in James Hillman, *The Myth of Analysis*, Harper Torchbooks ed. (Chicago: Northwestern Univ. Press, 1972,) p. 275.

16. Marcel Detienne, *Dionysos Slain*, trans. Mireille Muellner and Leonard Muellner (Baltimore: Johns Hopkins Univ. Press, 1979), p. 68.

17. Detienne, p. 68. Hillman phrases the concept of mystery a bit differently: "In Dionysus, borders *join* that which we usually believe to be separated by borders. . . . Dionysus presents us with borderline phenomena, so that we cannot tell whether he is mad or sane, wild or somber, sexual or psychic, male or female, conscious or unconscious. . . . Wherever ambivalence appears, there is a possibility for Dionysian consciousness" (p. 275).

18. Wendy Doniger O'Flaherty, *Women, Androgynes, and Other Mythical Beasts* (Chicago: Univ. of Chicago Press, 1980), pp. 196, 201.

19. O'Flaherty, p. 201.

20. O'Flaherty, pp. 283–84.

21. O'Flaherty, p. 284.

22. O'Flaherty, p. 312.

23. G. Wilson Knight notes that the "dream is loaded with suggestions of incest and cruelty," but he ascribes it to "an over-emphasis of power-instincts to the exclusion of sexual health; to the domination of ancestral authority; and to sadism." *The Burning Oracle* (London, 1939; rpt. Folcroft, 1974), p. 255. Elledge also remarks on the "strong suggestion of incestuous passion" in the nightmare, but he finds the point of it "obscure unless it is intended as another example of bestial wantonness" (p. 125).

24. O'Flaherty, pp. 284–86.

25. Jerome McGann, *Fiery Dust: Byron's Poetic Development* (Chicago: Univ. of Chicago Press, 1968), pp. 236–39.

26. Knight, p. 254.

27. Elledge, p. 125.

28. "Silkworm," *OED*.

29. B. G. Tandon, *The Imagery of Lord Byron's Plays*, "Salzburg Studies in English Literature: Poetic Drama and Poetic Theory," No. 31 (Salzburg: Universität Salzburg, 1976), pp. 113–14.

30. William Wordsworth, Preface to Lyrical Ballads, *The Lyrical Ballads 1798–1805*, English Classics ed. (London: Methuen, 1940; rpt. 1959).

31. Lionel Trilling, "The Fate of Pleasure: Wordsworth to Dostoevsky," in *Romanticism Reconsidered*, ed. Northrop Frye (New York: Columbia Univ. Press, 1963), pp. 75–77.

32. Trilling, p. 77.

33. Trilling, pp. 78–79.

34. Trilling, pp. 89–90.

35. Much of the problem in interpretation here may be attributed to the ambiguity attached to the word *voluptuous*. Its connotations in English are largely nega-

tive. It denotes the "sensuous enjoyment as a chief object of life, or end, in itself." It may even be personified pejoratively as a female deity. "Voluptuous," *OED*. As Trilling notes, however, the original Latin term *voluptas* was neutral, lacking moral implications (p 75). *Voluptuous* is actually an ideal word-choice for the drama because, in its almost opposing meanings, it demonstrates the dialectical struggle between pleasure and unpleasure.

Byron Representing Himself against Southey

Edward T. Duffy

As to "Don Juan"—confess—confess—you dog—and be candid that it is the sublime of *that there* sort of writing—it may be bawdy—but is it not good English?—it may be profligate—but is it not *life*, is it not *the thing*?

—Byron to Douglas Kinnaird

In *A Vision of Judgment*, Robert Southey speaks as if he had the eye to look down on history *sub specie aeternitatis*, the ear to catch snatches of heavenly music, and the lips to trumpet forth the last word of final divine judgment. Granting himself such capacities for seeing, hearing, and adjudicating, Southey does not hesitate to gather his lately deceased sovereign up into heaven and to damn Byron (in the poem's preface) as the archfiend of the Satanic School of Poetry. In his mock-visionary response to Southey, Byron will call these characteristically exaggerated claims of the poet laureate "a libel— / No less on History than the Holy Bible" (*The Vision of Judgment*, 687–88).[1] Southey may think he can take any and all of the materials of history and force them into the closure of some absolute anagogic significance, but his satiric respondent knows better. He knows that Bob Southey has been repeatedly rash in his accounts of people, acts, and events, and repeatedly pretentious in his elevation of politics and party to the marble constant of the highest absolute significance.[2]

The pretentiousness of Southey's *A Vision of Judgment* is immediately evident from its opening, where the poet laureate assimilates his sitting down to grind out a piece all but required of his
position to: a rush of the Pentecostal spirit, Dante's onset of vision
at the beginning of the *Commedia*, and the bodily assumption of the
Virgin into heaven. Southey's spiritlessly mechanical invocation of
some of our more prestigious literary and spiritual signifiers
stretches to absurdity Coleridge's dictum that poetry should make
evident in the symbols of time the translucence of eternity. Southey
is so eager, and thinks it so easy, to read the sempiternal into the
quotidian that he cannot help but put himself ludicrously out of
touch with the world around him. The result is that what he would
present as a flight of vision looks like nothing so much as a gaping
abyss of the inappropriate and the absurd.

Abhorring such pretentious cant, Byron would, as the Horatian
epigraph of *Don Juan* puts it, attempt to speak rightly of common
things, an ambition all the more difficult because any would-be
singer of the ordinary and everyday inevitably finds himself surrounded by a repertory of significant forms and mythologies, each
one offering itself, pat and on cue, as the true and definitive essence of what is unrolling in the muddled disguises of the temporal
and the contingent. Byron knew that his own wording of the world
could not avoid mythology as a means of textual production. To
name is to place, and this holds true whether the placement is the
rudimentary one that makes some given physical artifact in *Don
Juan* count as a *bed*, or our highly civilized sense of arrival when, in
reading Byron's *Vision of Judgment*, we enter into its concluding den-
igration of Southey as the myth of Phaeton come to life in Regency
England (*Vision*, 828). The fact remains, however, that with its simple root meaning of *story*, a myth can ring as false as a badly chosen
individual word. A story invoked can be *just* a story, a tale too tall
by far, whose effect is not a myth brought to life but life abandoned
in favor of the fabulous and the absurd. With the example of
Southey glaringly before him, Byron was acutely aware that the
generalizing moves of mythology or typology could be the snare
and delusion of a form too easily achieved.

In *A Vision of Judgment*, Southey betrays his mania for gathering
everything up into one true ball of meaning by the way he con-
scripts virtually all the heroes of English history into a heavenly
welcoming party for George III, a welcoming party that includes
even John Milton, the republican apologist for regicide. This talent

of Southey's for libeling English history into an "authorized" and totalist version was not, however, up to making John Wilkes and Junius one with the cause of the Hanoverian king. For them Southey employs another tactic. He has these historical critics of George III summoned to do the devil's bidding of accusation only to reveal that they have nothing to say either against the king or for themselves. In Southey's poem they are *abashed, dumb, speechless* (*A Vision*, 17,18).[3] Southey also contrives to make Junius as nonexistent to the eye as to the ear. As the eternally fixed sign for this anonymous "slanderer," "masked . . . in his life," he invents what must have seemed to him a Dantesquely appropriate "visor of iron / Rivetted round his head [and] . . . abolish[ing] his features for ever" (*A Vision*, 18). The poetics of Southey's vision are the poetics of casting out and abolishing feature: any opposition to the riveted steel trap of his judgment will either not exist or be cast out into the realm of the

> many-headed and monstrous . . .
> Fiend with numberless faces,
> Numberless bestial ears erect to all rumours, and restless,
> And with numberless mouths which [are] fill'd with lies as
>   with arrows
>
> (16)

Southey's horrified imagination of the numberlessly spawning beast—this "hircine host obscene"—takes a distinctively discursive turn when he describes the satanic targets of his judgment as bristling with "numberless bestial ears erect to all rumours." Byron does not so much deny this characterization of the Satanic beast as make it his own. For the Byron at play in *ottava rima* presents himself as exactly what terrorizes Southey: an ear erect to all rumors, an ear always alert to all the confusing voices of all sorts and sexes, an ear always ready for what does unaccountably fall out, what does in fact happen. Against the legitimate world of the laureate and his king, the Byron of *Don Juan* and the *Vision* obtrudes himself as ready to stand up for the disowned bastards of the random, the surprising and the anomalous. For "if a writer should be quite consistent, / How could he possibly show things existent?" (*Don Juan*, XV, 87).

In his *Vision* Byron brings to judgment a poetaster whose endless libels on history and the Bible reveal that in an infinitely various world calling for nimbleness of mind, Southey is rigid in conception and correspondingly lumbering in execution. *The Vision of Judgment* is Byron's *Dunciad*, and as the antithetical occasion for the spriteliness of his own wit, he pillories what funds the laureate's art of sinking in poetry: a lumpish heaviness that strains the left wing of the angel hauling him up to heaven's gate and impedes him from ever getting his "foundered verses" unstuck and off the ground:

> [He] stuck fast with his first hexameter,
> Not one of all whose gouty feet would stir,
>
> But ere the spavin'd dactyls could be spurr'd
>   Into recitative, in great dismay
> Both cherubim and seraphim were heard
>   To murmur loudly through their long array;
> And Michael rose ere he could get a word
>   Of all his founder'd verses under way,
> And cried, 'For God's sake stop, my friend! 'twere best—
> "*Non Di, non homines—*" you know the rest.'
>
> (*Vision*, 719–28)

As if in satiric antistrophe to Southey's making Junius and Wilkes speechless, Byron has Michael call a halt to the worse than jog trot of Southey's verse. The clear suggestion is that the poet laureate is so heavy and dull as to be unhearable and unreadable.

Byron's *Vision* subjects Southey to not just one but two pratfalls. And when he makes "multi-scribbling Southey" try to intone his *Vision* yet a second time, the laureate proves himself even more egregiously ineffective. He does not just turn his audience off. In a grand farcical climax, he drives it away:

> Those grand heroics acted as a spell:
>   The angels stopp'd their ears and plied their pinions;
> The devils ran howling, deafen'd, down to hell;
>   The ghosts fled, gibbering, for their own dominions—
> . . . .
> Michael took refuge in his trump—but lo!
> His teeth were set on edge, he could not blow!
>
> (*Vision*, 817–24)

In again endeavoring to blow the trump of his vision, Southey only persists in the folly of a dunce. Of his own intrusive and blundering weight, he will "sink to the bottom—like his works." He will be his own undoing, he will be "quite a poetic felony '*de se'* " (751).

By making Southey damn himself out of his own leaden mouth, Byron articulates his own voice of opposition. By nimbly picking up on what Southey has seen fit to write, he can make the instruments of Saint Peter's authority serve Southey not as keys to the kingdom but as a theatrical hook to shut him up and get him off. Let Southey try to silence someone, and Byron will empower him with voice. Let Southey rivet Junius into an iron mask "abolish[ing] his features," and Byron will counter with an "epistolary 'iron mask' " displaying not a dearth but a wealth of features. Let Southey call the devil "multifaced," and Byron will throw back at him his own exuberant version of the Satanic "late called 'multifaced' / By multoscribbling Southey." Let Southey tediously go on about the metrics of his *Vision*, and Byron will sting him with gibes about "gouty feet" and "spavined dactyls." Byron's title, different by only an article from Southey's, sets the pattern for these mocking reversals, as does the epigraph from *The Merchant of Venice:* "A Daniel come to judgment! yea, a Daniel! / I thank thee, Jew, for teaching me that word."

These reversals all work toward shutting up a writer whose name Byron made rhyme with *mouthy*. Their complement is the way Byron brings the laureate-silenced Wilkes and Junius to verbal life, the way he endows these two historical accusers of George III with the kind of verbal, ethical, and personal power he would deny to Southey and claim for himself.

How Byron represents himself in Wilkes is fairly straightforward. Against the heavily vindictive judgmentalism of Southey, Wilkes is a figure of forgiveness. In his own small way, he would call a halt to the world's infernal machine of an eye for an eye.[4] In Byron's *Vision* the stridently insistent Wilkes of history is a merry voice of forbearance coming from a "cockeyed curious looking sprite," who, in letting bygones be bygones, has the verbal agility to make the simplicity of "I have forgiven" rhyme with the wit of "I vote his 'habeas corpus' into heaven" (*Vision*, 567–68).

With Junius, the other of Southey's tongue-tied Georgian accusers, the countermove of bestowing voice and feature is intimately connected with how Byron would represent himself as born for opposition against Southey and his king. The portrait of Junius owes both its dazzle and its bravura length to the availability of this historical mystery as a protean form, along the shifting features of which Byron could let play the quicksilver of his own improvisational way of being and writing in the world. Junius represents the frequently noted mobility of Byron. "Quick in his motions, with an air of vigour," he is all Proteus and quicksilver, a "wight mysterious" who changes his countenance as often as people formulate his identity, which is very often indeed:

The man was a phantasmagoria in
Himself—he was so volatile and thin!

The moment that you had pronounced him *one*,
   Presto! his face changed, and he was another;
And when that change was hardly well put on,
   It varied, till I don't think his own mother
(If that he had a mother) would her son
   Have known, he shifted so from one to t'other,
Till guessing from a pleasure grew a task,
At this epistolary "iron mask."

(Vision, 615–24)

The power Byron here deploys and enacts is that of Keats's chameleon poet, who, having no identity of his own, can become any and every thing by turns. The star he reckons by is not a Miltonic beckoning toward the closures of *mythos* and *typos* but the *presto* of quick and nimble transformation. The persona of *Don Juan*, writes Carl Woodring, becomes "a kind of metaphor for volatility";[5] and Junius is Byron's representation of what, as against Southey, he can nimbly do both with the volatile stuff of words and with the world(s) that these words would articulate.

That figures in Byron's poetry are the author's often knowingly displaced self-respresentations is hardly news, but to my knowledge, no one has argued this specifically for the Junius of *The Vision*. If it was Southey's initial judgment to make Wilkes and Junius the tongue-tied accusers of the deceased king, I would argue that it was Byron's identification with this early and formidable critic of the same long-lived sovereign that prompted him into his elaborate presentation of Junius as an emblem of mobility, a "phantasmagoria in himself."

At the time of Southey and Byron's competing visions, interest in Junius was high. From Venice in the spring of 1818, Byron mentions him three times to English correspondents, each time in connection with the (most probably correct) theory that Junius was Sir Philip Francis.[6] What sounds in each case like a response to literary gossip from home undoubtedly stems from the recent publication of John Taylor's *The Identity of Junius with a Distinguished Living Character Established*, a piece of sleuthing that appeared several years after the important "Woodfall" edition of the letters in 1812, and now, more than a century later, authoritatively characterized as "the most important single work in the search for Junius."[7]

Already, in 1814, Byron had written of Junius, "I like him;—he was a good hater."[8] The liking was based on a firm bedrock of similarity. A full half-century after Junius had entered the arena of political polemic in behalf of John Wilkes, Regency England still had in place both the same king to oppose and the same grounds for opposition: a system of political corruption that made wordmen into paid trimmers like Southey and ministers into utensils like Grafton, whom, wrote Junius, "the wildest spirit of inconsistency . . . never once betrayed into a wise or honourable action."[9] What unprincipled Grafton was to Junius, Southey's pen of all work was to Byron: a fiercely personalized focus for the witty and particularized demolition work of Augustan satire, a form of writing made for the good hater and a rubric under which Junius and the "satiric" Byron have both often been considered. (In addition to these general affinities, The Vision's repeated assertion that George was the puppet of his ministers might well derive from the same insinuation as it appears in Junius's most notorious piece of king-baiting, Letter 35 of 19 December 1769. More specifically still, Junius could also have prompted The Vision's actual naming of Bute and Grafton (564), the two most prominent targets of Junius, one of whom Byron's poem elsewhere (340) belittlingly refers to only as a nameless minion, an epithet drumming its contemptuous way through Letter 35's acerbic footnote about "the Princess Dowager and her favorite the Earl of Bute").[10]

Whatever the nature and force of these similarities and echoes, it is clear that for taking his own swipes at the "Geordian knot" (Don Juan XVI, 74) of the monarchy and its men, Byron could have learned much from, and seen much of himself in, Junius. Besides the basic political and stylistic congruence between the two, there is a clear indication that, in Byron's mind, the two of them were paradoxically similar in that each could rightly be called a phantasmagoria. To the extent that Byron's Junius is amenable to summation, the phrase used to sum him up is "a phantasmagoria in / Himself so volatile and thin"; and at just about the same time Byron entered into his Detached Thoughts for 15 October 1821, a catalogue of all the comparisons and identifications he himself had been subjected to, one of which was "the phantasmagoria," still taken as a proper name, "invented," says the OED, "for an exhibition of optical illusions produced chiefly by means of the magic lantern, first exhibited in London in 1802." The phantasmagoria was one comparison that Byron did not find demeaning and inadequate because, unlike most of the others that would have reductively formulated him into a phrase or name, phantasmagoria was, internally as it were, a name for infinite and nimble variety. It was a name for his and Junius's uncanniness, a sign that no one could pluck out the heart of this mystery because "the object of so many contradictory comparisons must probably be like something different from them all,—but what *that* is, is more than *I* know, or anybody else."[11] What Byron says in the prose of his *Detached Thoughts* and with bemused delight about his own elusiveness is translated to *The Vision* as a verse catalogue of all the sworn and certain identifications of Junius, by which, it is gleefully reported, "the puzzle only was increased" (614).

The Byronic Junius is a fantasy on Byronic mobility, and on this subject Jerome McGann has analyzed how one of Byron's earlier representations of Southey also counts as Byron's confessing and partially making amends for his own easy submissions to the winds of fashion and the attractions of power. Without disagreeing with McGann's meticulous analysis of how, in *Don Juan* III, Southey figures as "the dark shadow cast by the mobility of the spontaneous Romantic poet,"[12] I would add that in the *Vision* Byron goes one reflective and critical step further. In it he confronts the signifier *mobility* with the human actions and phenomena it has named or could name, because in the figure of Southey he finds himself called out—provoked—into distinguishing between his own mobility, to be prized, and the turncoat mobility of the laureate, to be abhorred. Proud of his quicksilver mind, Byron is no less proud of the steadfast disdain with which

> 'Tis that I still retain my "buff and blue."
> My politics, as yet, are all to educate,
>   Apostasy's so fashionable too,
> To keep *one* creed's a task grown quite Herculean,
>   Is it not so, my Tory ultra-Julian?
>
> (*Don Juan* Dedication, 17)

Because his mobility is so obviously different from Southey's "pen of all work," Byron must, by the process Coleridge called *desynonymization*, retain *mobility* as his own badge of honor and power while excising from it such perfidious lack of principle as could make Southey go from the champion of Wat Tyler to the official canonizer of George III.

As a displaced self-representation of Byron, the portrait of Junius wears its mobility with a sharp edge of difference from Southey's politics because it also enacts for Junius a fixity or *immobility* that is to be sharply distinguished from Southey's poetic art of sinking by his own dead weight. This Byronic fixity is a steadfastness founding itself not on ponderous self-importance but on a firmly principled integrity, and to discover it in Byron's Junius, the

195

reader of the *Vision* need only move from its words portraying Junius to its words invented for Junius to speak, words both the content and the style of which epitomize steadfastness. Junius utters very few words, but words like "What I have written, I have written: let / The rest be on his head or mine!" (665–66) trenchantly drive home the accent of *Here I stand, I can no other.* That accent is, in a general way, ill suited to the traditional materials, rhythms, and resources of *ottava rima;* but when he needs it as a rebuke to Southey's backsliding, Byron knows how to make his form receive it and bear its stress. In Satan's most extended speech (305–400), for example, Byron uses such instruments for trenchancy as antithesis, anaphora, asyndeton, and ellipsis to hammer out masculine rhymes and imperative moods into the apodictic and peremptory demonstration that George III was a very bad king indeed. (By contrast, Junius's medium invites the tone of conviction; it was something external to Junius's style, the prolonged guessing game of who he was, that made him available to Byron as an emblem of mobility.)

Immovable in his way as Southey has been in his, Byron develops Southey in such brilliantly particularized dramatic detail that if this renegado ultra-Julian should ever dare to say, "Here I stand, I can no other," it would strike the ear as a remark not about his commitments and allegiances but about his spavined dactyls. There is a time and a way to be immobile and a time and a way to be mobile, and that Southey gets it all backward, with his commitments wavering and his verses "foundered," antithetically defines the self-representing parodist who would claim both the quicksilver seen in the mobility of his Junius and the apodictic trenchancy heard in his (and the devil's) summation against George III.

In the end, Byron claims the *Idem semper* (*Don Juan* XVII, 11) of steadfastness for himself and fixes onto Southey both the heavy immovability of his verse *and* the empty lightness of a corrupted intelligence:

> He first sunk to the bottom—like his works,
>   But soon rose to the surface—like himself;
> For all corrupted things are buoy'd, like corks,
>   By their own rottenness, light as an elf,
> Or wisp that flits o'er a morass.

(Vision, 833–37)

With its root of "broken up," this "*corrupted,* thing" of light and rotten Bob Southey is the final antithesis against which Byron defines his own form of integrity. Clad in the armor of a quicksilver mind that will not be "a Poor Thing of Usages" (*Don Juan* XIV, 23),

Byron defines himself by opposition to a Southey who took his words so lightly that they were bound to shift and veer with the winds of power. Only a committed liberal, still retaining his buff and blue, could instill this wit with so much real passion against the bought pen of a laureate. Only a superior verbal agility could so deftly hit upon this sinking / rising image so as to bring the high station and worldy success of the laureate into revelatory conjunction with the full biological, moral, and political range of *corruption*.

How Byron is alert to the many lives and turns of *corruption* is also evident in the way he plays on *brass*. When Junius / Byron claims that "My charges upon record will outlast / The brass of both his [George's] epitaph and tomb" (*Vision*, 657–58), the claim is the familiar Horatian one that poets and prophets have often lodged against devouring time: that "aere perennius exegi monumentum." But lest this claim appear too ponderously delivered, Junius uses a monument's figurative brass of endurance and its conceivably literal brass of inscription to score a palpable hit at both the supposed monument of brass that Southey's verses will build for George, and the real effrontery of all this visionary emptiness as it attempts "to canonize a Monarch, who, whatever were his household virtues, was neither a successful nor a patriot king."[13] In trying to be a creator of brass, Southey only reveals his brazenness. (This mocking use of *brass* Byron had already turned on the royal family in his letters: "The Braziers, it seems, are preparing to pass / An address, and present it themselves all in brass— / A superfluous pageant— for, by the Lord Harry, / They'll find where they're going [to Queen Caroline] much more than they carry.")[14] One reason Junius's claim to lasting words rings true is that Byron is right now reenacting these words, right now bringing back to vivid life just this antimonarchical stance. In the dedication to *Don Juan*, Byron grandly and scornfully asks what Milton, if living at this hour, would write of the newly deceased king and his sixty-year reign, but in the *Vision* it is Junius come back, not "heavy" Milton.[15]

The Vision's play on *brass* does not stop here, for Byron's claim that Junius's perduring words will constitute a monument of brass is subsequently and hilariously joined with how he makes *brass* the sign under which Southey blunders into the farce of his second attempt at obtaining a heavenly hearing for his *Vision*. Byron starts Southey down this path of the reiterated ridiculous when he represents his unseemly eagerness to recruit Michael as a patron for his biographical "pen of all work." To that end Southey assures the archangel that

[I] would make you shine
Like your own trumpet; by the way, my own
Has more of brass in it, and is as well blown.

But talking about trumpets, here's my Vision!"

(798–801)

The *brass* of Southey's *Vision*, here so wittily put into a mouth in the very act of blowing its own horn, exploits a range of meanings that includes not only *brazen* impudence but all the suggestions in *brassy* of the meretricious, the cheap, the showy, and, above all, the loud and overdone. If the exaggerated show of George's funeral is like the "mockery of hell to fold / The rottenness of eighty years in gold" (79–80), then *a fortiori* the exaggerated brass of Southey's *Vision* is another and similar piece of devilishness. It is a show of gilding that, like embalming spices, works but "to prolong decay" (88). The connection between this specious glitter and the real corruption beneath is what makes this comedy about cant so passionately serious. The visionary gilding of Southey lets things subject to at least some control go to the limit of their entropic force, unchecked by any pertinently accurate grasp of human understanding.

As if assuming the intimate symbiosis between world and word, Byron exultantly said of *Don Juan*, "is it not good English? . . . is it not *life*, is it not *the thing?*"[16] The life and liveliness of this English also circulates through *The Vision of Judgment*, and it is maintained by, and manifested in, the protean shifts of semiotic and semantic feature playing on the surface of words like *corrupt* or *brass*. The world and the language's mercurial play of meanings, forces, and combinations calls out for a fidelity to be proved in the limber and pertinent handling of the multiple valencies to be found in words like these (or even more brilliantly in a simple but politically charged word like *place* as it is found in *Don Juan* XVI, 72–79). Unlike a poet laureate loyal to his king, a self-representing Byron would be loyal to what, following Wittgenstein, Stanley Cavell has recently called "the human form of life which is the life of language."[17] Only to the lively of mind and agile of tongue do there come such decisive mockeries as naming Southey a writer of "blank verse and even blanker prose" (783–84). By such moves is English kept up and cant put down. But it is a process in the forming and reforming of our world(s) that is constantly threatened by a stiffening of articulation into the ready-made forms of our various pre-understandings and mythologies.

The dedication to *Don Juan* locates potent writing in the Miltonic sublime. It contrasts the laureate's time-serving prostitution of

198

his pen with the way an earlier English poet, who has made "the word *'Miltonic'* mean *'sublime,'* " would have (if come back to England in 1819) arisen "Like Samuel from the grave, to freeze once more / The blood of monarchs with his prophecies" and would not have obeyed "the intellectual eunuch Castlereagh" (stanza 11). As a running contrast to the weak words of Southey, *Don Juan* presents itself as a different kind of potent writing. Insisting on authorial potency as the one thing needed, Byron exposes Southey as a writer whose very insufficiencies have made him the tool of that "intellectual eunuch" Castlereagh, a ministerial power whom Byron repeatedly neuters into the icy, passionless *it* of a "state thing," its parliamentary oratory of such an inert "set trash of phrase" that

> Not even a *sprightly* blunder's spark can blaze
>   From that Ixion's grindstone's ceaseless toil,
> That turns and turns, to give the world a notion
> Of endless torments and perpetual motion.

(Stanza 13)

Everything said here of Castlereagh's speeches is applicable (in Byron's mind) to Southey's poems, and Byron's placement of them in the joylessly grinding hell of Ixion reflects how they grind out words to order, grind out phrasing that is trashy precisely because it is set. With his endless production of self-styled epics, the laureate was truly "representative of all the race" in the way he was continually neutering such mythologizing and typologizing lines of force as were so powerfully present in Milton, in the way he was continually cheapening the heroic stance and force of the Miltonic line. With his epic ambitions and his self-importance, Southey was, like Phaeton, an emblem or myth of constant impotence and fiasco:

> And then you overstrain yourself, or so,
>   And tumble downward like the flying fish
> Gasping on deck, because you soar too high, Bob,
> And fall, for lack of moisture, quite adry, Bob!

(Stanza 3)

If ideally mythology can gather event toward significance and raise it into epiphany, it was (to Byron's ear, at least) the excessive mythological practice of Regency England that was dispersing into the inanity of meaningless cant both the tools and the achievements of mythology. "Set trash of phrase" was not only letting the real historical experience of Regency England get away from those living it. It was also blunting those very verbal and semiotic forms that could turn the Regency's accounts of itself away from cant and to-

Edward T. Duffy

ward "the life" of *Don Juan*. Facts were the "grand desideratum! / Of which, howe'er the Muse describes each act, / There should be ne'ertheless a slight substratum" (*Don Juan* VII, 81); and when a canting community was given to sliding over these facts, when it abridged the stuff of that life and homogenized its grain, then it was bound to strip it of the force and point necessary to test and counter, and therefore to *develop*, the established discursive formations of its language and culture.

As the only begetter of a performance the very name of whose hero means sexual potency, Byron displays his power in a new key, the mythologized totem for which is Don Juan, that prodigy of promiscuous dissemination whose vigorously dispersed energies are not simply different from, but opposite to, the gathering mythological and typological productions of Milton. If Wordsworth fervently wanted to hear old Triton blow his wreathed horn, then as counterstatement to this call for a mythological ingathering, the Byron of *Don Juan* sought to expose the brassy (and often corrupt) trumpery of most such holds on Proteus, most such graspings toward a totalizing and identifying form of human experience. Toward the performance of such demythologizing work, a characteristically volatile Byron mythologized himself into a Don Juan of the spirit and into a Junius of mercurial feature; but the *idem semper* of these equally protean self-representations was Byron's fidelity to what the discursive formations of cant always threaten: the revelatory but slippery play of words, the form of life that is the life of the language. Against the paid intellectual eunuchs stitching together formulas into a set trash of phrase, Byron's demythologizing presents itself as a potent mythology of self, provoked or "called out" by such writers as multiscribbling Southey. Against a monolith indistinguishably literary and political, *Don Juan* and *The Vision of Judgement* would play out our energies not for gathering phenomenon and word up into the identities of *mythos* and *typos* but for articulating and deploying their play of differences in a manner so "quick in its motion with an air of vigor" that Byron could not contain himself from exulting, "is it not good English? . . . is it not life, is it not *the thing?*"

Notes

1. I cite Byron's poems as they appear in *Byron: The Complete Poetical Works*, ed. Jerome J. McGann (Oxford: Clarendon Press, 1980–). Because *The Vision of Judgment* has not yet appeared in this edition, I quote the text given in the *Byron* volume in the Oxford Authors series, ed. Jerome J. McGann, 1986. Citations are given parentheti-

cally in the text by line number, except for *Don Juan*, where canto and stanza numbers are given.

2. A succinct summary of the longstanding quarrel between Byron and Southey can be found in Frederick L. Beaty, *Byron the Satirist* (DeKalb: Northern Illinois University Press, 1985), 180–83.

3. Quotations from Southey's *A Vision of Judgment* are taken from *Opposing Visions: Byron's and Southey's Vision of Judgment*, ed. Henry J. Donaghy (Pocatello: Idaho State University Press, 1976) and are referenced by page number in this edition.

4. On the persistent theme of forgiveness and its difficulty of achievement in Byron, see Jerome J. McGann, *Fiery Dust: Byron's Poetic Development* (Chicago: University of Chicago Press, 1968), 42, and *Don Juan in Context* (Chicago: University of Chicago Press, 1976), 49.

5. Carl Woodring, *Politics in English Romantic Poetry* (Cambridge, Mass.: Harvard University Press, 1970), 212.

6. *Byron's Letters and Journals*, ed. Leslie Marchand (Cambridge, Mass.: Harvard University Press, 1973–82), VI, 18, 19, 35.

7. The 1812 edition is *Junius: Including Letters by the Same Writer under Other Signatures (Now First Collected)*. 3 vols. [Ed. J. Mason Good.] (London: Woodfall, 1812). Taylor's book was first published in 1816 by Taylor and Hessey. A supplement appeared the following year and a second edition in 1818. Thanks largely to the work of Alvar Ellegard, *Who Was Junius?* (Stockholm: Almquist & Wiksell, 1962), this identification appears settled to every informed inquirer's satisfaction. In his critical edition of the letters, John Cannon develops a hedged but nonetheless convinced and convincing case for Francis as the author: *The Letters of Junius* (Oxford: Clarendon Press, 1978) 547–72. The authoritative characterization of Taylor's book is that of David McCracken, *Junius and Philip Francis* (Boston: Twayne Publishers, 1979), 152.

8. *Byron's Letters and Journals*, III, 215.

9. *Letters of Junius*, 68.

10. *Letters of Junius*, 160.

11. *Byron's Letters and Journals*, IX, 11.

12. Jerome J. McGann, *The Beauty of Inflections: Literary Investigations in Historical Method and Theory* (Oxford: Clarendon Press, 1985), 274.

13. *Byron*, ed. McGann, 940, in Byron's preface to *The Vision of Judgment*.

14. *Byron's Letters and Journals*, VIII, 68.

15. *Heavy* and *weighty* are the words Byron used to describe, somewhat disparagingly, Milton to Medwin. See Ernest J. Lovell, Jr., *Medwin's Conversations of Lord Byron* (Princeton: Princeton University Press, 1966), 164.

16. *Byron's Letters and Journals*, VI, 232.

17. Stanley Cavell, *Disowning Knowledge in Six Plays of Shakespeare* (Cambridge: Cambridge University Press, 1987), 17.

The Positive Good
of Sheer Quirk:
Byron's Resistance of Myth
in The Vision of Judgment
Shirley Clay Scott

In May 1821, shortly after the death of the deranged, blind George III, Southey, in his office as poet laureate, announced the beatification of the king in the pretentious twelve-part poem cast as the poet's own vision of the heavenly event. The poem's only claim to notice now is that it was, largely because the Preface by awkward contrivance included an attack on Byron and his "Satanic school" of poets, the efficient cause of the poem that many of Byron's critics consider Byron's finest work, *The Vision of Judgment*.[1] But Southey, despite his corpulence, was too much a moral lightweight to be the final cause or ultimate concern of Byron's poem, a fact acknowledged in the imagery that finishes with him. The laureate falls from the celestial heights into the lake near Skiddaw, where first he sinks to the bottom "like his works" and then rises to the surface "like himself," buoyant as a cork (833–34). And though, as Andrew Rutherford has shown, Byron does base elements of his narrative on the events of Southey's *Vision*,[2] he accomplishes more than a travesty of Southey's grandiloquent poem. Northrop Frye, one of the few critics to point out the classical precedents of the poem, has

202

argued that *The Vision of Judgment* is Byron's most original and therefore his most conventional, his most serious and therefore his wittiest, poem.[3]

Frye's assessment, despite its too-perfect oxymoron, seems to me accurate, and I would like to use all of its terms in order to argue that the wit of the poem derives from a serious concern with history and that the conventions of mock apotheosis—a subset, of course, of mock-heroic conventions—allow Byron to make a highly original, even idiosyncratic, proposition about the necessity of resisting visionary or mythic treatments of historical fact.

In *The Vision of Judgment*, Byron treats historical events and figures, but he refuses to grant either events or persons the grandeur of heroic action or the status of myth. Instead he systematically undercuts the possibilities for the aggrandizements or universal features of myth. The French Revolution with its dismal aftermath is reduced to the "Gallic era eighty-eight" (5) affording a comic rhyme with "celestial gate" (1) and deflecting attention from the potentially symbolic or mythic events of 1789. The "mystique" of king, piously resuscitated by Southey in his vision of the uncorrupted royal vaults, is reduced to the "rottenness of eighty years" preserved "in gold" (80); and George III is presented as neither Rex Britannicus nor Albion's Angel but simply as "an old man / with an old soul and both extremely blind" (181–82). Even John Wilkes, who for his reputation as a firebrand of revolution and for his determined opposition to George and his ministers might have deserved the stature of mythic hero, is presented as merely an indefatigable campaigner with the innate decency not to carry either political or personal grudges beyond the grave.

The reasons for Byron's stance toward his materials are several. He had as a first target, of course, Southey and the pseudo-mythologizing of history in his poem, and mock-heroic was the appropriate weapon—at least for Byron. (Blake customarily chose a more "mythic form" even for satire or invective against "spiritual enemies.") Second, Byron knew that Southey's vision of judgment and the version of history he had been promulgating since *The Poet's Pilgrimage to Waterloo* was simply a particularly "impious" specimen of the "cant" that was the exhausted but still official myth of the English establishment. His second target was, then, as it was in *Heaven and Earth* (also written in 1821), the insidious power of an ideology that passes as religious piety and moral rectitude to be an instrument of social control and political repression.[4] He therefore enlists the wit of his poem to expose the societal assumptions that

203

align God and priest and king: the angels are solicitous of the "royal manes" in their charge because, as the narrator reminds us, "by many stories, / And true, we learn the Angels all are Tories" (207–8). To this extent Byron's poem fulfills one of the Romantic tasks of poetry, the calling back of repressive projections and outworn myths. But Romantic mythopoeia was usually twofold, visionary as well as analytical, myth-creating as well as myth-destroying; and the goal of poets like Blake, Shelley, and Wordsworth was to offer, for the systems of belief or thought that they deposed, new structures of imaginative "belief" or new possibilities for hope in history.[5] In *The Vision of Judgment*, Byron offers no new myth to replace the one he undoes. Instead, his diminutions of the mythic are designed to call into question mythmaking itself.

Byron had, then, not one but several aims in *The Vision of Judgment*. As Frye observes, he had precedent and model for the comprehensive poem he wanted to write in Seneca's *apotheosis per saturam* of the Emperor Claudius,[6] and a rereading of Byron's poem is enhanced by a review of Seneca's. In 54 A.D. Seneca had countered the Roman Senate's decree of the apotheosis of an irresponsible and murderous emperor with an *"apocolocyntosis,"* or *"gourdification,"* of the shambling, stammering Claudius, who, as Seneca has it, is so insentient a creature that he does not realize that he is dead until, on his way from Olympus (where entry had been denied him) to the underworld, he happens upon his own funeral procession. The *Apocolocyntosis* gives vent to Seneca's not inconsiderable personal animus against Claudius, but it goes well beyond that to pass judgment on the Senate's easy compliance with Agrippina's hypocrisy and political machinations, to mock the idea of divinization, and to scoff at the hagiography of officially correct historiography.

Seneca's work begins with the ascension to heaven of Claudius, attested to by the infamous witness who testified, at the behest of Caligula, to the translation of Caligula's sister and lover, Drusilla. It then features a disorderly council of the gods that, like those in the satires of Menippus, parodies the serious deliberations of the gods in epic poetry. It ends with a comic descent to an underworld filled with Claudius's own victims and guarded not by the three-headed Cerberus of Virgil but by the more grotesque *"belua centiceps"* or hundred-headed Cerberus contrived by Horace.[7] A narrating persona who is an incompetent but ambitious poet historian allows Seneca many of his ironic or comic effects. Throughout the poem the narrator's naïve comparisons of things above with things below work to the discredit of both, and his inappropriate or incongruous application of epic language and epic conventions to the events of his narrative explode the pretensions of men and gods alike.

There are numerous point-for-point correspondences between the first-century model and the nineteenth-century variation. The *Apocolocyntosis* opens in the language of official Senate business— used here to record the official proceedings on Olympus. Similarly, Byron enjoys the image of the Recording Angel's "black bureau" (20) and of an angel-clerk so busy that he must strip his own wings to keep himself in quills. Claudius makes his way up the sky "non passibus aequis," the phrase having been lifted from Virgil's tender description of the steps of Ascanius measured against the heroic stride of his father to offer the ridiculous image of the god-to-be dragging his foot into heaven. Byron, far less vicious toward George, nevertheless allows the old king's blindness, feeblemindedness, and speech impediment to persist in the afterworld; Southey had seen to the healing of all these earthly imperfections. Claudius's progress is halted at the entrance to the heavenly Senate because none of the gods recognize him as a human being let alone as a Roman emperor. Byron's keeper of the heavenly gate likewise fails to recognize George—and in fact has not even heard of him. When Claudius is finally granted an interview, he exercises his well-known pedantry and introduces himself by means of one of Odysseus's speeches. The pedantry is harmless, but the passage Claudius quotes resounds with unpleasant truth: "The wind, bearing me from Ilium, brought me to the Cicones / where I sacked the city and destroyed the people" (5:4). In the comparable passage in *The Vision of Judgment*, Byron grants George a similar harmlessness of avocation and charges him with a similar destructiveness of the nation and people he was meant to govern: "A better farmer ne'er brush'd dew from lawn, / A worse king never left a realm undone" (61–62).

Seneca presents a number of mythic figures in his work, but only in diminished or debased forms of themselves. For instance, the Three Fates, though addressed as "the Cruelest of Women" (3:1), carry out their spinning and shearing like common housewives; and they are agreeable—even affable—in their willingness to help Claudius "gurgle out his life" (4:2) and generous, if irresponsible, in their decision to provide such a gregarious fellow with companions for his postmortem journey. Their impersonal arbitration of human fate turns out to be a matter of alphabetical order— they pick first an "Augurinus" and then a "Baba" to go along with

Claudius. (3:4)[8] Though the arbiters of human fate, individual or collective, are not among the dramatis personae of Byron's poem, their presence and nature can be inferred from their effects: "So many conquerors' cars were daily driven, / So many kingdoms fitted up anew; / Each day too slew its thousands, six or seven"(35–37). The irresponsibility of the passive verbs of the first two clauses and the inanimate subject of the third clause, coupled with the chilly indifference implied by "thousands, six or seven," suggests that whatever these fates or forces may be, they are at least as cavalier as Seneca's spinners and less benign. In Seneca's poem Hercules, because of his wide travels and experience with monsters, is sent out by the gods to interview the new candidate for admission to Olympus. He is not, however, the demigod of myth and tragedy but Hercules as he appears in Aristophanes *The Frogs*—a cowardly, blustering buffoon who nevertheless takes himself seriously and holds forth in the exalted language of his tragic persona. The gods who debate, or, more accurately, squabble, over the issue of Claudius's suitability are the Olympian equivalents of Roman senators and consuls, and they are morally indistinguishable from their earthly counterparts. Janus, only recently in office, is garrulous and chiefly concerned to preserve the godly prerogatives; Diespiter is a money changer who also traffics in the perquisites of citizenship, and he is willing, for a fee, to vote Claudius's admission. Even the deified Augustus is not particularly august, and, apparently bored with divinity, he has not been moved to take part in Olympian politics until now. His speech, with its epic locutions and common exempla, is both bombastic and vulgar; but he is the spokesman for the most serious charges Seneca has to bring against Claudius, and those charges are particularly effective in the mouth of the ruler whose precepts for governance Claudius violated. As Andrew Rutherford has shown, Byron makes the case against George most powerful by demonstrating that Michael, though a "Tory," is willing to convict George if he is proved to have been a foe to the principles of liberty.[9]

Claudius manages to bribe Hercules to work on his behalf, and the unabashed venality and unembarrassed toadying of the demigod as he switches sides and takes up Claudius's cause may have helped to inspire Byron's portrayal of the turncoat laureate proffering his services as a biographer first to Satan and then to Michael. In Claudius's case the labor of Hercules is lost, and the gods dispatch the emperor to the underworld, where he is sentenced to a poetically just but not particularly hellish *contrapasso* as an amanuensis to one of his freedmen. Byron's moral and artistic triumph, of course, is that though he too demonstrates his candidate for heaven unfit for the honor, he refrains from remanding him to eternal punishment.

But my argument is not so much that Byron imitates or borrows from Seneca, but that he appreciates the demystifying and demythologizing properties of the form that Seneca brought to realization. The immediate effect of both poems is to explode the cynical or sycophantic mythologizing of king or emperor, but there are ulterior effects as well. Apotheosis as an imaginative form derives from the radical of myth, from the most visionary of man's intuitions (or, depending on one's point of view, the fondest of man's illusions), the identification of man and god. Mock apotheosis has, then, the potential not only to undo decadent or cynical variations on the theme but also to subvert the mythic impulse itself. Byron recognized and exploited that capacity. Seneca had set his poem against pseudo-heroic historiography and the heroic poetry of Homer and Virgil. Byron, by means of frequent ironic allusions and pointed references to *Paradise Lost*, sets his poem against the pseudo-visionary poetry of a poet like Southey and, more ambitiously, against the tradition of visionary poetry that derives from Milton. His narrator insists throughout on his composition of clay, admits his earthly and earthy limitations, and relies upon a "telescope" rather than the more sublime "optic tube" of the Miltonic poet. Yet he insists his vision is as true as any other vision—and Gleckner is surely correct when he suggests that Byron refers not only to Southey's poem of that title.[10] Seneca had made his mythic characters "overly anthropomorphic" and his historical figures insufficiently mythic. What Byron aptly called his "finest, ferocious Caravaggio style" is an adaptation of this technique.[11] For instance, the angels are quite "humanly" incapable of their assignments as recording secretariat of mortal history or as maintenance crew of an obstreperous cosmos; the saints are deficient in sanctity (Peter still resents the "parvenu" Paul); and the demons—even Milton's awesome Asmodeus—appear to be sociable spirits.

But unlike Seneca, Byron reduces from god to man, from mythic to mortal, not to discredit humankind or to disparage human effort in history, but to make a plea for the merely human and to allow for the positive good of sheer quirk. It is here that Byron is at his most original. The deflationary gestures required by the form become the agency for a serious contention with the deleterious effects of mythmaking. For instance, Peter, elevated to sainthood and mythic stature and supplied the keys to the kingdom instead of his earthly sword, is robbed of his ability to respond to injustice in the impulsive but salutary way native to his human and historical personality. He is, in his emasculated condition, forced to accept the entry of Louis XVI and George III into heaven without protest in the disheartening knowledge that it is the inexplicable "custom" of heaven to overthrow "whatever has been wisely done below" (167–68). It is not until the laureate's tedious recital rouses Peter's natural instincts that he is able to act in a humanly satisfying way: using his keys as a weapon, he clouts the poet on the head and tumbles him out of heaven.

George III is likewise the product of myth. Having taken to himself the inflated idea of "king," he failed to see through the myth of majesty to the opportunity he had to be a responsible constitutional monarch. Jack Wilkes's explanation that George's conduct was but "natural in a prince" (560) is precisely Byron's point, and he makes no effort to disguise his disgust that such a mythic view of office should have been grafted to so demotic an execution of duty and to so pusillanimous a conception of human excellence. As a monarch, George was content to be a puppet or tool of his ministers; as a man, he settled for the neutral virtues of household abstinence and constancy to an ugly queen.

Even Satan has been imposed upon by mythmaking. Cast by Christian vision as the archagent of evil instead of the fallen Castilian nobleman he prefers to affect, he is forced rather clearly against his will into apocalyptic contest with Michael, who left to *his* own inclinations, would remain the most deferential of civil servants. Were it not for their responsibility to myth, His Darkness and His Brightness would remain old acquaintance, now of differing political parties.

The demythologizing of Satan is a brilliant stroke on Byron's part, for Satan bears unmistakable resemblance to the melancholy *isolatos* that were Byron's self-dramatization and his legacy to the nineteenth century. Though some of the poem's critics have argued that Byron cast Satan as a noble figure to be taken altogether seriously,[12] it is more accurate to recognize that the poem offers a critique of Satan and of the Byronic rebel he represents. Satan is in part the victim of his own morbid psychology: "Where he gazed a gloom pervaded space" (192), and he is in part the perception and half-creation of a heavenly reading public apparently as avid for sensational figures mad, bad and dangerous to know as Byron's earthly readers. (In his letters Byron had complained, perhaps a bit

208

disingenuously, that his actual personality had been overtaken by that of the Byronic hero and wondered if the public imagination would ever allow him to doff his sable garb.[13] In the poem it is quite clearly Satan's public reputation and nothing that he says or does during his visit to heaven that puts Saint Peter into his apostolic sweat.) Such moral ascendency as Satan has in the poem derives from the fact that he has demystified himself and has trimmed his own ego in the knowledge that the evil in the cosmos is far too great to be of his making or subject to his control. Byron's Satan knows he is *not* Milton's Satan—and that is his strength.

The inference to be made is the proposition, Lucretian in implication, that myth—*any* myth—deprives men and women of their flesh and blood potential to contend with the conditions of existence. Byron's sense of what those conditions are informs the opening stanzas of the poem. The imagery, comic though it is, intimates an irrational, indifferent universe to which the mind may not be reconciled by myth, a collective history difficult enough to embrace without the burden of hope imposed by visionary poetry, and a mortal fate austere enough without any delusive intimations of immortality, whether Christian or Romantic. Myth, like the embalming spices used to retard the decay of the king's body, exacerbates rather than alleviates the pain of mortality:

> So mix his body with the dust! It might
>> Return to what it *must* far sooner, were
> The natural compound left alone to fight
>> Its way back into earth, and fire, and air.

(81–84)

Byron's opposition to myths of deliverance had been censured by Blake as imaginative failure, by Francis Jeffrey as philosophical irresponsibility, and by Shelley as a form of intellectual pride and estrangement from the common lot.[14] But in this poem, Byron's refusal of myth is a strength and not a limitation. Byron was, almost constitutionally, incapable of sustaining hope, and a number of scholars have traced in his works a pattern in which every effort to move from despair to hope succumbs to a deeper despair.[15] It may be that such a pattern was not restricted to Byron, for the history of the Romantic poets suggests that hope founded upon heroic demands of the human or chiliastic expectation for human endeavor is always perilously close to despair. Wordsworth and Coleridge had once felt themselves prophets of hope and "co-laborers" in the work of man's deliverance, and the quiescence and conservatism into which they subsided may be read as a manifestation of the despair that overtook them. Shelley, who recognized and struggled to quell the "anarchy of hopes and fears,"[16] nevertheless followed *Prometheus Unbound* with *The Triumph of Life*.

Byron therefore defends against hope by substituting a long view of history for the visionary power of the mythmaker. This long view forces Byron to acknowledge that human history is and will remain "the Devil's Scripture" (689), forever at variance with human desire, forever failing of the aspirations of the prophets. The lines in which Asmodeus declares Southey's puling verse a libel on both the "Devil's Scripture," history, and Michael's Bible, history as written by desire, evince a bitter deference to things as they are and at the same time betray a certain wistfulness for the visionary, for the Shelleyean; but Byron has no more hope than his recording angels who throw down their pens in "divine disgust" (39) that the good time will come.

He defends against the despair that might well attend such a long view by an act of imagination that his antivisionary, antimythic stance allows. Byron shifts from mock-heroic satire into what, using Michael G. Cooke's term, might be called "counter-heroic" comedy.[17] He converts history into humor and imagines a human and natural resiliency in which to repose his trust. The marks of this counter-heroic comedy and its burden are discernible in the energy of the narrative drive, the high-spiritedness of the rhythm, rhymes, and images, and in a number of passages. I will isolate only a few. First of all, despite seven verses that portray the failure of the French Revolution and the horror of the Napoleonic wars, Byron refers to 1820 as "the first year of freedom's second dawn" (57), and nothing in the poem or in what we know of Byron's interest and involvement in the insurgencies in southern Europe suggest that there is any irony in that phrase. In fact, the idea of a *second* dawn protects against irony; for the struggle for freedom is not the result of heroic aspiration or awakened vision, as it is in Wordsworth's "Bliss was it in that dawn to be alive," but the function of a diurnal natural force. If the visionary poet yearns for release from nature into imagination, Byron seeks refuge from vision in the old dependency of night and day.

Second, there is in verse I the mock-epic description of the angels at their cosmic maintenance project. It begins in a parody of the music of the spheres, then alludes to the deist's watchmaker's universe, and ends in what seems certainly a variation on Milton's epic simile that depicts a night-foundered seaman who anchors his skiff in the sea-beast, Leviathan, misdeeming it "some island."

> The Angels all were singing out of tune,
> And hoarse with having little else to do,
> Excepting to wind up the sun and moon,
> Or curb a runaway young star or two,
> Or wild colt of a comet, which too soon
> Broke out of bounds o'er the ethereal blue,
> Splitting some planet with its playful tail
> As boats are sometimes by a wanton whale.

> (9–16)

The immense, entropic universe evoked by this stanza and by details in stanzas LII, LV, LVI, and XXIV is not the best of all possible worlds of the *Essay on Man*, nor the fallen but providentially sustained universe of *Paradise Lost*, nor the universe pervaded by spirit of *Tintern Abbey* or *Mont Blanc*. But despite its disorderliness and its indifference to man, its energy and vitality appeal to, and even rouse, a responsive human energy. Energy seems in and of itself a good, and despite the fact that the angels are insufficiently angelic in their power to control their cosmic organism, their acceptance of the task is attractive and a model for disabused human engagement. It is a model that offers no sense of the final effectiveness of ameliorative action, but it suggests that the cosmos would be in considerably worse shape without the effort. In the first canto of *Don Juan* (stanzas CXXIX–CXXXII), Byron had suggested that ameliorative action and the recalcitrance of the human condition to any amelioration hold each other in perpetual standoff: "One makes new noses, one a guillotine, . . . the small pox is gone out of late; / Perhaps it may be followed by the great." The *Vision of Judgment* does not deny that assessment; in fact, "Heaven's" overturning of righteous human action confirms it, but it entices one to side with action nonetheless.

John Wilkes—or Jack Wilkes, as Byron terms him—is likewise a testimony to resilience and engagement. Southey had tried to make Wilkes appear sinister by refraining from mentioning his name, identifying him only by alluding to his slant eye, so Byron uses that same physical feature to suggest a benign idiosyncrasy that is connatural with his irrepressible energy and his capacity to withstand tyranny. He is "a merry, cock-eyed, curious looking Sprite" (521) who is "Dressed in a fashion now forgotten quite" (523). He assumes the occasion is a demand for an election and offers himself still "a candidate with an unturned coat" (535). He is, of course, the center of value of the poem because he did not wait for death to level king and common, because he refuses "to rip up old stories" (559), and because, against all odds, he beat George III "hollow at the last, / With all his Lords and Commons" (557–58). That Wilkes did in point of historical fact win his seat in Parliament supports Byron's imaginative re-creation of his efficacious humanity.

It is to Wilkes that Byron grants the line that condenses the moral and intellectual thrust of the poem: "For me, I have forgiven, / And vote his habeas corpus into heaven" (567–68). George III is allowed to slip into heaven, not, as Peter J. Manning has argued, because there is behind the scenes the figure of the Omnipotent Father who tolerates George's entry into heaven,[18] but because Jack Wilkes, Byron's representative of the humanly possible human, imagines something better than the king's consignment to the "immortal fry / Of almost everybody born to die" (119–20). Wilkes's swerve from the myths of his culture is Byron's as well, and his triumph here is not only over Southey, who, as Byron put it, was "a good Christian and vindictive" (Preface) but also over whatever vestigial power Christian visions of judgment had for Byron himself. The psalm that George rehearses in preparation for eternity is the One-hundredth. That psalm extols the mercy of the Lord, which is "everlasting." In *The Vision of Judgment*, Byron knows, with Blake, that mercy, or any other virtue that makes human life possible, has a human face; and for Byron that face might be a fit subject for Caravaggio, cockeyed and curious looking, flawed, unheroic, but the best there is to be had. Untrammeled by either the hope of "heaven" or the despair of "hell" (Wilkes and his peers make their abode in neither realm but are simply at large in eternity), a mere mortal may be capable of the local and temporal victories that the poem celebrates.

Notes

1. Leslie Marchand, *Byron's Poetry* (London: John Murray, 1965), p. 235; Andrew Rutherford, *Byron: A Critical Study* (Stanford, Cal.: Stanford University Press, 1961), p. 220; Robert F. Gleckner, *Byron and The Ruins of Paradise* (Baltimore: Johns Hopkins University Press, 1967), p. xi.

2. Rutherford, pp. 220–22.

3. "George Gordon, Lord Byron" in *Major British Writers*, ed. Walter J. Bate, et al., (New York: Harcourt, Brace & World, 1954, 1959), pp. 158–59.

4. See, for instance, Daniel P. Watkins, "Politics and Religion in Byron's *Heaven and Earth*," *Byron Journal* (No. 11, 1983), pp. 30–39; Rutherford, "Byron: A Pilgrim's

Progress," *Byron Journal* (No. 2, 1974), p. 8; Jurgen Klein, "Byron's Idea of Democracy: An Investigation into the Relationship between Literature and Politics" in *Byron: Poetry and Politics*, ed. John D. Jump (Salzburg: Institut Für Anglistik und Amerikanistik Universität Salzburg, 1981). p. 58.

5. See, for instance, Meyer Abrams, "English Romanticism: The Spirit of the Age" in *Romanticism and Consciousness*, ed., Harold Bloom, (New York: Norton, 1970). Abrams asserts that Romantic visionary poetry fuses "history, politics, philosophy, and religion into one grand design, by asserting Providence—or some form of natural teleology—to operate in the seeming chaos so as to effect from present evil a greater good" (p. 103).

6. I have relied throughout on the introductory materials and helpful notes provided by P. T. Eden in his edition and translation of the *Apocolocyntosis* (Cambridge: Cambridge University Press, 1984).

7. Eden, commentary to *Apocolocyntosis* 13.3, p. 138.

8. Eden takes care to establish this point in the commentary to *Apocolocyntosis* 3.4, p. 74.

9. Rutherford, p. 231.

10. Gleckner, p. 329.

11. The appropriateness of Byron's comparison of his technique to Caravaggio's (mentioned in a letter to Hobhouse, 12 October 1821) has been discussed by Frances M. Doherty, *Byron* (London: Evans Brothers, 1968), p. 143. Doherty cites Bernard Berenson's description of canvases attributed to Caravaggio that presented anachronized and vulgarized figures, lewd and obese, posing as Christ and his disciples. Byron's characterizations are not necessarily vulgar or blasphemous, but they are, like those of Caravaggio, decidedly demythologizing.

12. F. R. Leavis, "Byron's Satire," in *Byron: A Collection of Critical Essays*, ed. Paul West (Englewood Cliffs, N.J.: Prentice Hall, 1963), p. 86; Rutherford, pp. 228–29; M. K. Joseph, *Byron the Poet* (London: Victor Gollancz, 1966), p. 139.

13. Letter to Moore, 10 March 1817, in *Byron's Letters and Journals*, ed. Leslie Marchand (Cambridge, Mass.: Harvard University Press, 1976) V: 185–86.

14. I follow Ann Barton in thinking this to be the significance of Blake's dedication of his last work, *The Ghost of Abel*, to "Lord Byron in the Wilderness." See Barton on the significance of the epigraph to that poem in *Byron and the Mythology of Fact*, Nottingham Byron Lectures (Nottingham: University of Nottingham, 1968), pp. 3–4; Francis Jeffrey's comments are to be found in "Lord Byron's Tragedies," *Edinburgh Review* (February 1822), pp. 288–89; Shelley's most succinct criticism of Byron is, I believe, to be inferred from the discussion of Count Madallo in the headnote to *Julian and Madallo*.

15. Gleckner, throughout; but see especially pp. xvi, xviii–xxi, 70; John W. Ehrstine, *The Metaphysics of Byron* (The Hague: Mouton Press, 1976), especially pp. 2–6; George Ridenour, *The Style of Don Juan* (New Haven, Conn.: Yale University Press, 1960), p. 45.

16. The phrase is from Shelley's sonnet "Political Greatness."

17. Cooke discusses Byron's "counter-heroism" as a blend of stoicism and humanism that eschews both heroic and antiheroic definitions of the human in *The Blind Man Traces the Circle* (Princeton, N.J.: Princeton University Press, 1969) pp. 181 ff.

18. *Byron and His Fictions* (Detroit: Wayne State University Press, 1978) p. 16.

Beatrice Cenci
and the Tragic Myth
of History

Stephen C. Behrendt

History and myth converge in Shelley's deeply political tragedy *The Cenci*, whose compelling protagonist, Beatrice Cenci, dramatically embodies that crisis which occurs in human affairs when an intolerable situation of perceived injustice and oppression appears to offer no viable legitimized options for action. Voicing the instinctive desire for relief, the individual trapped in such a dilemma naturally responds, as Beatrice does, that "something must be done" (III, i, 86), and *The Cenci* records the nature and consequences of Beatrice's decision about just what is to be done. *The Cenci* is a play about revolution, and about the insidious combination of circumstances that engender it. Shelley's tragedy anatomizes a world ripe for the revolution that necessarily occurs, portraying the "sad reality"[1] of a moral, social, and political universe in which the ethical foundations of human institutions are undermined at their most primary level: that of the family unit itself. A familiar metaphor for political relations,[2] the family and its relationships supplied Shelley with a mythic paradigm grounded in a human reality that cuts across dis-

214

tinctions of audience and faction. Particularly in light of Shelley's practice in previous works of employing allegorical female figures to articulate his political philosophy, the chaotic state of affairs in the Cenci family and the role Beatrice plays therein bore implicit political relevance for the volatile England of 1819.

The course of action Beatrice pursues must be assessed against the backdrop of her incestuous father's unrelenting sadism and the grinding system of institutionalized patriarchal domination in which even the protagonist's surpassing virtue and innocence are insufficient to prevent her being, as Shelley declares in the play's Preface, "violently thwarted from her nature by the necessity of circumstance and opinion" (PP, 238). The audience cannot avoid being drawn into Beatrice's crisis: the power of both the circumstances and the action make that participation as irresistible as the compulsion to pass judgment. Shelley aptly assesses the phenomenon: "It is in the restless and anatomizing casuistry with which men seek the justification of Beatrice, yet feel that she has done what needs justification; it is in the superstitious horror with which they contemplate alike her wrongs and their revenge; that the dramatic character of what she did and suffered, consists" (PP, 240). Torn by our divided allegiance to the principles of humanity that dictate our sympathy with Beatrice and to the ethical discernment that requires our disapproval of her complicity in acts of murder and concealment, we are pressed inexorably toward Shelley's conclusion that the entire system that has placed Beatrice in her dilemma is both culpable and morally insupportable, a system of terrifying perversion in which, as Stuart Curran has written, "to act is to commit evil."[3]

The revolution in The Cenci fails because it is the wrong revolution. Eliminating a tyrant by enlisting his own methods against him merely perpetuates the violent system of revenge and retribution. The Cenci stands as Shelley's argument by analogy about the English nation's need to learn by studying the tragedies of fallen nobility of mind and spirit that the past furnishes, and to choose for itself the only acceptable alternative to the downward spiral of violence: not revolution, but reform of the entire inhering structure of society, its assumptions, and its institutions. To this end Shelley envisioned a stage production that would explore and exploit the social nature of the theater, and particularly the ritualistic function of historical drama as re-presentation of history (or the semblance of history). To the historian's task of recounting the past, however, The Cenci adds the poet's concern with influencing the present and shaping the future.

Shelley fully intended to capitalize in his play upon the same sort of "deep and breathless interest" in Beatrice Cenci that surrounded the Cenci legend as he encountered it in Rome, and that unfailingly combined "a romantic pity for the wrongs, and a passionate exculpation of the horrible deed to which they urged her" (PP, 239). By 1819 he apparently had encountered the story both in popular discussion and in print: in a manuscript fragment and in Vincenzo Pieracci's 1816 play, Beatrice Cenci.[4] The tale struck Shelley as exceptionally fitted to drama because of "its capacity of awakening and sustaining the sympathy of men" (PP, 239). "Sympathy"—the powerful principle of "the communication of passions" that arises not from reason but from human feelings— the skeptical tradition generally and Hume in particular had designated as "the chief source of moral distinctions,"[5] and the entire issue of relative success or failure, right or wrong, that this play examines is inextricably linked with Shelley's cognizance of the conflicting and often contradictory roles played by reason and passion (or "sympathy") in demonstrating the ultimate unattainability of absolute truth. The intellectual tradition of skepticism Shelley had absorbed especially from Hume and Drummond embraced the conviction that all hypotheses require continual testing, and this conviction governs the spectacle with which Shelley confronts his audience.

Shelley's play forces his audience to participate actively in Beatrice's moral and psychological testing and to discover in both her ordeal and their own a prototypical crisis of faith both in humanity generally and, more important, in the individual and autonomous moral and social self. In this interactive process, the audience is compelled to "go out of" its own nature (as discrete individuals and as collective social community) and, as Hume explains in A Treatise of Human Nature and Shelley recommends in A Defence of Poetry, to identify not only with "the beautiful which exists in thought, action, or person not our own" but also with "the pains and pleasures of [the] species" (PP, 487–88). The label Shelley attaches to this "great secret of morals" is Love, and his tragedy examines in painful fashion the failure, amid circumstances of overwhelming brutality and degradation, of a virtuous and innocent individual to sustain the love—both for others and, more important, for herself— that might bear her up were not all hope and support seemingly denied her.

Why Shelley elected to convey his message through the vehicle of drama is clear from another remark in the *Defence:*

> The connexion of poetry and social good is more observable in the drama than in whatever other form [of poetry]: and it is indisputable that the highest perfection of human society has ever corresponded with the highest dramatic excellence; and that the corruption or the extinction of the drama in a nation where it has once flourished, is a mark of a corruption of manners, and an extinction of the energies which sustain the soul of social life (*PP,* 492).

Shelley's view of the theater presupposes an audience willing to substitute for its customary passive spectatorship an active participation in a dynamic intellectual interaction with the playwright, a relationship mediated through the performance of the text both on-stage and in the consciousness of the audience. As Michael Henry Scrivener observes, Shelley envisioned *The Cenci* as "a catalyst for precipitating another kind of drama in the spectator," for whom the experience would yield important moral benefits.[6] Indeed, "truth must be understood in relation to one's social investments," as Jerome McGann concludes from the dialogic nature of Plato's works.[7] Though Shelley's *Defence* links the rise and decline of societies to the relative vigor of the arts throughout history, his dissatisfaction with the contemporary English stage (and its preference for spectacle and sentiment over substance) mirrors his increasing disaffection with English audiences generally. Moreover, Shelley's view of classical tragedy interestingly anticipates the later twentieth-century view of the culture that produced the great Greek tragedies, a view that discovers there not so much serenity, proportion, and rationality as "turbulence, dissonance, and an ambivalent morality that plagues action and passion."[8] Shelley believed that tragedy might function to "help us determine who we are and what we are doing to ourselves and others, while making it clear that such questions are never fully answered or finally resolved."[9] He extended this conviction also to historical drama, and particularly to that species of historical drama which bears visible implications for contemporary events.[10]

The *Defence* was composed in February and March of 1821, after Shelley had in 1820 secured publication of *The Cenci* when it had become clear to him that his tragedy would not be staged at Covent Garden as he had intended. Hence his comments on the historical decline of national theaters are not free of personal grievances. Nevertheless, they underscore Shelley's convictions about drama's implicit universal moral significance. Coming as it did after he had

217

completed the significant restructuring of myth evident in the first three acts of *Prometheus Unbound* (which was *not* intended for any temporal stage), *The Cenci* traces—as had both the lyrical drama and Shelley's longest poem, *Laon and Cythna* (*The Revolt of Islam*)—the stages of a revolution. Like *Laon and Cythna*—and unlike *Prometheus Unbound*—*The Cenci* is the record of a failed revolution, a rebellion that proceeds to its catastrophe from that most traditional, mythic spring: the conflict between generation and generation, between parent and child. That Shelley chose for his subject the history of the Cenci family, in which the revolutionary activity centers in a female protagonist, is not without significance for Shelley, either as liberal reformer or as husband of Mary Wollstonecraft's daughter. Beatrice's dilemma parallels those both of women during Shelley's era (whose advocate Mary Wollstonecraft had sought to be) and of the British populace generally (on whose behalf and for whose edification Shelley had for nearly a decade endeavored to speak in support of reform). Hence her situation and the choices she makes are invested with a significance far greater than the merely historical.

Beatrice Cenci is more than the protagonist in a protohistorical play: she is the central figure in a moral and ethical parable that functions on several interrelated levels. At the level of surface narrative, her role is historical and dramatic. At the level of moral and ethical significance, it is essentially allegorical. And at the level most directly relevant to Shelley's private thoughts and public intentions as he completed his play in 1819, her role is mythic, although Shelley criticism has routinely overlooked the explicit emphasis the poet places in the play's Preface upon the Cenci story's archetypal pattern of myth.[11] Shelley weaves these roles into the fabric of a tragedy that elevates history to the level and status of myth, creating a moral and political exemplum designed to reveal dramatically the inevitable destruction from within of even the noblest and best-intentioned society—epitomized in its most paradigmatically virtuous representative—when that society permits, and participates in, the subversion of the morally and imaginatively informed integrative choice to love, and revels instead in the pernicious proclivity toward brutality, domination, revenge, and retribution. Mary Shelley had only just recently explored the effects of this misdirection of impulse in *Frankenstein;* but to present in its most powerful and devastating fashion the terrible tragedy of such a misdirection of all that is noble and divine in humanity requires not a grotesque creature but rather a protagonist of surpassing

218

beauty and greatness, of tragic grandeur. Beatrice Cenci would seem to be just such a figure.

Beatrice clearly possesses external grandeur, both of social status (the Cenci are a powerful aristocratic family) and of moral character (she is, both by report and by initial behavior, extraordinarily virtuous). Indeed, in the play's Preface Shelley twice expands upon her moral and physical beauty, remarking at last that both in the historical account of her character and in her portrait (attributed at the time to Guido Reni) at Rome, "there is a simplicity and dignity which, united with her exquisite loveliness and deep sorrow, are inexpressibly pathetic. Beatrice Cenci appears to have been one of those rare persons in whom energy and gentleness dwell together without destroying one another: her nature was simple and profound" (PP, 242). Moreover, she is intellectually acute, capable of drawing minute and sophisticated moral and intellectual distinctions.

Shelley envisioned Beatrice being acted at Covent Garden by the lovely and dynamic Eliza O'Neill (1791–1872), the Irish actress who from her first appearance there in 1814 in the role of Juliet had increasingly been acclaimed the worthy successor to the great Sarah Siddons. Shelley wrote to Thomas Love Peacock that the part was so "precisely fitted" for her that "it might even seem to have been written for her," and that to see Miss O'Neill play the role would "tear my nerves to pieces." Clearly it was vital that Beatrice be represented by the actress who could most compellingly convey her many excellences on the stage.[12]

Beatrice's experience as Shelley presents it in his play bears out Aristotle's stipulation that the cause of the hero's reversal "must lie not in any depravity but in some great error on his part," some "error of judgment."[13] Aristotle's formulation precisely defines Beatrice, whose "great error" lies—as Blake might have put it—in becoming what she beholds. Her reversal stems from a terrible error of judgment that occurs in a situation of enormous stress; it engenders an internal depravity that comes to mirror with increasingly chilling irony the external depravity that prompted it. Shelley placed at the center of his tragedy the greatest of taboos, incest, an act so morally and socially repugnant that his audience could not but react with revulsion toward Francesco Cenci. In Act III Beatrice is unable to find a word for his crime:

> there is none to tell
> My misery: if another ever knew
> Aught like to it, she died as I will die,

And left it, as I must, without a name

. . . .

If I could find a word that might make known
The crime of my destroyer . . .

(III, i, 114–17, 154–55)

Moreover, Shelley refers in the Preface to Cenci's "capital crimes of the most enormous and unspeakable kind." The unspeakable, unnamable quality of Cenci's offense suggests, in fact, not just incest but also sodomy.

Echoing the Pauline doctrine passed down by the church fathers, William Blackstone, in his *Commentaries on the Laws of England*, had referred to sodomy as a subject "the very mention of which is a disgrace to human nature" and "a crime not fit to be named," and had called it a "capital" crime whose prohibition he deemed "an universal, not merely a provincial, precept."[14] Similar references to sodomy as unspeakable and unnameable, which abound in the later eighteenth and earlier nineteenth centuries, must have been familiar to Shelley and his audiences, who reasonably could have been expected to understand the extent to which Cenci's crime is in fact identified by the very fact that no one will name it. The implication is historically accurate in any event, for the account of the Cenci story that Shelley had studied indicates that Francesco Cenci had three times escaped the death sentence for sodomy by bribing the pope, Clement VIII.[15]

Shelley intensifies the agony of Beatrice's position, making it clear that Cenci's is a brutally calculated plan of domination and degradation that is intended to include still greater horrors at the Castle of Petrella. With acute psychological insight, however, Shelley incorporates into Beatrice's thinking an element of misplaced blame that has frequently been the lot of victims of sexual abuse. He locates the germ of her "error of judgment" in the despairing attitude of "polluted victimization"[16] she assumes in Act III after the assault, an attitude that recalls that of Coleridge's Christabel, who awakes after her nocturnal encounter with Geraldine convinced that "Sure I have sinn'd!"[17] Persuaded that the vicious and demeaning physical and psychological outrages to which she has been subjected have necessarily compromised and incriminated her in both physical and moral / ethical terms, she chooses to retaliate in precisely the terms in which she has been wronged: by a physical attack upon the body of her oppressor. In plotting her father's murder and in employing assassins to execute the deed, she adopts in herself the behavior she has condemned in others. In this she exceeds even Count Cenci: though the play's first conversation makes it clear that Cenci arranges for the murder of his rivals, Scene iii reveals that he is apparently not physically implicated in the deaths of his sons Rocco and Cristofano—something of a technicality since he has prayed earnestly for their deaths. Beatrice escalates the scale of actual violence, though; though her father's assaults upon morality generally are despicable, Beatrice's complicity in murder is ethically no less despicable despite the appeal presented to the audience's sympathies by the extenuating circumstances that surround her actions.

This matter of calculated *intention* is in fact central to the moral errors to which father and daughter alike fall victim, for in discussing the nature of the passions, Hume had written that "by the intention we judge of the actions, and according as that is good or bad, they become causes of love or hatred. . . . An intention is requisite to excite either love or hatred."[18] This passage enables us better to appreciate the error implied in the final authority to which Beatrice turns in determining "what is to be done":

> I have prayed
> To God, and I have talked with my own heart,
> And have unravelled my entangled will,
> And have at length determined what is right.
>
> (III, i, 218–21)

Once Beatrice internalizes her crisis and refers it to her own will for adjudication and counsel, the catastrophe becomes inevitable. So too does the return of mental calm and apparent rationality, which transformation itself reflects Hume's observation that "when a passion has once become a settled principle of action, and is the predominant inclination of the soul, it commonly produces no longer any sensible agitation."[19] Hence, in the final act, she is able coolly and apparently without compunction to sacrifice the soul of one of the assassins, whom she essentially consigns to hell by sending him to his death with a grave lie upon his soul.

In making her own will the final arbiter, Beatrice in effect appoints herself judge, jury, and executioner, assuming the ego-inflating posture of domination associated with the retributive God of wrath of the Old Testament, of Jehovah the destroyer, who is the figurehead for the whole patriarchal establishment against which Beatrice has been forced to struggle.[20] In doing so she rejects the paradigm of self-sacrifice and forgiveness of sins represented in the passion and death of the God of love of the New Testament, of the

221

Jesus Christ who gives his life as exemplum of fidelity to principles of nonviolent response to—and forgiveness of—even the most unmerited wrongs. More immediately, Beatrice reverses the response of Shelley's Prometheus, whose repudiation of revenge the poet had only just finished celebrating in the first three acts of *Prometheus Unbound*. Indeed, the variations Beatrice sounds on her "I have borne much" theme (I, iii, 111) are variations as well upon Prometheus's anguished cry of "I endure" early in the lyrical drama (I, 24).

In the Preface Shelley clarifies the issue, drawing at least a tentative distinction between apparent disgrace and real dishonor: "Undoubtedly, no person can be truly dishonoured by the act of another; and the fit return to make to the most enormous injuries is kindness and forbearance, and a resolution to convert the injurer from his dark passions by peace and love. Revenge, retaliation, atonement, are pernicious mistakes." Beatrice's error lies in her deliberate violation of the specific injunction of Romans 12.19: "Dearly beloved, avenge not yourselves, but rather give place unto wrath: for it is written, Vengeance is mine: I will repay, saith the Lord." Hers is the tragic flaw of hubris, the deadly sin of pride that impels her to arrogate to herself a function that is presumably God's alone. That she is a Roman Catholic in a Catholic country, and, moreover, that her father is barely dead by her devices when the emissaries of the pope arrive to arrest him in the name of the church (and hence of God) adds the crushing weight of cosmic irony to the gravity of her crime. Guilty not just of parricide, she sins doubly in blaspheming as well.

As the play progresses, it becomes increasingly clear that we must distinguish in Beatrice two significantly different voices. One is that of the virtuous woman we see initially and who is the unarguably innocent victim of both her father's abuse and the irresponsible earthly and heavenly patriarchy that tolerates it. The other is that of the skillful rhetorician whose increasingly profound self-delusion ironically increases in direct proportion to the fervency of her exercises in self-justification. Were the issues of right and wrong, of innocence and guilt, as clear-cut as these formulations imply, though, *The Cenci* would be little more than a formulaic morality play. But Shelley shrewdly enlists theater's immense emotional potential to complicate the audience's task by arranging matters so that the audience instinctively sides with Beatrice. It is no surprise that Shelley longed to have Count Cenci acted by the greatest of all Romantic actors, Edmund Kean, even though he admitted the impossibility of any such arrangement.[21] Although he disliked Kean's violent acting style enough to walk out of a performance of *Hamlet* in 1814,[22] Shelley fully appreciated its powerful impact in live performance. The heightened pity and terror that an actor like Kean might have elicited from a theater audience would necessarily have reinforced their bond of sympathy with Beatrice and made them party to the hubris that in these desperate circumstances seems to sanction actions that would ordinarily be condemned. Rendered emotionally defenseless by the horror of what Beatrice suffers, the audience is naturally primed to accept and endorse vengeance upon her oppressor. Shelley's strategy is to force the audience to recognize how easy and naturally they—like Beatrice—slip into sympathetic complicity in activities of which they normally would rationally disapprove. This unsettling recognition is central to the process of reeducation that Shelley has in mind: the audience must learn to resist and repudiate the longing for vengeance upon an oppressor that is itself the origin of Beatrice's fall. More important, it must reject the entire system of human behavior that makes violence and retribution an attractive and even desirable option. Beatrice's passion for what Curran calls an "ethical absolute," however noble or "right," is as futile as her father's pursuit of the sort of epitome of depravity we encounter also in Flannery O'Connor's violent Misfit, who declares that there is "no pleasure but meanness."[23]

Shelley expects his audience to make difficult and momentous moral and intellectual choices in dealing with *The Cenci*, however distasteful those choices may prove to be. This expectation underscores the rhetorical nature of the play and its grounding in the tradition of the skeptical debate, in which truth is never absolute but only relative. Shelley confronts his audience with that most difficult of dilemmas: the need to reconcile intensely subjective emotional responses with objective reasoning and discrimination in coming to discoveries that are at once relevant to the self-knowledge both of each individual member of the audience and of that audience taken as a political body, as a community in which the potential for action is great. The process of recognition at which Shelley aims must arise, furthermore, not from any overt moralizing by the author through his characters but rather from the plot itself. In this matter Shelley again follows Aristotle, who asserts that "it is the action in it, i.e., its Fable or Plot, that is the end and purpose of tragedy"; for "the most powerful elements of attraction in Tragedy, the Peripeties and Discoveries, are parts of the Plot" (*Poetics*, 1461). The relevance of this dictum to political fiction is underscored by Irving Howe's observation that because ideology is abstract it is not easily accommodated in the political novel, whose preoccupation is necessarily with the quality of concrete experience: "It is precisely from this conflict that the political novel gains its interest and takes on the aura of high drama. . . . [The political novelist's] task is always to show the relation between theory and experience, between the ideology that has been preconceived and the tangle of feelings and relationships he is trying to present."[24] Shelley declares similarly that "there must . . . be nothing attempted to make the exhibition subservient to what is vulgarly termed a moral purpose" (*PP*, 240). Hence although Shelley considers Beatrice's desire for revenge "morally condemnable," he tries to show her "as she was,"[25] leaving it for the audience to judge her from her actions.

Aristotle distinguishes between poetry and history on the grounds that poetry's statements "are of the nature rather of universals, whereas those of history are singulars" (*Poetics*, 1464). Hence the author of a tragedy is advised to "first simplify [his story] and reduce [it] to a universal form, before proceeding to lengthen it out by the insertion of episodes" (*Poetics*, 1472). Shelley's Preface indicates that he has pursued just this strategy with the Cenci story, for "anything like a dry exhibition of it on the stage would be insupportable. The person who would treat such a subject must increase the ideal, and diminish the actual horror of the events, so that the pleasure which arises from the poetry which exists in these tempestuous sufferings and crimes may mitigate the pain of the contemplation of the moral deformity from which they spring" (*PP*, 239–40). In short, history must be made into poetry, or, to paraphrase Aristotle, "the thing that *has* happened" must become also the "kind of thing that *might* happen" (*Poetics*, 1463; italics added). In this fashion a story of such universal dimensions as that of Beatrice Cenci becomes more than just poetry, however: it assumes the nature and significance of myth. Moreover, it participates in that element of prophecy which Shelley associated throughout his career with patriotism and the desire to play a part in the renovation of humanity and human institutions.

By the summer of 1819, Shelley had already published *Laon and Cythna*, and had (he thought) completed *Prometheus Unbound* in three acts. The former develops a personal mythology, and the latter restructures familiar mythological materials. The viability of myth and mythic consciousness depends upon an audience's participation in both the formulation and the endowing with significance of that myth or mythic consciousness. In *The Cenci* Shelley labors in perhaps the most artistically "cramped" vehicle of all, creating a work tied at least in part to both the shape and the details of history, a work that, because it has no narrator, assigns its audience greater responsibility for both the "telling" and the interpretation of the story. As Joseph Wittreich observes, however, though prophets (like epic poets) may recount history, they do so "less to record it than to bring it to an apotheosis."[26] Like the prophet Wittreich describes, Shelley explores the past in his works in an attempt to liberate humanity from that past, and from the cycle of recurrent error of which history furnishes sad record.[27]

Shelley's choice of historical subject matter is important here. To choose the subject of the Cenci family is to accept that "this happened," that the actual "shape" of the events cannot be profoundly altered (however much the *details* might be altered, embellished, or suppressed) but can only be observed and assessed. Shelley wanted his audience to be no less knowledgeable about the story and its catastrophic culmination than were the spectators at, say, *Oedipus Rex*. Indeed, he even suggested publicizing details of the play's plot in advance, partly to arouse interest, of course, but also to replace the customary concern with *what* happens with the greater one of *how* it happens.[28] In the ritualistic playing-out of this familiar story, Shelley wants his audience to discern the relevance *as analogy* of the Cenci story, to get beyond the individual tragedy of the historical Beatrice Cenci and to perceive the inherent horror of the superstructure of custom and belief that leads Beatrice to choose such a terrible course of action in the first place. Shelley believes with Blake that error must be given form and recognized before it can be repudiated, and *The Cenci* is properly regarded as a complex and unrelenting embodiment of a misguided and oppressive patriarchal system and the self-consuming monsters it spawns. Such a fallen state of affairs produces no-win situations in which even the virtuous inevitably become scorpions (to use Shelley's image) stinging themselves to death.

It is upon this point of prophetic significance that Shelley's own position in 1819 bears greatest relevance to the mythic dimensions of Beatrice Cenci and of Shelley's play as a whole. By 1819 Shelley had settled in Italy, a self-exiled liberal reformer whose previous poetry and prose everywhere counsels against the desire for revenge of real or imagined wrongs in human affairs. Like his father-in-law, William Godwin, Shelley feared the bloody consequences of any repetition in England of the sort of radical alteration of the social and political structure that had occurred with the French Revolution. Conditions were indeed ripe for revolution in England during the latter years of the Regency: crop failures and political repression had aggravated the already acute socioeconomic dilemma arising from a postwar economic recession, the mechanization of the trades and industries, and the return to the work force of war-weary soldiers who found no jobs to which to return. In August of 1819 came the bloody action against the crowd of reformers at Manchester, to which Shelley responded from Italy with the series of impassioned poems that proved too hot for the cautious Leigh Hunt to publish in the *Examiner.*

The *Examiner* in fact sheds interesting light upon the ground occupied by Shelley and other liberal reformers in 1819, as they contemplated the approaching crisis in English domestic affairs. In the first issue of the *Examiner* for 1819, Hunt had written: "A spirit is abroad, stronger than kings, or armies, or all the most prominent shapes of prejudice and force. . . . This spirit is knowledge[:] that gigantic sense of the general good which has awaked for the first time in the known history of the world. . . . All classes feel that something, as the phrase is, must be done."[29] By late July, though, by which time Shelley had completed *The Cenci,* Hunt's tone had darkened considerably: "It is a fact, notorious and *undeniable,* that the present possessors of power are in the daily habit of violating the constitution; and it is a fact, undeniable and *awful,* that the suffering classes know it, and feel it, and will not let the consideration go out of their hearts."[30] The volatility of the situation in England was a recurrent theme in the *Examiner* in 1819, as well as in those other liberal journals with which Shelley had asked Hunt to keep him supplied. It is therefore not unreasonable to see in *The Cenci* an attempt to enlist the vehicle of live theatrical performance in the poet's attempt to play an active part—even from the distance his departure had imposed—in the stabilization, the reformation, and the reorientation of English society and values. It was as live theater, Shelley obviously believed, that *The Cenci* held the greatest potential for educating the public and providing the necessary brake to the speeding vehicle of public unrest that increasingly threatened to become a runaway as had happened in France thirty years earlier.

Beatrice Cenci's "great error," then, consists in her deliberate subscription to the impulse toward vengeance and retribution for injuries inflicted by a powerful and vicious oppressor. This is not to say that she has failed to give more acceptable alternative measures their fair chance to work on her behalf. As she declares publicly to the guests at Cenci's banquet in Act I,

> I have borne much, and kissed the sacred hand
> Which crushed us to the earth, and thought its stroke
> Was perhaps some paternal chastisement!
> Have excused much, doubted; and when no doubt
> Remained, have sought by patience, love and tears
> To soften him, and when this could not be
> I have knelt down through the long sleepless nights
> And lifted up to God, the father of all,
> Passionate prayers.
>
> (I, iii, 111–19)

Later in the play the duplicitous Orsino tempts Beatrice at her moment of crisis with a series of brutal questions calculated further to undermine her instinctive virtue:

> Should the offender live?
> Triumph in his misdeed? and make, by use,
> His crime, whate'er it is, dreadful no doubt,
> Thine element; until thou mayest become
> Utterly lost; subdued even to the hue
> Of that which thou permittest?
>
> (III, i, 172–77)

In imputing blame for Cenci's survival to an act of omission and weakness on her part, Orsino plays upon precisely that self-doubt which has led Beatrice to consider herself implicated in, and corrupted by, her father's vice. Shelley more than once raises in his poetry and prose the suggestion that, in failing to resist it, the oppressed participate in their own oppression. Shelley paints himself into something of the same corner into which he paints Beatrice, however, for the line separating principled passive resistance from practical submission in the interest of surviving is a fine and infinitely flexible one. The shift from absolute rejection of revolutionary violence in Shelley's early works to the qualified (or, occasionally, the wholehearted) acceptance of it as a practical means to an end in later works like *Swellfoot the Tyrant*, *Hellas*, and "Ode to Liberty" indicates that, though he staunchly resisted such violence in England, he gradually and reluctantly abandoned his aversion to its employment in service to liberty elsewhere.

Orsino's temptation of Beatrice with a rhetorical vision of Cenci's triumph over the forces of good directly echoes the Furies' temptation of Prometheus with the vision of the crucified Christ in

Act I of *Prometheus Unbound*, and it is undertaken for the same purpose. Both visions are invoked to intensify the protagonists' self-doubts by misrepresenting history, and both find a significant antecedent in Satan's temptation of Jesus atop the pinnacle of the temple in *Paradise Regained*. Prometheus recognizes in the visions conjured up by the Furies Jupiter's own insidious designs: "I close my tearless eyes, but see more clear / Thy works within my woe-illumed mind" (I, 636–37). He concludes, furthermore, that his strength—indeed, his salvation—lies not in revenge but in self-sufficient endurance:

> The sights with which thou torturest gird my soul
> With new endurance, till the hour arrives
> When they shall be no types of things which are.
>
> (I, 643–45)

Beatrice Cenci responds to her temptation in exactly the opposite fashion, determining to endure no more but rather to be revenged upon her tormentor. With a mastery of terrible irony, Shelley has her declare, as we have seen, to "have at length determined *what is right*" (III, i, 221; italics added). In a world in which best options are merely the least of evils, "what is right" can exist only in relative terms. This is precisely why *The Cenci* is about "a sad reality," as Shelley's dedication to Hunt proclaims, rather than about "my own apprehensions of the beautiful and the just" (*PP*, 237).

Of course, Shelley does not mean to suggest that Beatrice (or any other victim, for that matter) is abjectly and unresistingly to accept brutality and oppression. But he agrees with Christ's counsel to Peter in the garden of Gethsemane: striking off the ear (or the life) of the offender does no good and indeed merely perpetuates an intolerable cycle of violence. What is called for is not revenge but rather a sympathetic and informed understanding of the weakness and complexity of human nature that enables the victim to appreciate that the oppressor is the ultimate, unwitting victim of his or her own cruelty. Prometheus understands this, as had Jesus on the Cross ("Father, forgive them; for they know not what they do" [Luke 23.34]). In pitying the Furies, Prometheus effectively disarms them, even as he recants his curse partly because it had constituted a momentary lapse in his ability to be "king over myself, and rule / The torturing and conflicting throngs within" and partly because he so fervently wishes "no living thing to suffer pain" (I, 492–93, 305). In short, genuine liberty and dignity can never be taken away: they can only be surrendered, rashly, blindly, irrationally.

The self-poisoning nature of the lust for vengeance is a theme that had preoccupied Shelley from the earliest stages of his career. Already in *Zastrozzi*, for instance, the beautiful Matilda plots the murder of Julia, her rival. When the scheme miscarries, Matilda murders Julia herself and brutally mutilates the corpse, exemplifying the hideous atrocities to which the lust for revenge of perceived slights can drive the individual.

More important is Shelley's *Address to the People on the Death of the Princess Charlotte* (1817). Ostensibly written on the occasion of the princess's death, the pamphlet in fact excoriates the government's conduct in entrapping and executing—on the day following the princess's death—three members of the abortive Derbyshire rebellion of 1817.[31] Shelley's pamphlet concludes with a funeral procession that appears at first to be that of the dead Princess Charlotte. But in a daring rhetorical maneuver, Shelley shifts his reference:

> A beautiful Princess is dead:—she who should have been the Queen of her beloved nation, and whose posterity should have ruled it for ever. . . . LIBERTY is dead. . . . Let us follow the corpse of British Liberty slowly and reverentially to its tomb: and if some glorious Phantom should appear, and make its throne of broken swords and sceptres and royal crowns trampled in the dust, let us say that the Spirit of Liberty has arisen from its grave and left all that was gross and mortal there, and kneel down and worship it as our Queen.[32]

Only a few months after completing *The Cenci*, Shelley included among his responses to the Peterloo Massacre *The Mask of Anarchy*, whose apparatus includes the chariot of the Phantom of Liberty prefigured in the conclusion of the *Address*. Beatrice Cenci is, in fact, the most prominent and compelling among a considerable number of politically allegorical female figures in Shelley's works, including Ianthe *(Queen Mab)* and Cythna. Like the two phantoms in particular, she is a figurehead for the oppressed, for Liberty soiled and subjugated by irresponsible patriarchal power and authority.

But unlike the Princess Charlotte (who dies naturally in childbirth), the "Princess" Liberty (dead of neglect and abuse in England), and the Phantom of Liberty (who rises triumphant, even apocalyptic, from the carnage), Beatrice Cenci is her own worst enemy, her own destroyer. Like Oedipus, she sentences herself by and to her own hand. But unlike Oedipus, she proceeds not to "justice," truth, and self-knowledge but rather to vengeance, prevarication, and self-deception. Shelley suggests that the essence of Beatrice's tragic fall—and the locus of the genuine pathos her circumstances elicit from us—is her failure to live up to her heroic *potential*. In failing to remain steadfast in the humanizing principles of love and integration, she rejects society itself in an act of tragic self-aggrandizement. The underlying mythic design here is that of the Fall. Beatrice succumbs to the temptation to commit an act—murder—that is expressly forbidden by God. In determining within her own will "what is right," she becomes in fact her own tempter, her own Satan, responding in the fashion of the oppressor, returning injury with injury.

Shelley had to force his audience to rethink their allegiance to Beatrice, finally, and to recognize—however reluctantly—the error of the choices she has made. He uses the fate of the hired assassin Marzio for this purpose. When Beatrice confronts him in Act V after he has named her to the authorities under torture, Marzio finds himself so overwhelmed that he cannot repeat his accusation. In a speech combining dramatic irony with massive self-deception, Beatrice swears a false oath as prelude to her question:

> Think
> What 'tis to blot with infamy and blood
> All that which shows like innocence, and is,
> Hear me, great God! I swear, most innocent,
> So that the world lose all discrimination
> Between the sly, fierce, wild regard of guilt,
> And that which now compels thee to reply
> To what I ask: Am I, or am I not,
> A parricide?

$$(V, ii, 149-57)^{33}$$

Through Beatrice, Shelley challenges the audience also to distinguish between appearance and reality—between what "sympathy" prompts and what rational analysis dictates—and to comprehend the actual facts of what it has witnessed, lest it too "lose all discrimination."

Moreover, Marzio's response to Beatrice's question ("Thou art not!") implicitly dooms him to an eternity in Hell, for that response is an outright lie, a lie that he never recants but bears to his death on the rack, where he holds his breath resolutely and dies of suffocation.[34] His answer, like all of his final speech, indicates the degree to which he has been seduced by Beatrice's rhetoric, even as Eve had been deceived by the Serpent. That she is subsequently implicated by her own brother and mother makes even more poignant this needless sacrifice of Marzio's eternal soul. Whether we judge his death suicide or death-by-torture, Beatrice cannot be absolved of responsibility. Though she could not have known he would take his own life (for a Catholic, yet another mortal sin), she chooses to let his torture proceed, even as, having settled upon a course of action and determined that Cenci must die, she was unswerving in her dedication to that end. Her attempt to exonerate herself at Marzio's expense is occasionally regarded as a last desperate attempt to escape that "demonstrate[s] her valor in the face of hostile destiny."[35] But however much he might wish to "save" Beatrice, Shelley cannot, bound as he is both by history and by the ethical design of his tragedy. What he wishes to demonstrate to the audience is, in fact, the tragic erosion of valor. So consistently does Beatrice misstate fact and misrepresent reality after the crisis of Act III, Scene i, that her rhetorical maneuvering increasingly reinforces her conviction that she is blameless, free of responsibility in her father's death. Shelley requires that his audience face up to the universal truism that the greatest crimes against humanity are fraught with self-delusion and self-justification.

In terms of political allegory, then, Beatrice Cenci might have stood as an important warning to the theater audience Shelley hoped most to reach. In the explosive climate of 1819, the notion of real evil attractively packaged (or disguised) as apparent good held particular relevance. The bloody lesson of the French Revolution was still fresh in the English mind and, especially for a Godwinian gradualist like Shelley, the great moral *and patriotic* imperative was to stave off in England the natural and seemingly justified thirst for violent redress of wrongs on the part of the people generally. Like Beatrice Cenci, the later Regency Englishman and Englishwoman could not but feel the painful "generation gap" that was becoming ever more apparent as the official "father-figure" (both the government in the abstract and the profligate prince regent, who substituted for his apparently mad father) tried to maintain an ever-weakening grip on power by means of oppression and intimidation. Nor could the fate of the petition for assistance and intervention that Beatrice and her family address to the pope, which the scheming Orsino deliberately withholds to further his own designs,[36] fail to suggest to some the similar fate of the floods of petitions submitted—with apparently equal lack of success—to Parliament by the advocates of reform during the Regency.

Both as metaphor and as myth, the history of the Cenci family was germane to English affairs. Like Francesco Cenci, the English royal father figure might be perceived as an irresponsible disciplinarian who had conspired in the deaths of his sons by committing them to protracted and often unpopular wars (against France and, earlier, against the American colonies). His cruelties against the "mother country" are manifest, from the destruction of her sons and daughters to the plundering of her national dowry. Finally, if we permit ourselves to regard Beatrice at least on one level as Liberty—as *An Address to the People on the Death of the Princess Charlotte* gives us reason to do—we can appreciate how a liberal reformer like Shelley could see in the England of 1819 a tale of brutality and incest not unlike that which had decimated the Cenci family. Aristotle claimed that the best dramatic situation for the tragedian is one in which "the deed of horror" is contemplated within a family unit, and in which the protagonist makes a discovery—typically of kinship—"in time to draw back" (*Poetics*, 1468–69). Beatrice has several such opportunities, but she fails to acknowledge what should be a "discovery": that, like the violence of which she is the victim, murder is an unnatural act that violates the universal "kinship" of humanity. But Shelley wants his audience to discover their own emotional *and sociopolitical* kinship with Beatrice, whose situation is in so many ways analogous to their own, and to temper their own behavior in accordance with what that discovery reveals, both about Beatrice and about their own potential for self-destruction. For like Beatrice, England stood in 1819 on the brink of committing the sort of national parricide and ethical suicide to which France had recently fallen victim. But *unlike* Beatrice Cenci—and France—the English people had not yet taken the fatal step. Therein, finally, lies the real point of Shelley's great political drama. Shelley would have his country reclaim and preserve the grandeur of its greatest heroine—Liberty—before that grandeur becomes a tragic one.

Notes

1. Dedication of *The Cenci*, in *Shelley's Poetry and Prose*, ed. Donald H. Reiman and Sharon B. Powers (New York: W. W. Norton, 1977), p. 237. Hereafter cited in the text as "*PP.*"

2. See Stephen C. Behrendt, "'This Accursed Family': Blake's *America* and the American Revolution," *Eighteenth Century: Theory and Interpretation*, 27 (Winter 1985), 30–52.

3. Stuart Curran, *Shelley's "Cenci": Scorpions Ringed with Fire* (Princeton, N.J.: Princeton Univ. Press, 1970), p. 132.

4. See George Yost, *Pieracci and Shelley: An Italian "Ur-Cenci"* (Potomac, Md.: Scripta Humanistica, 1986). Yost's introductory essay offers compelling evidence for

regarding Pieracci's play, published in Italian in Florence, as an important source for *The Cenci*.

5. C. E. Pulos, *The Deep Truth: A Study of Shelley's Scepticism* (Lincoln: Univ. of Nebraska Press, 1954), p. 23. See David Hume, *A Treatise of Human Nature*, ed. L. A. Selby-Bigge (Oxford: Clarendon Press, 1888), p. 398.

6. Michael Henry Scrivener, *Radical Shelley: The Philosophical Anarchism and Utopian Thought of Percy Bysshe Shelley* (Princeton, N.J.: Princeton Univ. Press, 1982), p. 188.

7. Jerome J. McGann, *Social Values and Poetic Acts: The Historical Judgment of Literary Work* (Cambridge, Mass.: Harvard Univ. Press, 1988), p. 29.

8. J. Peter Euben, "Preface," *Greek Tragedy and Political Theory*, ed. J. Peter Euben (Berkeley: Univ. of California Press, 1986), p. x.

9. Euben, p. xii.

10. It is worth noting Shelley's abortive efforts in 1822 to produce another stageable, *salable* historical drama, *Charles the First*, whose subject was also directly relevant to the political and social climate of Shelley's time.

11. Curran, pp. 32–33.

12. *The Letters of Percy Bysshe Shelley*, ed. Frederick L. Jones (2 vols.; Oxford: Clarendon Press, 1964), II, 102; ca. 20 July 1819. Ironically, she had only a week earlier, on 13 July 1819, made her final appearance before retiring from the stage to marry William Becher.

13. *Poetics*, in *The Basic Works of Aristotle*, ed. Richard McKeon (New York: Random House, 1941), p. 1467; subsequent references are to this edition.

14. William Blackstone, *Commentaries on the Laws of England*, (4 vols.; Oxford: Clarendon Press, 1769), IV, 215–16. See also Louis Crompton, *Byron and Greek Love: Homophobia in 19th-Century England* (Berkeley: Univ. of California Press, 1985).

15. Yost, p. 11. Like others before him, Yost misses the point of Shelley's handling of the "unspeakable," concluding that the poet "drops the charge of sodomy" (p. 30).

16. Yost, p.27.

17. Christabel, l. 381.

18. Hume, pp. 348–49.

19. Hume, pp. 418–19.

20. For an interesting examination of the issue of the play's irresponsible patriarchies, see Eugene R. Hammond, "Beatrice's Three Fathers: Successive Betrayal in Shelly's *The Cenci*," *Essays in Literature*, 8 (Spring 1981), 25–32.

21. *Letters*, II, 102–3.

22. *Mary Shelley's Journal*, ed. Frederick L. Jones (Norman: Univ. of Oklahoma Press, 1947), p. 20.

23. Flannery O'Connor, "A Good Man Is Hard to Find," *The Complete Stories* (New York: Farrar, Straus, and Giroux), p. 132.

24. Irving Howe, *Politics and the Novel*, (1957; rpt. New York: Avon, 1967), pp. 22–23.

25. Kenneth Neill Cameron, *Shelley: The Golden Years* (Cambridge, Mass.: Harvard Univ. Press, 1974), p. 401.

26. Joseph Anthony Wittreich, Jr., *Visionary Poetics: Milton's Tradition and His Legacy* (San Marino, Calif.: Huntington Library, 1979), p. 34.

27. For a fuller discussion of this aspect of the prophet's role and function, see Stephen C. Behrendt, "'The Consequence of High Powers': Blake, Shelley, and Prophecy's Public Dimension," *Papers on Language and Literature*, 22 (1986), 254–75.

28. *Letters*, II, 120; 21 September 1819.
29. *Examiner*, No. 575; 3 Jan. 1819, 1.
30. *Examiner*, No. 604; 25 July 1819, 465.
31. For additional information about the event, see Newman Ivey White, *Shelley* (2 vols.; New York: Alfred A. Knopf, 1940), I, 545–46; Richard Holmes, *Shelley: The Pursuit* (New York: E. P. Dutton, 1975); and P. M. S. Dawson, *The Unacknowledged Legislator: Shelly and Politics* (Oxford: Clarendon Press, 1980), pp. 175–77. See also Scrivener's discussion of the pamphlet, pp. 133–37.
32. *The Complete Works of Percy Bysshe Shelley*, ed. Roger Ingpen and Walter E. Peck (10 vols.; London: Ernest Benn, 1926–30), VI, 82.
33. Significantly, while Cenci's is a crime that cannot be named but only referred to obliquely as "the act" or "the deed," Beatrice's crime *has* a name—parricide—that is repeatedly uttered explicitly in the play. I thank my student Kevin Binfield for pointing this out to me in the course of his own striking investigation of *The Cenci*.
34. Marzio's denial of the truth here, and his self-reproach at having named the person the audience knows to be the guilty party, recalls the manner in which Caleb Williams castigates himself for having revealed the murderer Falkland in Godwin's *Caleb Williams* (1794). Both are deluded in their faulty beliefs that those they accuse somehow do not deserve their punishment; both Marzio and Caleb strongly regret having revealed the truth to the respective authorities.
35. Yost, p.43.
36. Yost points out that though the manuscript record Shelley consulted (Es) indicates that Beatrice's petition to Clement VIII went unanswered, Pieracci, like Shelly, has the petition intercepted and suppressed by an intermediary, in this case Francesco Cenci's friend Aldobrando. Interestingly for the political dimension of the tale that Shelley explores, Pieracci calls the pope "the Sovereign" (*l Sovrano*); Yost, p. 35.

"The Mask of Darkness":
Metaphor, Myth, and History
in Shelley's
"The Triumph of Life"

P. M. S. Dawson

I wish to propose a reading of Shelley's powerful and enigmatic last poem that sees it as centrally concerned with the question of human history and how human beings envision that history. The poem offers a number of myths or metaphors concerning the ways in which human beings relate to time. What these metaphors have in common is a reference to repetition. The relevance of repetition to our understanding of history is brought out in Marx's famous comment, invoking the authority of Hegel, that "all the great events and characters of world history occur, so to speak, twice," with his own qualification: "the first time as tragedy, the second as farce."[1] It is no doubt at least partly the very fact of repetition that gives its farcical character to the second occurrence. At the same time, the sense of being condemned to repeat what has gone before in a now degraded form is itself tragic, part of that burden of the past which Marx characterizes so eloquently: "Men make their own history, but not of their own free will; not under circumstances they themselves have chosen but under the given and inherited circumstances with which they are directly confronted. The tradition of the dead generations weighs like a nightmare on the minds of the living."[2] For Shelley as for Marx, the thought that the future could only repeat the past was a "nightmare." Others might take a grim satisfaction in registering the limiting lessons of history. For Byron the "Chaos of ruins" that Rome offers is a universal emblem of human experience:

> There is the moral of all human tales;
>   'Tis but the same rehearsal of the past,
> First Freedom, and then Glory—when that fails,
> Wealth—Vice—Corruption,—Barbarism at last
> And History, with all her volumes vast,
> Hath but *one* page . . . [3]

Shelley might well have replied to Byron as his Christ replied to Satan in the Prologue to *Hellas:*

> Obdurate spirit!
> Thou seest but the Past in the To-come.
> Pride is thy error and thy punishment.[4]

But the force of repetition in human history could not be refuted this simply. The final chorus of *Hellas* moves from the prophecy of "A brighter Hellas" and "Another Athens" to lamenting the possibility that the renewal of the glory of Greece may simply mean the repetition of the previous cycle: "O cease! must hate and death return?" (1064–1101)

Shelley certainly did not deny the existence of this force, and his awareness of it is clear in the overtly historical references of the "Triumph." Rousseau's comment on Napoleon, who "sought to win / The world, and lost all it did contain / Of greatness, in its hope destroyed" (217–19)[5], identifies a self-contradicting tendency that echoes the apparently casual reference of the narrator to "Imperial Rome . . . When Freedom left those who upon the free / Had bound a yoke which soon they stooped to bear" (113, 115–16). But to continue seeking and enforcing such parallels could only support the gloomy conclusion of Byron, that "History . . . Hath but *one* page," and we can never hope to turn it. At Byron's preferred level of generality, where all history is used to point a moral and adorn a tale, his case is irrefutable.[6] Shelley's answer to the Byronic view of history takes the form of what we might call a microanalysis of repetition, an investigation of the human being's most intimate relations to time.

We may begin our consideration of this issue by recalling what must be for many readers Shelley's most telling account of repetition:

I knew

That I had felt the freshness of that dawn,
Bathed in the same cold dew my brow & hair
And sate as thus upon that slope of lawn

Under the self same bough . . .

(33–37)

The impact of these lines depends upon a shock of recognition; they are a description of dé jà vu that must strike us as itself an example of the phenomenon. The eeriness of the experience is reflected in a perceived ambiguity in the syntax, where tense and mood momentarily seem to be confused (in fact the ambiguity is only apparent). Readers initially may well read the second main verb ("Bathed") as if it were dependent on the first: "I had felt the freshness . . . Bathe . . . my brow." (In the manuscript there is no comma after "dawn.") The fact that it is a finite past form suggests a kind of pseudosyntax by which one could say things like "I heard him said" (strengthened by the existence of such constructions as "I heard it said," "I felt my brow bathed"). We immediately construe the sentence correctly, but the misreading cannot be entirely dismissed since the very subject is a present experience that somehow seems like a past one.

Shelley had a keen amateur psychologist's interest in such experiences, and earlier had discussed an example of dé jà vu in talking about dreams.[7] Its evocation in "The Triumph of Life," however, is not to be explained merely by the desire to mention a psychological curiosity. As an example of repetition, it is one of the thematic centers of the poem, as critics have recognized by offering explanations for the narrator's sensation, such as that he is literally repeating the experience of Rousseau. There are certainly strong similarities between the dawn scene at the beginning of the poem that precedes the narrator's "Vision" and Rousseau's description (from line 308) leading to his seeing "a new Vision never seen before" (411). Logically the narrator's experience must be seen as a repetition of that of Rousseau, who, as he reminds the narrator, "Before thy memory / . . . feared, loved, hated, suffered, did, & died" (199–200). But for the reader, it is Rousseau's account that seems a repetition of the narrator's. This ambivalence suggests that what is at issue is more than a local connection; both characters are repeating a pattern whose origin is not to be located with either of them. The narrator does not see the vision *because* Rousseau had seen it, any more than Rousseau sees it because the narrator had. What we see is rather a repeated cycle of experience, preceding and succeeding the two particular examples we are offered (the effect being strengthened by the strong reminiscences in both accounts of Wordsworth's "Immortality Ode," itself structured around a myth of reminiscence).

It is certainly suggested that the cycle need not always go the same way. Rousseau offers to tell the narrator his story "If thou canst forbear / To join the dance, which I had well forborne" (188–89). The narrator's forbearance is, of course, only a necessary condition of hearing the story; but the point of his hearing it is presumably that it will help him avoid Rousseau's error and his fate. But this possibility is undercut later, when Rousseau confesses his ignorance of the "Why" and the "Whither" of the whole process, and adds

> But follow thou, & from spectator turn
> Actor or victim in this wretchedness,
>
> And what thou wouldst be taught I then may learn
> From thee.

(305–8)

The participant cannot teach the spectator enough to dispense him from becoming a participant in his turn; perhaps it is only a participant who can learn the important lesson, which is that it would have been better to forbear participation. Can one escape the cycle? Yes, but only by joining it.

For Byron history has "but *one* page" because it is written by human beings according to the strict grammar by which they all, singly and collectively, live. History simply shows on a large scale the pattern of aspiration and defeat that is the law of all human existence. For Shelley it is rather our mistaken acceptance of this "law" that condemns us to repeat the past. In trying to learn from past mistakes we learn only that we must repeat them: " . . . the daily scene, / The flow and ebb of each recurring age, / The everlasting *to be* which *hath been*," in Byron's words, "Hath taught us nought or little."[8] Apparently it has taught him the futility of hoping to escape from a cycle that is as fixed and ineluctable as the tides. The casual association of the "law" of human history with a natural cycle is a rhetorical commonplace with Byron. Shelley's desire to free "to be" from what "hath been" prompts him in the "Triumph" to a much closer scrutiny of our relationship to such cycles and to their applicability to human affairs.

Shelley's poem turns out to be remarkably dense with allusions—pointed, passing, and metaphorical—to a number of natural cycles. This density is such as to constitute an interrogation of the assumption, adopted unquestioningly by Byron, that these cycles can be applied directly to human life. As we shall see, the applications, by their very profusion, involve contradictions, from which we can only extricate ourselves by a firm reminder that they are after all only metaphorical—a consideration that Shelley evidently wishes to enforce. The central cyclical reference, if only by its privileged status in literary tradition, I take to be the comparison between human life and the annual cycle of the seasons. At line 51 the narrator compares the multitude in his vision to "the million leaves of summer's bier." The simile is later echoed in Rousseau's account when he likens the parasitic shadows to "the dead leaves blown / In Autumn evening from a poplar tree" (528–29). The comparison could hardly be more traditional. Homer likens "the generation of leaves" to "that of humanity."[9] Virgil describes the souls of the dead as being "thick as the leaves of the forest that at autumn's first frost dropping fall."[10] In Dante the fate of "the wicked seed of Adam" is compared to the way that "in autumn the leaves drop off one after the other till the branch sees all its spoils on the ground."[11] And Milton describes his fallen angels as lying "Thick as autumnal leaves that strew the brooks / In Vallombrosa" (*Paradise Lost*, I, 302–3). Shelley's unique contribution to the tradition is to specify the trees as *poplar* trees. This is unlikely to be local color, and I suspect that Shelley intends a pun on "pop(u)lar," which would reactivate the universal implications of the metaphor in Homer and in Virgil, where the falling leaves are *all* men, not just the wicked as in Dante or devils as in Milton.

The comparison with autumn leaves invites an extension to the other phases of the seasonal cycle. Indeed, Homer proposes just such a comprehensive comparison:

> As is the generation of leaves, so is that of humanity
> The wind scatters the leaves on the ground, but the live timber
> Burgeons with leaves again in the season of spring returning.
> So one generation of men will grow while another dies.
>
> (*Iliad*, IV, 146–50)

This aspect of renewal through the annual cycle is stressed by Shelley in the "Ode to the West Wind." But the apparent optimism of that poem is tempered by its concluding interrogation of its own metaphor: "O Wind, / If Winter comes, can Spring be far behind?" (69–70). Spring comes immediately after winter in the cycle, and thus not "far behind" it; but for the individual progressing through the cycle, spring is indeed "far behind" when he reaches winter. The ambivalence of Shelley's rhetorical demand points up the essential pathos of the comparisons between human life and the seasonal cycle. The latter is repeated indefinitely, but human life is once around the track. In the "Ode" Shelley accepted his individual extinction as the condition of participating in the new growth. In the "Triumph," on the contrary, the possibility of such a return to life is given Gothic connotations of vampirism and demonic possession:

> the old anatomies
> . . . .
>
> laughed from their dead eyes
> To reassume the delegated power
> Arrayed in which these worms did monarchize
>
> Who make this earth their charnel.
>
> (500–505)

The renewal of the seasons is a natural process, but when humans thus outlast their deaths, it is either a perversion of the natural or a descent into the natural that is a perversion of the human—as with Rousseau, who is initially mistaken by the narrator for "an old root" covered with dry grass (182–88). If the seasonal metaphor is turned in the other direction and made to relate to a cosmic rather than to a human time scale, the implication is hardly more reassuring. The famous around the chariot are

> All those whose fame or infamy must grow
> Till the great winter lay the form & name
> Of their own earth with them forever low
>
> (125–27)

As early as 1816 Shelley had mused on "Buffons sublime but gloomy theory, that this earth which we inhabit will at some future period be changed into a mass of frost."[12] In this perspective the whole history of the globe could be seen as a single year, a one-off cycle which, like that of the individual human, ends in death.

Seen in this long perspective, the life of the individual is but a day. The daily cycle is touched on in the poem more often than any of the other cycles I have identified (I count nineteen references). One reason for this is its connection with the imagery of light and dark, whose (metaphorical) significance for the poem is well recognized. The daily cycle in its metaphorized form provides Shelley with one of his tersest comments on the self-frustration of human pretensions: "for the noon of truth they feigned, deep night / Caught them ere evening" (214–15).Under no circumstances could there occur naturally the vehicle of this metaphor, though the point of the tenor is clear and cogent. Once again the applicability of a cyclic metaphor to human existence reveals itself as problematic. This problematic nature is revealed at the outset of the poem where dawn is described as "the birth / Of light" (6–7), a metaphor linking the diurnal to the human life cycle. The opening description offers us an account of the dawn that does indeed make it seem unique, the first and only dawn, the very birth of light; but we hardly need the explicit reminder that the sun took on himself his daily labor "of old" (19). The dawn described is *particular* (the only one that was the occasion of the events of the poem), but it cannot be unique as the birth of a person is unique. But the paradox is both weakened and given a further twist by the fact that the human life cycle (including birth) can be imaged in terms of the daily cycle. This is the point of such an apparently casual reference as that to "The mighty phantoms of an elder day" (253; cf. "in his day"). If a "day" can be the length of a life or a generation, it can be even longer. The narrator faced with the dispiriting example of Napoleon is grieved to think "how power & will / In opposition rule our mortal day" (228–29). Is "our . . . day" merely the time of the narrator's own generation, a day that will pass? Or is it the time of all human history, ruled in opposition by power and will, as the natural day is ruled by light and dark? Rousseau certainly has more than a limited historical space in mind when he refers to "the sick day in which we wake to weep" (430). He seems rather to mean the recurrent condition of human life, the day(light) in which it must always be played out. Just as the invocation of the annual cycle suggests a view of all history as a single year that must end in the "great winter" of the world itself, so too can the daily cycle become a metaphor for all life. Rousseau certainly sees himself as existing within such a cycle, referring to "the morn" as the time when the pageant of Life began, and inviting the narrator to follow it "even to the night" (193–95).

His attempt to use the analogy of the daily cycle to understand the pattern of his own life leads him into serious error. Having compared the overpowering of the light of the "fair shape" of his vision by the "new Vision" of Life to the effacing of Venus by the coming of daylight, he goes on to express his faith in the continued presence of the shape and his confidence in its reappearance. This confidence rests on an explicit simile:

> as the presence of that fairest planet
> Although unseen is felt by one who hopes
>
> That his day's path may end as he began it
> In that star's smile, whose light is like the scent
> Of a jonquil when evening breezes fan it
>
> (416–20)

Venus is indeed both the Morning and the Evening Star; but even so the confidence in its reappearance is misplaced, for it cannot be both on the same day.[13] The appearance of Venus occurs according to a cycle that is different from the daily cycle, with which it intersects in different ways in the course of the annual cycle. In refusing to accept that the shape has departed from the cycle within which he has trapped himself, Rousseau commits himself to identifying the shape with the figure that has replaced it, Life.

> So knew I in that light's severe excess
> The presence of that shape which on the stream
> Moved, as I moved along the wilderness
>
> (424–26)

Some readers have followed Rousseau in this identification, and have concluded that the original shape was malevolent or at least maleficent. But this is another form of Rousseau's own error. The shape, like the dream maiden of *Alastor*, was a product of his own imaginative powers. His attempt to convince himself that she somehow continues to exist apart from him, within or behind the vision of Life, is itself a symptom of that failure of imaginative power that led to her loss. He handed over his own creative power to Life when he inscribed its productions within a merely natural cycle. His error receives an appropriately Dantean punishment when he is reduced to "an old root" from which nothing can grow.

Whether or not the narrator can avoid Rousseau's error and his fate, he does at least recognize that human activities need not automatically follow the daily cycle. In an apparently perverse way, he has remained wakeful through the night, falling into sleep and vision with the dawn. To invert the cycle is not necessarily to escape it. In refusing to emulate the sun as the whole natural world does, he imitates instead "the stars that gem / The cone of night" (22–23). He is following a stellar cycle that is merely the obverse of the solar cycle. But the reference to the "cone of night" is a powerful hint toward the real source of all the cycles we have considered. This cone is the shadow that the earth casts by intercepting the rays of the sun. It is only because of this shadow that it is possible for an earthly observer to ever see the stars at all. The cycle of day and night is produced by the earth's own rotation, just as Rousseau's shape is his own imaginative creation, and just as the vampiric forms that he describes tormenting those in the pageant of Life are originally their own "shadows" (481). In this poem and elsewhere, Shelley uses the imagery of shadows to describe those products of human action that can become alienated from the actor and appear to him as something external.[14]

The insight toward which "The Triumph of Life" strains is the recognition that all the cycles to which the earth and its inhabitants—"their own earth" (127), as Shelley significantly says—are subject are the product of its own motion. The earth seems to have attained some such recognition in Shelley's "Lines Written on Hearing the News of the Death of Napoleon" (1822). As the source of Napoleon, she does not end with his fall: "I feed on whom I fed" (32). Where the observers in "The Triumph of Life" tend to reduce all the eternal natural cycles to single revolutions with a final end, the earth knows that every end can be a beginning:

> Leave the millions who follow to mould
> The metal before it be cold,
> And weave into his shame, which like the dead
> Shrouds me, the hopes that from his glory fled.

(37–40)

The error of applying natural cycles to human life is also the reverse error, of reducing the infinite repetition of nature to the closed cycle of the individual life. To do this is to follow those who "mournfully within the gloom / Of their own shadow walked, and called it death" ("Triumph," 58–59). If human life were infinitely cyclic, however, it would be the nightmare of infinite repetition, in which the dead past refuses to allow the future to come to life. Either alternative would make man the slave of his own Spectre, to adopt Blake's terms. The sole way out is for him to acknowledge that it is his own shadow that lies over him. The recognition to which the figures in "The Triumph of Life" do not attain, at least within the poem as we have it, but which the poem offers to its readers, is that the history of which human beings seem to be the helpless victims is their own creation—*our* own creation.

243

Notes

1. *The Eighteenth Brumaire of Louis Bonaparte* (1852), in Karl Marx, *Surveys from Exile*, ed. David Fernbach (Harmondsworth: Penguin, 1973), p. 146.

2. Ibid.

3. *Childe Harold's Pilgrimage*, Canto IV (1818), Stanza cviii.

4. Lines 160–62; in *The Complete Works of Percy Bysshe Shelley* ed. Roger Ingpen and Walter E. Peck (10 vols., 1926–30; London: Ernest Benn, 1965), III. 15.

5. References are to the text in Donald H. Reiman, *Shelley's "The Triumph of Life"*: *A Critical Study* (Urbana: U. of Illinois P., 1965).

6. Byron himself echoes the Johnsonian tag (*The Vanity of Human Wishes* [1749], line 222) in the first line of the passage quoted.

7. See *Works*, VII. 67. According to Mary Shelley, this fragment was written in 1815.

8. "Ode on Venice" (1819), lines 57–60.

9. *Iliad*, VI. 146; in *The Iliad of Homer*, trans. Richmond Lattimore (Chicago: U. of Chicago P., 1951), p. 157.

10. *Aeneid*, VI. 309–10; in *Virgil*, with an English translation by H. Rushton Fairclough (2 vols.; London: William Heinemann, 1967 [Loeb Classical Library]), I. 527.

11. *Inferno*, III. 112–15; in *The Divine Comedy of Dante Alighieri*, trans. John D. Sinclair, I: *Inferno* (1939; London: Oxford U.P., 1975), p. 53.

12. *The Letters of Percy Bysshe Shelley*, ed. Frederick L. Jones (2 vols.; Oxford: Clarendon Press, 1964), I. 499.

13. See John A. Hodgson, "The World's Mysterious Doom: Shelley's *The Triumph of Life*", *ELH*, 42 (1975), 603–4.

14. See P. M. S. Dawson, *The Unacknowledged Legislator: Shelley and Politics* (Oxford: Clarendon Press, 1980), pp. 106–07.

Index

Stephen C. Behrendt is Professor of English and Graduate Chair at the University of Nebraska. He received the M.A. degree from Eastern Kentucky University and the Ph.D. from the University of Wisconsin. He is the author of *The Moment of Explosion: Blake and the Illustration of Milton,* and has edited an edition of Shelley's *Zastrozzi* and *St. Irvyne.* His articles have appeared in such journals as *Blake: An Illustrated Quarterly, Papers on Language and Literature, The Eighteenth Century: Theory and Interpretation, American Poetry,* and *Genre.*

The manuscript was prepared for publication by Robert S. Demorest. The book was designed by Joanne E. Kinney. The typeface for the text is Palatino and the display is Goudy Handtooled and Goudy Old Style. The book is printed on 55 lb Glatfelter text stock. The cloth edition is bound in Roxite A grade cloth; the stock for the paper cover is 10 pt C1S.

Manufactured in the United States of America.